The Dynamics of
Human Service
Delivery

The Dynamics of Human Service Delivery

by

Gilbert Levin
*Albert Einstein College
of Medicine*

and

Edward B. Roberts
*Alfred P. Sloan School
of Management, M.I.T.*

with

Gary B. Hirsch
Pugh-Roberts Associates, Inc.

Deborah S. Kligler
*Albert Einstein College
of Medicine*

Jack F. Wilder
*Albert Einstein College
of Medicine*

Nancy Roberts
*Lesley College, Graduate
School of Education*

Ballinger Publishing Company ● Cambridge, Massachusetts
A Subsidiary of J.B. Lippincott Company

This book is printed on recycled paper.

International Standard Book Number: 0-88410-132-0

Library of Congress Catalog Card Number: 75-46547

Printed in the United States of America

Library of Congress Cataloging in Publication Data

Levin, Gilbert.
   The dynamics of human service delivery.

   1. Social service. I. Roberts, Edward Baer, joint author. II. Title.
[DNLM: 1. Social service. HV40 L665d]

HV41.L444	361	75-046547
ISBN 0-88410-132-0		

Contents

List of Figures

List of Tables

Introduction

This is a book about the process of providing services to people. It attempts to bridge the gap between social theory and practice. That gap exists because theories have been too simple to do justice to the nuances and complexities of social behavior, whereas practice often appears too helter-skelter to be characterized systematically.

Sociologists and other social theorists may be interested in the book as a demonstration that a theory can be useful without sacrifice of rigor. To the social practitioner—anyone whose vocation, avocation, or personal commitment calls upon him to act constructively in a social system—the book offers a perspective that draws his intuitions and hunches into a coherent framework within which progress is possible.

PREVIEW

Chapter One develops the position that the usual static view of human service delivery must be supplanted by one that illuminates the dynamic (time-varying) character of that process. The dynamic viewpoint is used in Chapter Two to construct a theory of the relationship between a human service agency and its clients. The heart of any human service system lies in the interaction between care-needer and care-giver. Contact between these two is the vehicle by which care is delivered and also the basis for the relationship that evolves between them. Chapter Three shows how a variety of apparently disparate phenomena, during the life of a typical human service agency, can be explained by simple extensions of the theory.

Since our theory is so general, it can only be evaluated in terms of its specific applications. The applications presented in chapters Four through Nine address two related questions: (1) How faithfully does our general theory represent the human service delivery process? and (2) Of what practical use is the theory?

Thus the theory is applied to the areas of mental health (chapters Four and Five), education (chapters Six and Seven), and dentistry (chapters Eight and Nine). In each pair of chapters the first seeks to establish the validity of the theory for a specific human service delivery issue. That chapter provides an integration of existing empirical literature and develops the basis for a rigorous model. The second chapter in each area communicates analyses that have been carried out using quantitative computer simulation models derived from the theory. Although mathematical models and computer simulation analyses are employed, no technical training is required to understand the applications.

The appendices include brief explanations of the computer equations developed for carrying out each of the three quantitative application studies. This material will be of primary interest to the specialist who wishes to simulate policies and conditions not considered in this book and to the reader who requires a precise statement of the models. The reader interested in social science modeling will find the appendices useful for study in conjunction with the empirical discussions of chapters 4, 6, and 8.

ACKNOWLEDGMENTS

Portions of this book have appeared elsewhere in modified form. Chapters Six and Seven draw heavily from Nancy Roberts, "A Computer System Simulation of Student Performance in the Elementary Classroom", *Simulation & Games,* vol. 5, no. 3 (September 1974), pp. 265–90; and Nancy Roberts, "Parental Influence in the Elementary Classroom: A Computer Simulation", *Educational Technology,* vol. xv, no. 10 (October 1975), pp. 37–42. Chapters Eight and Nine reflect Gary B. Hirsch and William R. Killingsworth, "A New Framework for Projecting Dental Manpower Requirements", *Inquiry,* vol. xii (June 1975), pp. 126–42.

Donald Mandell and Christina Hoven provided helpful editorial assistance. Lisa Kunstadter assisted with typing and secretarial support marked by appreciated cooperation and efficiency.

The overall work was supported in part by the National Institute of Mental Health under Grant #16586. The application to dental manpower analysis was supported in part by the DHEW Bureau of Health Manpower, Division of Dentistry, under Contract N 01-DH-44091.

Part I

Theory

 *Chapter 1*

The Dynamic View

STATIC VERSUS DYNAMIC VIEWS

The delivery of human services is a dynamic process taking place in a changing environment. Traditional attempts to describe human service delivery are, however, overwhelmingly static, telling how things look but not how they work. The experienced observer of a human service program strives to penetrate beyond formal accounts in order to get at the "experience" to date.

The static view leads to emphasis upon discrete symptoms, such as:

The cost of providing service is high and increasing too rapidly.
Facilities are overcrowded and otherwise inadequate.
Too few trained workers exist, and they are badly distributed geographically.
Services are bureaucratic.
Those who need services most often get them least.
Services are not relevant to the needs of people.
Specific techniques do not work.
Politicalization interferes with service efficacy.
Research and development priorities are influenced too little by the needs of people.

Gaining insight into the underlying dynamic system structures that generate these symptoms is a difficult undertaking, partly because of gaps in knowledge about specific parameters and variables. More important, existing knowledge about service delivery systems is too highly compartmentalized and hence for practical purposes hidden from view. This compartmentalization exists because artificial boundaries between relevant scientific and technical disciplines create artificial domains of knowledge, with little cross-fertilization or integration.

Integrative thinking about human service situations is important, more difficult to achieve than is usually supposed, and too often omitted in favor of naive intuition. Given the growing complexity and interdependence of our social and technical systems and their frequently counterintuitive behavior, we can no longer put our trust in intuition. The intuitive solution to one social problem often causes another even more serious problem:

Federal assistance for construction of single-family homes alleviated the postwar housing shortage, but inadvertently contributed to today's urban problems by providing incentives for the middle class to leave the city and thus weaken its tax base.

The use of certain pesticides improves farm productivity but kills wildlife and birds and poisons waterways, ultimately decreasing food supply.

Highway construction eases traffic congestion but destroys neighborhoods, breeds more cars, and causes even more congestion.

Temporarily effective action against the import of marijuana from Mexico may have expanded the market for a more dangerous drug, heroin.

Why does the usual analysis fail to provide an adequate understanding of the human service delivery process? In our view, the major reason is that cause and effect are seen as operating in straight lines moving through time.

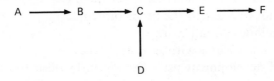

Figure 1-1. Some Condition *A* Elicits State or Condition *B*, Which Then Combines with *D* to Effect *C*. *C* Causes *E*, and *E* Then Causes the Ultimate Outcome *F*.

Experience from every discipline teaches us that life situations do not follow such linear chains. Instead the elements of such a chain themselves interact in loops and circles, so that along the way to producing an outcome the components affect each other. The outcome in turn affects the initial conditions, blurring any absolute sense of beginning and end. This interaction-oriented analysis is, we think, fruitful in considering social systems that are necessarily complex and in which feedback loops and causal circles connect the interacting elements. Thus, a better approximation of the interaction of variables through time might look like figure 1–2:

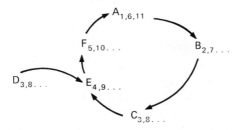

Figure 1–2. In Figure 1–2, Condition or Event *A* at "Time 1" Causes Condition or Event *B* to Occur at "Time 2". *B* in Turn Elicits *C* at "Time 3", and Then *C* and *D* Act Together to Cause (or Produce) *E* at "Time 4". *E* Produces *F* at "Time 5", and Then *F* Feeds Back into the System to Produce *A* at "Time 6".

DYNAMICS OF SOCIAL PRACTICE

In contrast with the static conception, the dynamic view accounts not only for the separate elements of a system, but also for the interactions between these elements as the system operates through time. Adopting this view helps us to better understand the behavior of social practitioners, be they hospital managers, politicians, teachers, parents, or therapists. When a social practitioner becomes involved in a dynamic process, he can be seen as an information-receiving and decision-making agent, continually interacting with a changing reality, as shown in figure 1–3.

The social practitioner views continuous streams of data which come to him from reality. Some of these data are quantitative and some are based on impressions; some are free from bias while others are heavily biased. The practitioner processes all of these data and fashions an imperfect approximation of "reality"; this we call his "account" of reality.

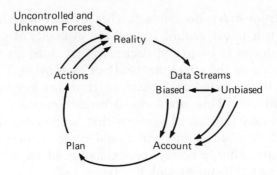

Figure 1-3. The Social Practitioner: A Dynamic View

The *account* of reality within the practitioner governs his propensity to sustain or to modify his *plan* which in turn affects the *actions* he takes. The *actions,* of course, flow back into *reality* and change it. At some later time when the practitioner receives and interprets new *data streams* he will rightly or wrongly attribute changes in data to his earlier actions. The changed data may require an altered *account* of reality which in turn affects his *plan* and then his new *actions*. Thus, the practitioner is continually conversing with reality. By processing *data streams* he conceives of a *plan* for *action* and then executes this plan. *Actions* change *reality* and cause it to emanate changed *data streams*—and so the conversation continues.

Although these elements are in constant operation, they tend to change character at very different rates. As a rule, plans and accounts are slower to change than the streams of data. But at any moment in time the practitioner acts on the basis of a present plan (which may be implicit) derived from a present account (which may be nonveridical). Even if the practitioner is dissatisfied with his current account of reality and is contemplating a change in it, the account remains in operation. Social practice never contains the condition that there is no account; the practitioner does not have the luxury of not knowing or not acting at any time. The social practitioner constantly makes decisions and acts on them based on an imperfect but best available account of reality. Let us stop to take a closer look at the elements of this system within which the social practitioner continuously processes information, constructs an account of reality and a plan for action, and acts.

The Account

Given the fundamental importance of the account of reality to the social practitioner's construction of his new plan for action, he wants to know what constitutes a "good" account. The chief aim of a scientific account is to achieve increased knowledge of and control over presently unknown and uncontrolled influences upon reality. However, since the aim of the social practitioner is to practice as effectively as possible (or as effectively as is presently feasible), he is less interested in a purely scientific account than in one that points the way toward appropriate action.

This difference in emphasis gives rise to differences in criteria for evaluating the account of reality. We look now at two aspects of the account's quality—precision and bias, and timeliness—and compare the requirements of pure science to those of adequate social practice.

The "Good" Account—Precision and Bias. In the domain of pure science, or scientific inquiry, the overriding purpose and greatest challenge is to construct an account of reality that corresponds maximally with reality itself. Other considerations are secondary. From the pure scientist's point of view, the *data streams* that are allowed to flow into a scientific *account* should be as pure as possible. A rising standard of purity accompanies the development of any science. Data that fail to meet this standard are considered not to exist. Thus, *no* present scientific accounts exist for many phenomena, because no body of data exists on which to build. To anthropologist Leslie White, the capacity to "not know" is the distinguishing feature of the scientific mentality.[1]

The social practitioner is in quite a different position from the pure scientist. If many studies ranging over a long period of time are needed to build a good scientific account of some social phenomenon, the social practitioner will probably not have time to wait. A social worker, policeman, or politician "knows" that poverty is a contributing cause of crime and that it plays a role in malnutrition. He "knows" these relationships without the benefit of carefully controlled research, and he is willing to overlook exceptions like the wealthy criminal or the successful executive alcholic suffering from severe protein deficiency.

For the social practitioner the criterion of richness of data is at least as important as that of purity. In contrast to the pure scientist, he never "not knows", but always uses whatever data he can to construct the best possible account of the aspect of reality that concerns him. Of necessity, the practitioner's standard of quality for data is flexible. His account may be influenced more by data of high relevance from a questionable source than by hard data of lower relevance.

The "Good" Account—Timeliness. The pure scientist is a knowledge-builder engaged in the scientific process, and as such he is relatively free of time constraints. Although it would not be accurate to say that the phenomena investigated by pure scientists are immune from societal influence (such as the availability of grant money), it is nonetheless true that many investigators foresee no immediate social applicability for their product. Even so the scientist has strong faith (substantiated by countless examples) that the product of his inquiry will one day be useful.

In the more usual case, applied scientific activity is stimulated or restrained by economic and social necessity. For these studies, time is of the essence, and the funding arrangements often reflect this by requiring that a social service accompany the research. Thus, when funding is made available for biochemical research on schizophrenia, money is also invested immediately in the day-to-day management of the illness.

The practitioner is concerned with a shorter span of time than the researcher. At every moment he must do something "next". In each area of action he must decide whether to step up, maintain, or decrease the vigor of his actions. He has no time to wait for guidance from pure research, which often lags one to three years behind. Thus, a program manager may rely more on the anecdotal observations of the community worker than on last decade's census figures or last year's attitude survey of area residents. In similar fashion, the psychotherapist's *plan* today may rely more on the patient's dream of yesterday than on the written personality test administered at intake.

The Plan

Based on his present account of reality, the social practitioner formulates a plan for action, a statement of what he intends to do and what he expects to accomplish in terms of system maintenance or system change. In terms of these objectives he must select a set of possible actions and decide in what order they should take place and at what rate of speed. Just as the reality with which he deals is in constant flux, so must the practitioner's plan be continuously responsive to the account of the changes.

The plan must be, above all, sensitive to the consequences that actions may have, so that the practitioner may have some clear and realistic idea of where the system will be at the next iteration of the action-reality loop of which it is a part. This sensitivity is crucial not only to the achievement of the particular objective of the system, but also to the maintenance of the system itself. Although goals are usually stated in terms of something real to be accomplished, the practitioner must never lose sight of the larger goal of maintaining either a state of dynamic equilibrium or an orderly growth or evolution of the system as a whole. Failure to keep the demands of system stability clearly in view invites the possibility of introducing instability and chaos, thus bringing about negative consequences not only for the immediate objectives but for the very life of the system.

Action

The social practitioner or manager who regards it as his mission to reduce some problem in "reality" takes specific actions, as outlined by his "plan", to accomplish that goal. He views his actions as "corrective", and in terms of his intentions they are. In terms of actual consequences, however, his well-intentioned actions may either amplify the problem or bring on new and different problems.

How can this happen? In part, the unforeseen consequences result from having perturbed one element of a complex network of interaction. Problems are rarely the product of simple causal sequences that can be interrupted, patched, and controlled. Problems in "reality" are usually complex problems involving a large system of interrelated components. To be able to foresee where one comes out of such a system when he enters it he must know the system or its map.

In large measure, however, the risk of amplifying a problem exists because a practitioner's action and its effect are not simultaneous; they are often separated by an appreciable length of time. Failure to perceive this time delay accurately may lead the problem-solver to act with inappropriate vigor or for too long a time—he "overcorrects" the situation and increases the original problem.

Contemporary life is filled with examples of ways in which "corrective" policies complicate the problems they were devised to solve.

Whoever has had the experience of trying to design and enact programs for alleviating problems in the environment, in education, job availability, or crime reduction, whoever has worked with programs designed to better the conditions of America's poor has already been introduced to the unanticipated consequences of "corrective" actions and to the crucial importance of the vigor of the action, its duration, and the time-delays between an action and its results. These very dimensions (vigor, duration, time delays) apply no less to the control systems involved in the operation of the economy and in industrial production-distribution systems.

A Case Example

Some of the mystery about problems that arise as the unintended result of corrective actions will disappear as we now take a closer look at a typical social practitioner, the manager of a human service agency.

The manager's most important job is to convert information, that is data streams, into actions that influence reality favorably in terms of the goals of the organization. He is an essential part of a system whose other component parts are constantly subject to the possibility of change. His success is determined, in large part, by the character of his responses to changing streams of data.

Let us consider a relatively straightforward managerial problem. The director of an acute psychiatric hospital service has responsibility for regulating the flow of patients into and out of the hospital wards. The high fixed cost of operating a hospital service inevitably puts the director under pressure to maintain a constant census at nearly full capacity. The principal data streams he attends to are: (1) the rate of patient applications for admission; (2) the current total census; and (3) the number of patients in process who are in varying stages of readiness for discharge. Based upon his reading of these variables, he constructs an account of the probable census at some time in the near future.

If the *account* of this probable future state approaches the system goal of full capacity, he constructs a *plan* that says: "Do nothing to alter present action, continue 'business as usual'." However, if the *account* of the probable future state differs by some critical factor from the system goal, the manager executes a *plan* that is designed to influence the streams of *action* in a fashion that he expects will maintain the census at or near to the desired level.

In most instances an altered paln will not affect action immediately. In part, this is due to the fact that some actions, like speeding up the rate of discharge, require time for accomplishment. A discharge scheduled for next Wednesday can often be effected by Monday without harm to the patient. However, it is most unlikely that half the ward's population could be discharged with a one-day notice without doing damage to the recovery process.

Another constraint on the director's (or any other social service manager's) strategy is the fact that the authority to implement decisions is usually not in his hands alone but is shared on either a formal or informal basis with other staff members. His responsibility, the welfare of the total service operation, is not (except under very special circumstances) accompanied by unlimited authority. Even the needed unlimited access to all relevant data required to make decisions that affect the welfare of individual patients is usually not present.

Depending upon a variety of factors, including personal style, the structure and politics of the organization, and its traditions and history, the human service manager attempts to motivate staff members to take the necessary *actions* to execute his *plan* by explaining the necessity of these actions, or by persuading or pressuring staff, or by other means at his disposal. If the manager is in a privately endowed independent hospital, he may be able to handle the management problem directly by immediately shutting off or turning on the flow of patients at its source. However, in publicly supported acute treatment services, announcing that no further patient admissions will be allowed is almost never possible.

The administrator might try to get around this by leaking information to "gate-keepers" that beds are scarce and urging them to raise the standards of admission temporarily, making alternative dispositions if possible. If the increase in the rate of incoming patients is not too great or too persistent this stratagem works, especially when coupled with simultaneous efforts to politely nudge patients toward discharge.

Naturally, similar problems arise when ward census or expected census drops below some critical level. Low census is an especially significant problem when reimbursement for services is based directly upon census, as it is, for example, in facilities operated by various states and cities. Such facilities often follow the common practice of holding patients longer than necessary during periods of inventory-taking in order to establish a claim for future budget.

The manager must not only cause others to alter the rate at which

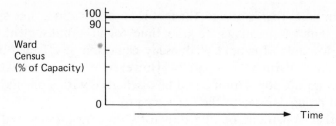

Figure 1–4.   Ideal Ward Census

critical action streams are allowed to flow, but he must also insure that the actions taken are of appropriate vigor and duration. For example, if the response to a slight increase in the number of patients seeking admission is to initiate immediately a policy of rapid discharge, he may soon be coping with a serious problem of the ward becoming under census. In turn, efforts to correct this condition may then cause the earlier problem to recur, and so set up an unsatisfactory oscillatory pattern.

The goal of management procedures in this situation is to approximate the condition depicted in the graph of figure 1–4.

Since the flow of patients into the service and out of it is inherently irregular, achieving this goal is literally impossible. The practical goal thus becomes the maintenance of census within a desired range, such as is indicated in figure 1–5.

Oscillatory behavior is a general characteristic of control systems that can be observed in the operation of the economy, in industrial production-distribution systems, in regulating the temperature of a shower, or in driving a car that is out of control. Once a ward census

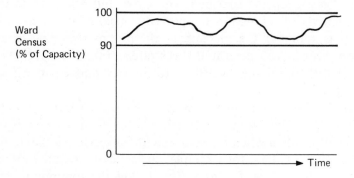

Figure 1–5.   More Typical Ward Census

moves into a phase of wide oscillation, bringing it under control is extremely difficult without resort to extraordinary measures. Faced with a ward that is far over census the ward director may be forced to make a Hobson's choice among unattractive alternative:

1. He may engage in wholesale dumping on another institution if one is available. For example, a municipal hospital may send its unwanted patients—old or new—to a state hospital. The effect of this action is to worsen the relationships with the other institution, which have probably been damaged already by similar past actions.

2. He may refuse service to applicant patients who clearly meet customary admission standards, thus damaging the service's position in the community and adversely affecting the morale of his own staff.

3. He may resign himself to operating beyond capacity for a period of time, thus antagonizing staff, providing inferior service, and risking that the temporary situation may become a chronic condition.

Anticipating the dangers of being caught up in a process that is out of control, some services arm themselves by explicitly or implicitly stratifying patients as they enter into categories, such as potential short-stayers and long-stayers. Staff are discouraged from becoming personally invested in the short-stay patients, who will be moved out as rapidly or slowly as is required by the inflow of new patients. Naturally such patients receive inferior service, the staff is aware of this, upset by it, and rendered less effective. Patients ticketed for long-stay are usually more fortunate. However, they too suffer as a result of their role in the system as a kind of buffer against the danger of temporary underpopulation.

In situations where the service has a statutory or contractual responsibility to admit all patients in a particular category, the stratification process is most prevalent, explicit and destructive in its consequences. These conditions inevitably exact a serious toll in the form of dehumanized staff attitudes toward patients and the consequent poor self-image of staff itself. In all probability the demands of census balance have contributed to the unhappy history of degradation of services in many state hospitals.

Managers of acute psychiatric services who feel compelled to make one or another of the Hobson's choices attribute the source of the problem to one or both of two conditions: (1) the total flow of patients seeking service is grossly in excess of capacity; and/or (2) the flow of patients seeking service is too variable to be accommodated without at least occasional recourse to extraordinary measures. A quick glance at a large, busy municipal hospital service lends credence to such views. However, the body of experience now emerging from the study of numerous complex systems challenges these views. Ineffective policies within the system appear to unintentionally complicate rather than control the problems created by the pressures that stem from sources outside of it.

In any event, the effective manager in our example is distinguished by his ability to discover ways to keep census under control without having to resort to measures that have unduly destructive consequences of the varieties discussed above. The particular data streams he chooses to monitor and the particular action streams he attempts to influence are of essential importance, as are the frequency with which he enters the streams, how rapidly he responds to altered conditions, and how vigorously he acts. Assuming that he has chosen the correct streams, his success seems to depend upon monitoring frequently and responding rapidly to changed conditions, but softly enough to avoid overcorrection.

The manager of a service program has many other problems to face besides controlling patient flow. Some of these problems, although more difficult to conceptualize in the quantitative terms of our previous example, are similar in character. The frustration of the program planner forced to make immediate decisions based upon decade-old census information, known to be out-of-date, provides further testimony to the generality of the phenomenon we describe.

Of course, some of the understanding needed already exists and is used by practitioners dealing with very small systems. For example, the experienced psychotherapist continually evolves hunches and makes use of his intuitions and insights about the interaction between himself and his client. He tries to anticipate how the client will respond to a particular behavior of his and to understand his own responses to changing signals from the client.

However, in larger systems, data that can be helpful to the practitioner usually take so long to surface that they are generally not available to him at the moment of need. The data tell the practitioner what aspects of the situation tend to co-vary, but shed little light on causal or continuously changing relationships.

The following chapters intend to show how such apparently unrelated phenomena fit together into a coherent human service delivery system structure, and how an appreciation of that structure can improve practice.

Notes to Chapter One

1. Leslie A. White, *The Science of Culture, A Study of Man and Civilization,* New York, Farrar Straus, 1949.

Notes to Chapter One

1. . . .

Chapter 2

A General Theory

The interaction between a service program and its clients is the essence of human service delivery. The two major sectors of the system, one representing the service program, the other representing the client or client population, are linked together through services that are rendered by the program in response to demands generated by the client, as shown in figure 2-1. The circles that represent the two sectors are, in reality, highly complex and differentiated; each contains many variables that operate through time and may cause the client to demand services, and the program to respond by rendering these services in varying quantity.

The system may lay dormant for years under a wide range of circumstances in the client sector. An individual may go through a life-

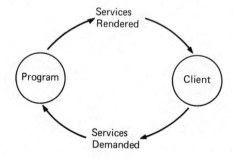

Figure 2-1. A First Approximation of the Theory

17

time without developing a need for a particular service. In these cases the program is not activated and services are not delivered. Yet, activated or not, the system remains potentially operative.

A variety of circumstances may call the system into active operation. Forces operating either within the client or impinging upon him from outside the system, such as economic emergency or serious illness, have the potential to produce a significant need for services. This need becomes expressed as some degree of demand for service. If this demand is large enough it stimulates the program to respond to the client demand by allocating resources. As a result, service is delivered that can satisfy the client's needs, and when satisfied the demand for service shuts off.

A service program is thus viewed as a negative feedback system governed by its operation to satisfy client need. The greater the client need, the greater the demand; the greater the demand, the greater the program activity, and the greater the services rendered, the less the client need. The system answers needs with services that reduce these needs, and consequently lessen the demand for services. The system goes into business in order to go out of business.

The addition of another causal link further elaborates our theory. The client not only signals his need for service but also cooperates actively in the service transaction, as shown in figure 2–2. He telephones the dentist for an appointment and later appears at the appointed time, willing to cooperate. He not only applies for service as a welfare client but also accepts and uses his welfare check on mutually agreed-upon occasions.

Thus, the rendering of service is an interactive process, requiring mutual actions on the part of program and client. Without this mutuality or contact, service does not occur. Allocation of resources by

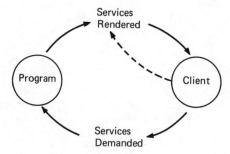

Figure 2–2. A Causal Link Is Added

the program for the client only results in service when the client cooperates. And client need for service is only met when the program perceives the need and responds to it.

Figure 2–3 makes explicit three factors that have a prominent influence on client behavior throughout a large range of human service systems. Recall that the client's need for service both signals the program into action and also involves the client in cooperating with it. As figure 2–3 illustrates, this need for service is itself dependent upon two other factors: the client's *level* of functioning and the client's *standard* of functioning. When the level of functioning is low, the client's need for service tends to increase. However, this increase in need does not necessarily trigger a visible demand for service. Demand for service increases only when the client's level of functioning is significantly at variance with his standard of functioning. Suppose for example that as a result of an illness the client's level of functioning has declined rapidly from some arbitrary value, say 100, to a new level of 80. His demand for service will increase only if at that point in time his standard of performance is sufficiently greater than 80 to materially affect the demand mechanism. The client's demand for service at any moment is based on the difference between his actual level of performance functioning and his standard of functioning.

In reality, the standard reflects not only the expectations of the individual client but also those of his family, his friends, and others in his immediate social environment. While a man in the act of assaulting his wife and disturbing his neighbors may not be violating his own present standard of functioning, he may be described as

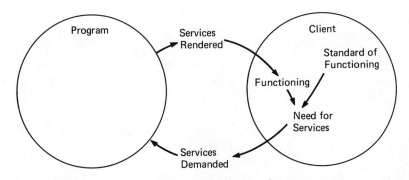

Figure 2–3. Each of the Two Major Sectors of the System Is Composed of a Number of Interacting Variables

needing service on the basis of the discrepancy between his behavior and the expectations others have of him.

A demand for services can generate several possible results depending on the manner in which the program meets the demands upon it. Consider the three scenarios shown in figure 2–4:

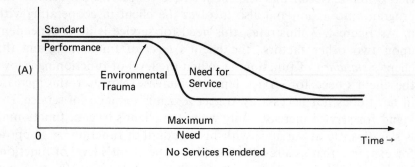

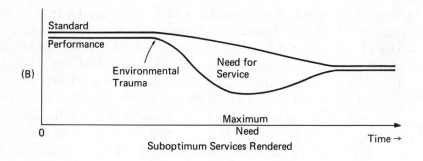

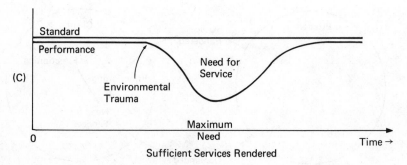

Figure 2–4.   Results Engendered by Three Levels of Program Response

Starting at time zero and extending for an initial period of time, the actual functioning and the standard are identical, generating no need for service. Then a crisis (the person loses his job, develops cancer, is injured in a car accident, becomes psychotic) causes a sharp decline in functioning. In (A) the environmental force is unrelenting and no effective services are secured. Equilibrium is restored by a gradual process of accommodation of standard of functioning to perfor-mance. After a time the discrepancy vanishes and the system is again stable. However, the person now functions at a reduced performance level. Note that the line representing performance drops precipi-tously following the environmental trauma, indicating that function is lost rapidly. The decline in standard does not fall so quickly; it lags behind and falls at a gentler rate. The size of the gap between the two lines indicates the client's need for service. Notice that this gap changes with time, small at first, then growing larger, and then shrinking again. The unfortunate outcome may be assumed to re-sult from the fact that the gap between standard and performance of this scenario is at its maximum too small and of too brief duration to generate sufficient care-seeking behavior to secure active agency response. We do not assign blame to either party in this interaction, but merely assert that the forces promoting their contact are not brought into play. Either a more demanding client or a more reactive agency might have produced more favorable results. The person in this scenario eventually adjusts to a new lowered level of stable operation.

In (B) we see that need is only great enough to elicit minimal program response. In this case, re-equilibration is achieved by a compromise between recovery of function and deterioration of standard. Of course, the most favorable outcome is the one described in (C). In this case sufficient need is generated to elicit a high level of demand upon the program. The program in turn renders sufficient services with the consequence of stable functioning at the pretrau-matic level. A variety of other outcomes is possible, depending upon the strength and duration of the environmental trauma, the time re-quired for changes in performance to be reflected in the standard, and the strength, rapidity, and duration of the program response.

Regulation of the intensity, frequency, and duration of a series of interactions between program and client is a central management objective in the delivery of any service. In various service systems the optimum intensity, frequency, and duration differ depending upon the character of client need and of program service. For example, education systems usually require intense and frequent contacts ex-

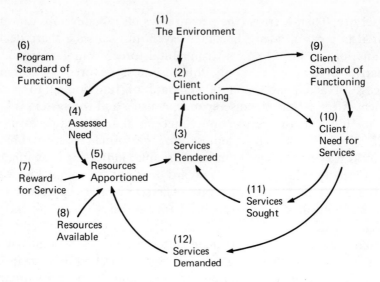

Figure 2-5. A More Complete Version of the General Theory

tending in duration for years. In contrast, immunization programs may require only a single contact in the lifetime of the client.

We now examine the character of the program's response to the client's needs. Figure 2-5 depicts a more complete picture of our analysis of a service delivery system. Look at the program or agency side of the diagram. Services rendered depend upon a pool of resources apportioned. Although the agency policy may not be explicit and the staff may not be aware of it, the apportionment of resources is controlled by four factors: assessed need (4), reward for service (7), resources available (8), and services demanded (12). Two of these, (4) and (12), are affected by the client sector. The linkages of the remaining two, (7) and (8), are not shown in the diagram and are here assumed to derive from exogenous sources. In some types of relationship between client and program—for example, fee for service medical practice—rewards must be considered within the system boundary, which is affected directly by the services rendered within the system.

Apportionment policy with respect to a given client or a population of clients is regulated in this fashion: The program compares the client's present level of functioning (2) with its standard (6), deriving an assessed client need (4). Thus, if the client is functioning at 80 and the program defines its standard of adequate functioning as 100, the client's need is 20. The resources deemed to be required to close this gap are then apportioned or reserved for the client. The actual intensity of treatment given each week or month also depends on the highly variable time period over which attempts are to be made to render the apportioned services. This time period is determined primarily by the total amount of discretionary resources resident in the agency at any moment (8), and secondarily by the size of the reward to the agency (7), and by the amount of pressure for services placed upon the agency by the client (12). If the combined strength of these forces is great, and resources are available, the program attempts to satisfy the assessed need rapidly. If these forces are weak, the rate at which attempts are made to render the needed service is extremely slow. The difference between these extremes in an actual service situation may be very great. The dentist setting up private practice in a suburban community who has only a few patients is able to satisfy their dental needs nearly instantaneously; a public dental clinic in an urban area may be subject to such heavy demands that extremely long waits for service are encountered.

Note also that in figure 2–5 structural boundaries distinguishing the program sector from the client sector have been omitted. Variables (1), (2), and (3) are at the interface between the two sectors and conceived of as integral to both. From a functional perspective, such boundaries are cumbersome and misleading. Also note that the environment has been acknowledged explicitly as a pressure that influences client functioning.

On the client side of the diagram a link has been added connecting client functioning to client standard of functioning. This expresses the premise that, in the long run, the client's standard of performance is a simple reflection of his actual past performances. In the short run a vast gap may exist between performance and standard, such as when a man is stricken with an acute illness. We have seen that precisely such a gap generates the need for service. The behavior of the system shifts from a steady state to a transient condition only when one or more of these gaps exist. The goal of this system, and of all negative feedback systems, is to eliminate the discrepancy, to re-establish a steady state. We have seen that the effectiveness of services rendered determines how close the final equilibrium comes to the original level of performance.

The greater the service, the greater the client functioning; the greater the functioning, the less the client need. Finally, the less the client need, the less the service. And, on the program side, the greater the service, the greater the functioning; the greater the functioning,

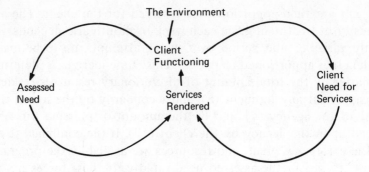

Figure 2-6. An Overview of the General Theory

the less the assessed need; the less the assessed need, the less the service. Thus, these two principal loops, as shown in figure 2-6, operate to maintain the client's functioning at an optimum level, via their control of services rendered.

The key relationships in our theory of human service are in reality identical to the economic conception of supply and demand in the operation of a market. The client sector of the two-loop system defines the general conditions of demand for human service. Supply is represented by the program sector.

Client demand derives from the client's perception of need for human service, just as consumer demand derives from needs for such goods as food, clothing, and shelter. The program represents the supply of human service. Profit opportunities play a role in motivating the private supplier to meet human service needs. The nonprofit human service agency is society's attempt to meet human needs in instances where profit opportunities are insufficient to generate a level of service that is deemed to be socially desirable.

The conception of supply and demand has proved useful in the analysis of a wide range of economic issues. Our intention is to show that our general theory illuminates some important issues in the provision of human services.

The theory can be applied to health, education, welfare, and other areas of human service at various levels of aggregation. It can treat the interactions between individual care-seekers and care-givers; illuminate the relationship between a community and the agencies that serve it; and contribute to the analysis of human service delivery at the level of national policy as well.

Chapter 3

Sense from Symptoms: The Life Cycle of an Agency

An extension of the general theory of program-client interaction provides a relatively simple explanation for a
number of apparently unrelated phenomena that are
commonly observed in human-service programs. Although most human services may be presumed to work, in the sense that benefits
result from a contact between an individual provider and an individual consumer, human service agencies are often less effective than
is desired.

The life cycle of many human service programs is illustrated in
figure 3-1. The process of growth and decay it displays might as
easily describe the behavior of a bacterial colony on a petri dish or
the rise and decline of an epidemic of influenza.

First, we see a short start-up period in which service efficacy grows
slowly as staff are hired and trained, and various operating procedures are established. This is followed by a longer period of exponential growth. The growth phase shifts gradually into a period of stable
mature functioning. The primary cause of this shift is scarcity of
resources relative to demand for service. At this point in its history,
the agency is forced either to increase its capacity or to reduce the
demand for its services. In privately financed practice, further expansion may be accomplished, as when a physician hires an additional nurse or takes in a younger physician associate. Raising his fee
or referring new patients to another physician or agency are effective
tactics for reducing the market. Other practices are employed by

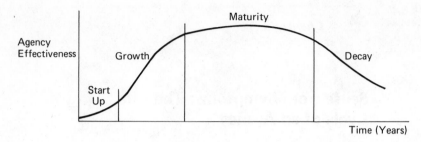

Figure 3-1. The Life Cycle of an Agency

public agencies: waiting lists, strict standards of eligibility, complicated registration procedures, unattractive waiting spaces, and inhos-
pitable behavior on the part of receptionists and other public contact
personnel have the effect of reducing the number of requests for
service. A discouraged client hesitates to return unless motivated by
greater needs, and may also discourage others from coming. Thus,
the period of stable mature functioning is characterized by lessened
attractiveness of the service agency. The villain in our example is not
the evil professional or callous administrative staff; what occurs is the
natural consequence of the underlying structure of the system. The
agency executive would argue, and correctly so, that the money
needed to maintain attractive waiting space, for example, is better
used for substantive client services. Although he is less likely to be
fully aware of it, he might claim with some justification that discouraging some clients is the only way to maintain acceptable service standards for those who are actually served.

The underlying condition that these efforts strive to control lies
in the relationship between service capacity and demand for service
shown in figure 3-2.

Consider the following scenario: A new public hospital is con-
structed to meet a gap in service, and it actually does so for a period.
Capacity grows quickly and in the process stimulates a latent demand
for service. The hospital responds by increasing its effective capacity
to the limit, but eventually capacity is overtaken by demand. This
stage is reached sooner if the hospital serves an urban population
whose alternate service resources such as private physicians are leaving the area faster than they are being replaced. It is ironic that an
ever-widening gap between demand and capacity is classically viewed
as a situation of opportunity by a profit-making program, yet this
same gap is necessarily viewed as a problem by most municipal

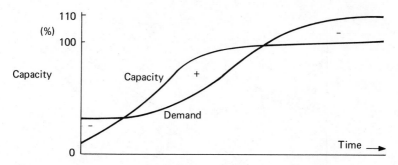

Figure 3-2. The Relationship Between Service Capacity and the Demand for Service

governments. They envision that scarce tax revenues will have to be used for capital construction. These are high costs with no return, since increased capacity is likely to stimulate even greater demand.

So far we have considered the primary effects of scarcity upon agency effectiveness. Efforts intended to correct the problem of scarcity often bring on a set of conditions that hasten the process of decay. Let us consider these secondary effects.

Reduction of the intensity of service rendered to each client

This is the natural consequence of increasing the period in which the client's need is to be satisfied. Imagine an agency whose model client is assessed to require 20 units of service. Suppose that under conditions of nonscarcity agency policy is to fill this need by providing 2 units of service per week. Given a growing shortage of resources, the agency may decide to provide service at half the rate for twice the total period. The assumption here is that the needed 20 units of service will be provided in a period of 20 weeks rather than 10. This tactic is satisfactory only if the rate at which services are rendered has a linear relationship to service efficacy, one possibility indicated in figure 3-3.

If the relationship is nonlinear then the stated policy change does not produce the expected 50 percent weekly benefit, but a benefit of say only about 15 percent. This means that in the long run, more than three times the estimated resources will be used to satisfy the original need. In real life, this situation would be approximated by a dentist who administered an anesthetic to his patient, opened a cavity, removed part of the decay, and then inserted a temporary filling, intending to continue this process in future visits. While

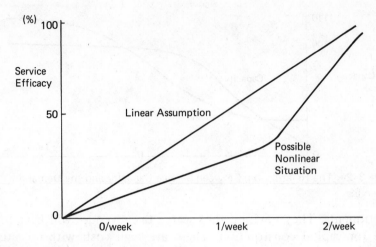

Figure 3–3.   Rate of Services Rendered

dentists do not function in this way, under some circumstances providers of other human services, such as welfare and mental health services, do. Experiments in the intensive short-term treatment of acute psychotic patients are predicated on the assumption of nonlinear benefits. Intensive and expensive short-term efforts are seen as having a long-term high cost-to-benefit ratio for acute psychiatric patients. The opposite assumption, that a little goes a long way, is made in many programs that treat chronic psychotic illness. Brief contacts and medication are the most commonly provided services for patients in this category.

The reason that scarcity does not cause the dentist to fill cavities in a grossly inefficient manner is that the performance criterion for his service is a relatively objective one. In the absence of unequivocal criteria of service efficacy, an agency may adopt this stretchout strategy with its untoward consequences of lessened efficiency.

Degradation of agency standard

In our general theory the mechanism postulated to explain the program's contribution to program-client contact differs in an essential respect from the client's mechanism. The relevant portion of that diagram is reproduced in figure 3–4.

The program's standard of client functioning, that is, the level of functioning at which the agency believes the client to require no service, is represented in figure 3–4 as fixed. Program standard is here

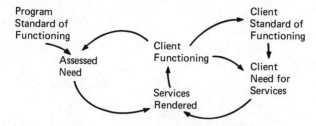

Figure 3-4. Program vs. Client Standard-Setting Mechanisms

assumed to influence system behavior, but to be unaffected itself by the rest of the system. Thus, this standard represents the agency's goal, an implicit statement that the job is to provide service to a client until he functions at some fixed level, X. The particular value assigned to X is assumed to derive from traditional norms currently supported by the several service professions, and ultimately is assumed to be based upon the sciences that contribute knowledge to professional practice.

On the other hand, the client's standard is recognized as changing gradually in the direction of his actual functioning. He withdraws from contact, either because his impaired condition is reversed or because his standard is adjusted to the worsened condition.

Under conditions of prolonged scarcity a similar dynamic adjustment process may develop within the program. If full achievement of service goals becomes the exception rather than the rule, the program standard eventually drops to reflect the actual lower achievement. The agency, for a period, will then more nearly approach its new more "realistic" goal. But if pressure for service continues, the standard will be readjusted again toward a new more realistic (i.e. lowered) goal, and so on in continuous fashion. The system structure that produces this insidious process is shown in figure 3-5.

The standard that actually governs behavior in a declining agency is a local one that derives from that agency's past performance in attempting to maintain the ideal self-regulated standard of its professionals in the face of pressure for service. To the extent that the agency is able to minimize the discrepancy between its contribution to client functioning and the contribution prescribed by the fixed professional standard (shown as "achievement gap"), it is able to maintain service standards. As the gap grows, the agency standard degrades.

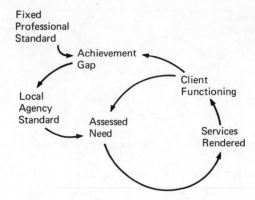

Figure 3-5. The Program Adopts More "Realistic" Goals

Decline of morale and its effect on service efficiency

Another positive feedback loop operates to the detriment of agency performance, as shown in figure 3-6.

High professional standards do not vanish as the practices of an agency degrade. To the extent that staff maintain their identification with the traditions of their profession, their morale is affected adversely. Then as morale declines, workers may underproduce and service efficacy may be reduced. Furthermore, the most productive workers tend to leave the agency for jobs that permit them to maintain high standards. They are replaced by more complacent individuals, who may be less effective service providers.

Client discouragement and underutilization of resources apportioned to him; occurrence of dropout or other forms of waste

Another system substructure must be described to explain this phenomenon. In the formulation shown in figure 3-7, two new variables are displayed as having a moderating influence upon the client's care-seeking behavior. The influence of habit is straightforward. A person who is not presently in a care-receiving relationship is unlikely to enter one unless his need for care is great. On the other hand, a person in such a relationship will tend to remain in it even after it has ceased to benefit him.

What benefit the client expects to derive from agency contact also affects the client's care-seeking behavior. Benefit expected varies on

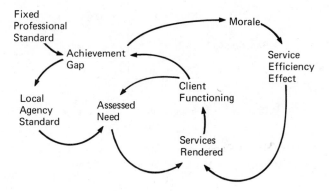

Figure 3-6. Falling Morale Contributes to Agency Decline

the basis of past experience with the agency; or before there has been a history of contact, benefit expected is based upon what one has heard about the agency or other anecdotal sources. Expectations are high if in the past the client has experienced improvement in functioning at times when there is a high level of contact with the agency. Expectations are low if the client has experienced declining function during episodes of contact. These resultants are indicated in figure 3-8. Care-seeking behavior is seen as regulated principally by the client's need for service, significantly modified by habit and expected benefit.

If the rate of services proferred by the agency is sufficiently low, as it may be under conditions of scarcity, drop-out or waste of resources results as a consequence of client discouragement. Either or both of the moderating variables may produce this phenomenon. If the client's present habit is not to seek service and if the quantity of services reduced by scarcity offered to him is too small, he will not

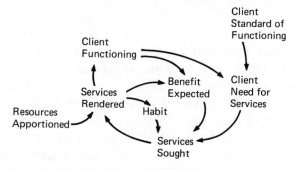

Figure 3-7. Client Experience Affects His Behavior

	High Contact	Low Contact
Functioning Improves	High Expectations	Moderate Expectations
Functioning Declines	Low Expectations	Moderate Expectations

Figure 3-8. The Client's Expectations Are Affected by the Degree of Contact Coincident with Variations in the Level of His Functioning

sustain his efforts long enough for a relationship to develop between him and the agency. For example, having to wait several weeks for an appointment may be sufficient to terminate all further efforts to establish contact. The mechanism of expected benefits functions in a similar way. If too low a quantity of service is offered to him, the client will not have the opportunity to build up a high enough set of expectations to sustain his efforts once his service need begins to be satisfied. In those instances where the client begins to be served while his functioning is still declining, he may remove himself from contact in the belief that the services rendered are making his condition worse.

In the extreme case discouragement produces client drop-out, which may be said to exist whenever a significant quantity of resources are apportioned to the client but no services are being rendered. A situation of waste exists when significantly less service is rendered than is apportioned. In addition to the direct consequences of waste, perception of waste within the agency may create additional pressures that further reduce morale and agency standard. Although these linkages are not shown, they may be readily inferred by the reader.

Environmental circumstances that produce conflict between an agency and its clients; short-run further degradation of system functioning

In order to understand this process of system decay, it is necessary to think of the client sector not as a person, but as an aggregate of many individuals, who, when organized effectively, can exert counterpressure upon the agency for more and better service. We may assume that the system substructures that generate political pressure are always present, but only under special circumstances are they triggered into actions as significant as the recurring conflicts between consumers and providers in the areas of health, welfare, and correction. The goals of political pressure are identified in figure 3–9. Several effects described earlier have been omitted for the sake of simplicity but may be assumed to remain in operation.

The desired effects of consumer political action are shown with dotted lines. Demand for service is converted into organized political pressure with three aims: (1) to increase the investment of community resources in the agency (e.g., through legislative lobbying); (2) to raise the agency's standard or service goal (e.g. by demonstrating that certain prescribed resources such as telephones are being withheld); and (3) to improve client performance directly. As clients succeed in affecting their economic, social, and political life, their competence or level of functioning consequently improves.

The causal structure that produces effective political pressure is approximated in figure 3–10.

Demand for services is translated into political pressure only if significant and effective effort goes into organizing activities. The amount of such efforts is determined largely by environmental influences outside of the system boundary that determine political climate. However, the state of the system is shown to influence the effectiveness of organizing effort. The total impact of client organizing effort in translating client demand for service into political pressure is summarized in figure 3–11.

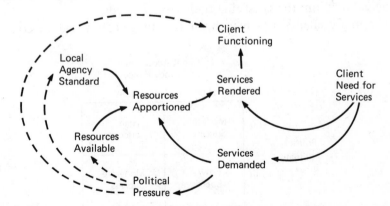

Figure 3–9. Consumer Pressure Aims at Increasing Resources, Raising Agency Standards, and Increasing the Competence and Control of the Client Population

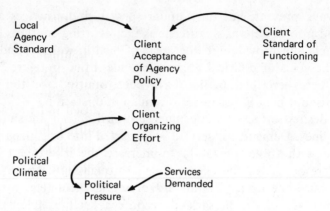

Figure 3-10. The Causes of Political Pressure

The source of client acceptance of agency policy remains to be explained: As agency standard of client functioning declines, through the mechanisms described earlier, a gap eventually develops and widens between it and the typical standard that the client population sets for itself. The greater the gap, the less the client acceptance of agency policy.

The real situation is of course more complicated. It may be argued that the client standard, which has been described as variable rather than fixed, also deteriorates over time, perhaps quickly enough to prevent a gap from developing between it and the agency standard. However, we are considering the total client population. The argument is valid for those clients who continue to use the agency as the principal medium for satisfying their service needs.

The many clients who have been discouraged from agency contact

		Client Acceptance of Agency Policy	
		High	Low
Political Climate	Hot	Moderate Success	High Success
	Cold	Low Success	Moderate Success

Figure 3-11. The Success of Efforts to Organize Clients is a Function of the Political Climate or of Client Acceptance of Agency Policy

by the processes described earlier are subject to a great many influences operating outside of the system boundary. Their standards may have remained high as a result of finding other more effective means of meeting their needs. Another significant factor not represented here is when in the agency's life cycle a client has his contacts with the agency. The irregular user may get what he needs during the growth phase and return years later expecting more of the same, only to be shocked by what he is offered. A very similar phenomenon may distinguish the attitudes of the younger generation of clients who are appalled by agency practices from the attitudes of their parents who have accommodated to them.

It is also plausible to assume a linkage between organizing efforts and client standard such that a small quantity of such effort increases the deteriorated client standard significantly. This latter may be construed as a partial account of the process of political radicalization. Further exploration of this issue would lead inevitably to a discussion of a much larger topic which deserves to be treated on its own. The essential point is that in a client population mechanisms exist to account for the development of a significant gap between client and local agency standards during the agency's phase of decline.

Whether the long-term objectives of political strategies aimed at improving system performance will work remains to be seen. Given the obvious difficulty of improving the performance of the declining agency, it would be difficult to deny that they deserve a try. The short-term effects of these efforts, however, appear necessarily to further degrade system performance. Agency resources in the form of time and effort are inevitably diverted from client service into activities that protect the agency from its attackers. Even the pressures exerted by clients toward funding sources, when successful in increasing the flow of funds into the agency, are unlikely to benefit clients immediately. Staff salaries are likely to be increased first until they pass some threshold before service improves. During a phase of decline, poor agency performance is often compensated by poor salaries and working conditions. As the composition of its work-force shifts from a predominantly "professional" one to one that accepts the local variable standard of client functioning, it becomes unable to demand a professional level of compensation. Since they are objectively undercompensated and since there is client pressure for even higher performance from them, the workers have a

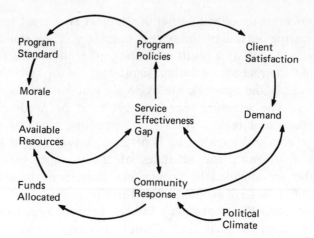

Figure 3-12. Overall Structure Underlying an Agency Life Cycle

natural claim on additional funds allocated to the agency. Staff are closer to the source of funds than clients, and as a homogeneous natural interest group more readily organized to pressure for greater compensation. Of course, in the long run, higher compensation for staff will tend to benefit clients. Higher, more competitive wages will bring in and hold new workers whose standards may be dominated by professional ideology, eventually boosting the local agency standards.

Client groups are aware of this, and in some instances apparent pressure for better service is actually pressure for jobs and/or control of agency funds. Since the short-term effect is greater compensation for staff, not better service for clients, conflict develops and competitive interest groups vie for a share of the added wealth.

Summary

As the gap grows between demand for service and resources available, the rate of rendering service is reduced, which beyond some value reduces service efficiency. As service efficiency declines the agency inevitably adjusts its standard of performance downward to a more realistic value. This affects morale, and increases turnover of employees, resulting in a further decline in service efficiency. Waste increases due to client discouragement. Through these mechanisms, demand for service is kept under control; costs increase, but the value of the services rendered continues to decline.

Demand for services is controlled not by rendering the needed services, but through the secondary mechanisms described. Given a hot political climate, unmet service needs can become the driving force behind efforts to reorganize the service delivery system structure. The short-term effects are chaotic and not uniformly productive of better services; the long-term effects are not known.

The general theory augmented by the system substructures described in this chapter are sufficient to account for the growth and decline of a "typical" service-rendering agency. The structure may be summarized very roughly as indicated by figure 3-12.

Part II

Applications

Chapter 4

The Causes of Patient Drop-out from
Mental Health Services

In this chapter we apply the general theory to the phenomenon of drop-out from treatment in a comprehensive mental health facility. Our causal account or model of the
drop-out phenomenon describes the interaction of key factors or
variables within and between "the program", that is, any staff mem-
ber(s) in any service component of a facility, and "the client", that
is, the patient. The vehicle for their interaction is, of course, the
psychiatric service or "treatment" rendered to the patient by the
staff. The operational definition of a "drop-out" that underlies this
analysis is the patient who ceases to make efforts to get care while
the staff still judges him to be in need of it and, in fact, is still making treatment sources available to him. The type of patient used in
this example is a typical chronically ill psychiatric patient, someone
who has periodic exacerbations of his illness and usually has residual
disabilities between such episodes. As will be apparent, however, the
model also has considerable applicability to other types of patients.

The diagram of this structure, shown in figure 4–1, parallels very
closely that of the general theory presented in figure 2–5 (p. 22). A
few of the names of variables have been changed to terms more common in psychiatric practice; for example, the "client" is here called
the "patient". In addition, two variables in the Patient Sector (Habit
and Benefit Expected) which were introduced only as a system substructure to the general theory (figure 3–7, p. 31) have been retained
in the drop-out model as critical elements. Within the Program Sector

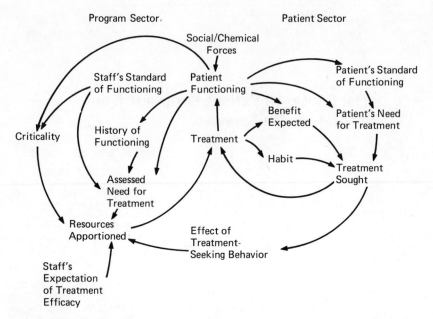

Figure 4–1. The Causal Structure of Treatment Drop-out

the several differences from the general theory reflect the differences in the problems under study. Thus, two variables (Reward for Service and Resources Available) were included in the general theory as relevant to the problem of agency effectiveness and scarcity of resources, but have been eliminated from the treatment drop-out model, inasmuch as the "scarcity" factor is not central to this analysis. Conversely, several variables have been added to the Program Sector that relate specifically to the functioning of staff in a mental health facility in their interaction with patients—"History of Patient Functioning", "Criticality", and "Staff Expectation of Treatment Efficacy"—all of which influence professional assessment of the client's need for help when the problem is one of mental illness. The import of each of these variables will be clarified in the discussion below.

The model is dominated by two major causal feedback loops. On the patient side, a decline in his functioning produces efforts to secure treatment that, in proper intensity, restores functioning to his pre-episodic level. In the program sector, the staff perceives the drop in the patient's functioning, and allocates resources so as to produce treatment in the amount needed to effect the restoration.

Return to the pre-episodic level acts to "shut off" the system by eliminating the need for treatment until such time as another drop in the patient's functioning of sufficient magnitude sets the system into motion once again.

Even this skeletal view of the model depicts the dropout as a dynamic rather than a haphazard occurrence. As did the general theory of program-client interaction, it makes very clear that the rendering of treatment depends not only on the staff's assessment of the patient's need for treatment and the allocation of resources for this purpose, but also on the patient's collaboration, i.e. his willingness to seek or receive service.

To understand the system behavior that generates the type of drop-out under study, we shall first examine its separate components and the ways in which they interact to produce this particular phenomenon.

PATIENT SECTOR

Patient Functioning has been chosen as the expression of the mental health of a chronically ill psychiatric patient in preference to an intrapsychic or psychosocial formulation. As such, this variable refers to the individual's ability to function independently, for example, socially and vocationally, in accordance with general norms for behavior. The model postulates that this level of functioning is influenced by two factors, treatment and social and/or chemical forces (figure 4–2).

The model assumes that treatment always has a positive effect on the patient's functioning, and furthermore that the greater the amount of the treatment given, the greater is the resulting improvement in the patient. Little consensus exists in the literature on the

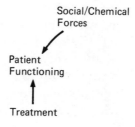

Figure 4–2.

nature of the link between amount of treatment and amount of patient improvement. On a simply mechanical level, "amount" of treatment may be defined in terms of the overall duration of the therapeutic relationship, the number of contacts with staff, the total time spent in such contacts, and the frequency of contacts between patient and therapist. Utilizing the more common "number of sessions" criterion for amount of therapy,[1] investigators report findings that range from direct positive relationships between amount of treatment and outcome[2] to no association at all[3]. Errera et al.[4], for example, in 1967 found no significant difference in results of treatment between short- (6 to 10 visits) and long-term (more than 21 visits) psychotherapy clinic patients. Similarly, in a study of brief and extended casework, Reid and Shyne[5] reported, contrary to their expectations, that both staff and clients assessed the planned short-term service as more immediately helpful than continued service, and that no difference was found between the two groups of clients in retention of treatment gains at follow-up.

Even those studies that find a direct positive relationship between treatment and outcome, however, cannot speak to the question of the incremental value of ever increasing additional amounts of treatment. Do X number more therapeutic hours beyond some given point produce proportionally more benefit to the patient? If not, then at what point does the ratio begin to level off, or perhaps diminish?

The question is hardly new or academic: it is raised in practice by the proponents of brief therapy, and in research by investigators who report neither a simple positive nor a negative association between amount of treatment and outcome, but rather a curvilinear one. The curvilinear finding describes a relationship in which incremental patient improvement results from higher doses of treatment up to a level beyond which more treatment is no longer helpful and may hinder the patient.[6]

Cartwright[7] makes an interesting observation about the relationship between amount of treatment and outcome. He detected a "failure zone" in the outcome curve, i.e. improvement accompanies increase in amount of treatment up to a certain point (in his study, 12 interviews), then drops off and does not resume until after the twenty-first interview. He suggests that this occurs because short-term clients are aided quickly and leave the therapeutic process early, thus accounting for the initial positive association between

Positive Linear Relationship

Figure 4-3.

amount of treatment and improvement, whereas the patient with long-term personality problems must work out considerable resistance before resuming improvement from his therapy.

Examples of possible relationships between generic treatment "units" and functional improvement are expressed graphically in figures 4-3 through 4-6. A computer model makes possible experimentation with each of these assumptions about the impact of treatment on outcome, and makes possible examination of how a different assumption produces different behavior in both parties to the therapeutic relationship. Although it is unlikely that a simple positive linear relationship exists between treatment and outcome (figure 4-3), this "shape" was selected for the initial model simulations because of its simplicity. Experiments were then run using two of the curvilinear assumptions (figures 4-4 and 4-6), both of which were judged by the senior clinicians in the facility in which the actual study was conducted as representing the real world relationship between treatment and patient improvement.

Social and Chemical Forces, as well as treatment, affect the patient's level of functioning. They may operate either to improve or to impair his performance at any given point. Although they may be central to the course of the patient's illness, they may be conceptualized as aspects of the general theory's "Environment" which are

Curvilinear Relationships

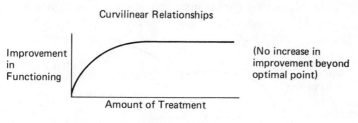

Figure 4-4.

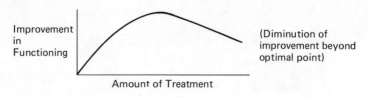

Figure 4–5.

particularly relevant to mental illness but which reside outside of any system structure that our present state of mental health knowledge permits us to construct.

This position is consistent with that taken by Meltzoff and Kornreich in their recent review, *Research in Psychotherapy:*

> Regardless of therapeutic intervention, the patient is a dynamic living organism functioning in and interacting with a fluid environment: a new job, a sympathetic teacher, a new love gained, an old family problem resolved.... Invariance of environmental milieu is often erroneously assumed.... Most theories of psychotherapy provide for the attempt to modify personality and behavior by altering the patient's experience (within the psychotherapeutic situation). The therapist believes that he is doing this systematically, and further believes that response to these alterations will be generalized.... However, the patient's experiences beyond the consultation room are fortuitous.[8]

This model defines these environmental factors as exogenous, that is, as not directly affected by other components in this particular program-patient system. The model acknowledges both but its operation depends on neither.

Patient's Standard of Functioning is the equivalent of the patient's expectations for his own level of functioning, that is, his present estimate of his maximum capacity to perform in the roles appropriate to his life situation. This estimate is based upon a long-term averaging of his actual functioning, as is shown in figure 4–7. Small

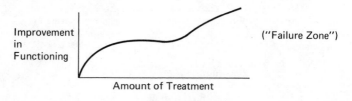

Figure 4–6.

Figure 4-7.

variations in functioning are reflected to a small degree in a patient's standard, but large and sustained changes in his performance over time have a substantial effect on his expectations for himself and on the standard of functioning to which he aspires. Thus, if improvement does not occur after a decline in performance, the standard eventually declines to accommodate the new lower level of functioning. In our later discussion of system behavior the term "eventually" will take on considerable significance, both as a source of variation among different kinds of patients and as a potential avenue for influencing their treatment behavior.

The model's variable of "standard of functioning" is closely related to the concept in psychology of "level of aspiration", which "denotes the goals or standards that an individual sets for himself".[9]

> The *level of aspiration* usually represents a compromise between the subject's evaluation of his ability with respect to the difficulty of the task and his desire to achieve a high level of performance, that is, between a judgment and a goal.
>
> *As a judgment,* the level of aspiration ordinarily tends to remain close to the actual level of performance. This tendency probably arises from the almost universally present need to keep in touch with reality.... Insofar as the level of aspiration is a judgment, it is largely determined by perceptual "anchoring points," of which the most influential is the subject's own past performance.
>
> *As a goal,* the level of aspiration tends to remain well above the level of performance in that it expresses the wishes to do well and to improve....
>
> The level of aspiration may be used to *improve performance* by being placed far enough above the actual performance to act as an incentive.... or to help *protect the ego from the effects of failure* by being kept resolutely high despite poor performance.... public refusal to admit that the failures are significant.... On the other hand, if the subject experiences a performance below his estimate as a severe threat to his self-esteem, he may keep his level of aspiration low to prevent such a situation from arising ... a method of avoiding tension or a way of avoiding the appearance of failure. Furthermore, successes and failures may not only influence the behavior of the level of aspiration in any one of its meanings, but may cause it to change from one meaning to another.[10]

In the three decades since Jerome Frank wrote this statement, a continuing accumulation of evidence indicates that past experience or performance determines the succeeding standard, or aspiration level.[11] Also, increasing attention has been given to such issues as how the standard is affected differentially by experiences of success and failure, and how individuals vary in the rigidity with which a given goal is adhered to in the face of actual performance.[12] This latter question will be easily recognized as the one already alluded to as having particular importance for our model, that is, how quickly after a decline in performance does the patient's standard decline to reflect the change?[13]

The interaction between performance and standard is particularly relevant to understanding the dynamics of chronicity in psychiatric patients in which the cycle of impaired functioning and declining expectations is especially evident.

Patient's Need for Treatment refers to the discomfort experienced by an individual and others in his environment when a discrepancy exists between his actual level of performance and the expectations (or standards) concerning how he should be functioning in his life roles. When these two are equal, no discomfort is felt and no need for treatment is perceived. When, however, actual performance falls below the standard, a need arises. Take, for example, a housewife (and her family) whose standard, based upon past experience, is high enough to warrant the belief that she can manage the household and care for her children. Should her present performance fall below this standard, some measure of discomfort or need for corrective intervention will develop.

This formulation, indicated in figure 4-8, is consonant with the view of motivation as a product of "discrepancy". Peak finds that the persistence and intensity of behavior appear to arise "when disparity exists between two or more psychological events or states which are associated and therefore mutually activating . . . seen at once as disparate and similar in some way. It is essential that the

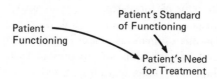

Figure 4-8.

events or processes involved must be seen as related or belonging to the same framework if the discrepancy between them is to produce a motive structure as, for example, when disparity occurs between perceptions and attitudes about the self, motivation is likely to be set up."[14]

The literature addressed specifically to the motivation of patients for treatment generally agrees that psychological distress is a necessary condition for motivation. Whether psychological distress is in itself a sufficient condition for motivation of treatment is, however, more controversial. Ripple, for example, is cited[15] as suggesting that "one must attend both to the impelling forces of psychological discomfort and the seducing qualities of hope; she speaks of the 'push of discomfort' and the 'pull of hope'." This latter position parallels that of the model, in which the "push of discomfort" is represented by the discrepancy between the patient's standard of functioning and his actual level of performance, and the "pull of hope" by the benefit he expects to reap from treatment.

Benefit Expected refers to an explicit or implicit forecast by the patient of the change in his level of functioning that he expects to experience if he continues to accept treatment from the program. The patient's initial set of anticipations about the value of treatment is influenced, once in treatment, by a continuing appraisal of the impact on his level of performance of the treatment received thus far (figure 4-9). Although changes in functioning during treatment may originate in social and chemical forces outside the treatment relationship (see figure 4-2), it appears doubtful that the patient can precisely attribute them to the appropriate source. The model assumes, therefore, that the patient attributes the changes—regardless of their actual causes—to the treatment process in proportion to its present intensity. For example, if his performance is improving while treatment intensity is high, more of the improvement is attributed to treatment than if treatment intensity was low at that time. The result of such attribution is an increase in the Benefit Expected by the patient from continued treatment. Conversely, should the patient

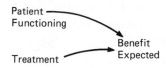

Figure 4-9.

experience a decline in performance coincident with a period of intense treatment, he associates that decline with the treatment process and reduces his expectations of benefit from further treatment.

The importance to the course of psychotherapy of patient expectations has been noted, frequently by both practitioners and students of the field, but only rarely has the issue been treated with the kind of clarity and explicitness helpful in the construction of a mathematical model. An exceptional attempt to systematize thinking in this area was contributed by Goldstein, who made a very useful distinction between "prognostic" and "participant role" expectancies.

A prognostic expectancy is an outcome that is looked for with the belief, faith, confidence, or conviction of being found. It is essentially a prediction anchored in belief that may or may not be warranted. Therapeutic expectancy has an object, a direction, an instrumentality, and a temporal schema. The object is symptom relief, conflict resolution, or attainment of some positive state, or the expectations can be of failure. Its instrumentality is that which brings about the anticipated goal. It is the person or processes in whom the belief or faith is placed. It may be the patient himself, the therapist, the therapeutic process, or external forces alone or in combination. . . . Another characteristic of expectancies is their time dimension, how long it should take to achieve the object.[16]

This formulation corresponds closely to the model variable, "Benefit Expected", which excludes those patient expectations (or "Participant Role Expectancies") specifically about the kind of treatment he will receive (e.g. medication, advice, intercession with others), or about how he and the therapist will interact to solve his problem. "Benefit Expected" is concerned only with the patient's forecast, whether correct or incorrect, as to how helpful the process will be in closing the gap he perceives between his present functioning and the standard of functioning that he holds for himself.

The patient approaches a therapeutic program with an initial set of beliefs about the benefits he may expect to reap from it. Some of these beliefs originate in the ideology and customs of his social group and others from his own personal contacts with helping agencies. For example, is a facility regarded by his social network as helpful for certain kinds of problems, or is it viewed with suspicion and as a last resort? Regarding prior experience, Ludwig and Gibson,[17] addressing themselves to the seeking of medical care in general, discovered that recent contacts by patients with welfare agencies generated a negative orientation to helping systems as a whole (in our terms, a low or negative initial level of "Benefit Expected"), and thereby increased reluctance to seek medical care when needed. Similarly, a study of Veterans Administration psychiatric patients by Dengrove and Kutash revealed that "There is often a carryover from the armed services to the V.A. The slightest repetition of the veteran's service experiences enhances his hostility, substantiates his prejudices and sends him out of the clinic."[18] Once he is in treatment, however, according to the model, the patient's expectations of benefit change to reflect his assessment of how helpful treatment is for him, whether or not this assessment is an accurate perception of the objective facts. No empirical studies have been made of the change in expectations over the long course of therapy,[19] but an application of level of aspiration data suggests that actual experience is a potent modifier of expectations through time.

In the model, the importance of "Benefit Expected" lies in its contribution to the patient's motivation to seek treatment. The greater the benefit he anticipates from it, the more likely he is to participate in a therapeutic program. Literature and research relevant to this relationship between "Benefit Expected" and continuation in treatment is sparse. Studies of patient expectations, which use continuation in treatment as outcome, often focus on "participant-role expectancies" rather than on "prognostic expectancies". In other words, they explore the patient's initial understanding of the particulars of treatment, and of how he and the therapist interact, and usually demonstrate that lack of complementarity between patient and therapist expectations is associated with premature termination of treatment.[20]

Research on "prognostic expectancy", on the other hand, seems most often to be concerned with its implications for final therapeutic outcome. Fewer studies address themselves to the relationship between "prognostic expectancy" and continuation in treatment, specifically. Although Ripple and Alexander[21] found that clients with high hope continued treatment more than those with low hope, Heine and Trossman[22] reported no relationship between the initial degree of the patient's conviction that treatment would be helpful and his continuance in treatment. This latter finding seems to contradict accumulated academic[23] as well as folk wisdom about the significance of hope in human endeavor. Furthermore, "hope" is not a static quality. Our model allows for the fact that the level of conviction that treatment will help is subject to continual modification by

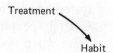

Figure 4–10.

the patient's ongoing experience in treatment. Thus, if a patient with an initially high level of conviction about the value of treatment finds his first contacts less beneficial than he expected, his level of conviction will diminish and he may indeed drop out of treatment. Conversely, a patient with an initially low level of hope may find his first therapeutic contacts more beneficial than he had anticipated, may increase his expectations of being helped by treatment, and may be encouraged to continue.

Habit refers to an "inertial" effect that asserts simply that a person with little or no recent treatment experience is not likely to seek it out in the absence of very pressing need, while a person presently involved in treatment is likely to continue in that relationship even after he has ceased to derive benefit from it. This momentum factor is a function solely of the prevailing rate of treatment, illustrated in figure 4–10.

Furthermore, "habit" is conceptualized here as a threshold-type phenomenon, that is, resistance is overcome (or "habit" is established) at a level of engagement in the treatment process. More intensive participation beyond that level is not seen to make the habit correspondingly more potent. The relationship between the rate of treatment and the development of the treatment-habit may be visualized as in figure 4–11.

The notion of a "breakthrough" in the patient's treatment behavior clearly evokes analytic analogues of working through resistances to therapy and developing necessary transference in the therapeutic relationship. Although these processes are undoubtedly involved, the dynamic postulated here is more grounded in learning theory than in psychoanalytic formulation: turning to a mental

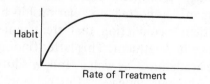

Figure 4–11.

health resource for help with a perceived problem may be viewed as a type of behavior that must first be learned, and then may tend to become perseverative.

The habit of seeking help from a particular program may have to be learned de novo within the context of that program, or may derive at least in part from other experiences. Thus, for example, Frank et al.[24] reported in 1957 that patients were more likely to remain in treatment if they had at least 6 months of previous psychotherapy. Similarly, Lipman and coworkers, in a study of "Neurotics Who Fail to Take Their Drugs",[25] found that patients who deviated from the drug program were less likely to have had previous treatment experience with psychotropic medication.

But the individual's reluctance or readiness to form a treatment-habit is influenced not only by his particular experiences as a client or patient, but also by the experiences of his social network. Thus, in his discussion of illness behavior, Mechanic draws specific attention to "the person's learned behaviors for dealing with symptoms", and cites a study of 614 students in which Jews and Episcopalians showed a significantly higher inclination to use medical facilities than did Christian Scientists or Catholics.[26] In relation to psychotherapy specifically, Charles Kadushin has made a persuasive case for the relationship between the patterns common to one's "social circle" and the likelihood of turning to psychotherapy for help.[27]

Let us return now to our model of the treatment-behavior of a patient in a mental health facility. The model postulates that a patient is subject initially to certain constraints, produced by unfamiliarity with a particular program, which operate to inhibit his turning to that program for help. Achievement of a certain level of contact, however, serves not only to eliminate this constraint, but to establish a behavior "set" whereby participation in the program becomes a kind of habit.

The literature on drop-out from psychotherapy always speaks to this issue, even if not explicitly, when it raises the question of when in the treatment process a patient really becomes a patient—inasmuch as the concept of "drop-out" is meaningless without a definition of patienthood. The empirical research in this area most commonly employs a given amount of contact as the criterion of patient status. Some studies define as a patient anyone who has been accepted for treatment, whether or not they have begun it.[28] Most, however, classify as patients only those who have actually been seen in treatment, and defines drop-outs as those who discontinue therapy. Although the cut-off points employed vary from one to twelve visits, all of these latter studies obviously assume—as does our model—that some minimum degree of contact must occur before a person is really engaged in the therapeutic process as a patient. In their research on patient discontinuation as it relates to the various stages of the treatment process, Phillips et al. differentiated five phases of treatment: application for help; beginning of evaluation; completion of evaluation; recommendation of therapy; and beginning of therapy.[29] His finding of a drop-out rate of 40 percent during stages 2 to 4, compared with one of 10 to 20 percent in stage 5 supports the need to distinguish between those who have reached a given level of engagement in therapy and those have not not. Those who discontinue treatment before that point may be seen as never having developed the necessary "habit", and their dropping out raises different issues. In his article "Predicting Client Discontinuance at Intake",[30] Krause makes precisely this point: "The longer a client is in treatment before he decides to discontinue, the more complex is likely to be the cause of his action."

A second assumption made in the model about the habit factor is that, once established, its force does not increase correspondingly with an increase in the intensity of treatment. The habit factor in a patient seen ten times a week, for example, is not necessarily stronger than that in a patient seen five times a week in treatment. This assumption coincides with what we observe in practice, where an intuitive belief seems to exist that the optimum intensity of patient contact falls somewhere in the range of one to five contacts per week. Therapists operate as if intensity of contact beyond this level does not generate sufficient incremental benefits to justify it. It is difficult to know, of course, whether this judgment is based on belief about limits on how fast "healing" can take place, or on assumptions about what is needed by way of contact to solidify and maintain the therapeutic relationship, or perhaps on both. The result, however, is behavior that supports our assumption that a saturation effect becomes operative at a certain level of contact—beyond which there is no significant increase in the patient's propensity to continue in treatment.

Treatment Sought refers to all efforts exerted by the patient, or by others acting on his behalf, with the aim of obtaining professional help. These efforts include both the behavior involved in the initial search for help and in the ongoing cooperation with staff in order to enable the appropriate rate of treatment to be given. The magnitude of these efforts is a product of the interaction of three variables already discussed: the need for help, the estimate of the value of treatment, and the habit of contact with the program (figure 4-12).

Each of the three variables contributing to the patient's treatment-seeking behavior has been noted by others. They closely parallel three tenets of traditional learning theory: (1) habit operates according to the principles of association or contiguity; (2) benefit expected represents a cognitive-economic view; and (3) patient's need for treatment is formulated as a drive-reduction reinforcement mechanism. Frank et al., in their excellent study "Why Patients Leave Psychotherapy", isolate six personal attributes of patients and three aspects of the treatment situation that they regard as important.[31] Their list for remaining in treatment includes the "degree of the patient's expressed distress" (our variable "Patient's Need for Treatment"), experience with psychotherapy (our variable "Habit"), and a positive view of psychotherapy (our variable "Benefit Expected"). They also address themselves to the patient's personal quality of perserverance, which is closely related to our earlier discussion of the patient's ability to maintain his "Standard of Functioning" in the face of an impairment in his actual performance.

The present authors build on the contributions and insights of Frank and others in at least two ways: first, by helping to identify the relative importance of each factor that influences treatment-seeking behavior; and second, by showing how the factors interact to produce the phenomenon of interest. As Bernice Eiduson noted in her sensitive article, "Retreat from Help": "Whether or not a patient continues seems to be the function of a number of conditions taken

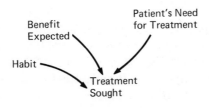

Figure 4-12.

together. As yet, no study shows how a series or group of factors combine to move a patient toward dropout or continuance."[32]

PROGRAM SECTOR

Parallel to the patient's personal standard of functioning, staff behavior in a treatment program is also influenced by standards of patient functioning. The model reveals, in fact, that the staff is subject to not one, but two standards—one more universalistic in its application ("Staff Standard of Functioning"), the other specific to each particular patient ("History of Functioning").

Staff Standard of Functioning, the first of these standards, refers to the level of functioning that the staff believes, based on its training and experience, is needed by any patient to maintain a minimal community adjustment. This standard is a general one and has its origin in sources apart from the individual patient. It tends to be highly stable for any single professional group, and any change occurs only over a very long period of time, and not as a consequence of any one particular staff-patient interaction.

A staff standard of functioning may be said to be operative whenever a "diagnosis" is being made, in the sense that the various aspects of a patient's condition are being measured against some generally held criteria of "normalcy" or "health". This standard originates outside the model and operates within the treatment process as one of the determinants of how the staff assesses the patient's need for treatment. By defining a "floor" under which patient functioning should not be allowed to fall, it triggers another mechanism called "criticality".

Criticality, diagrammed in figure 4–13, refers to the discrepancy between the patient's actual performance at a given time and the staff standard of functioning, the fixed estimate of the level of performance required for a person to maintain a stable community adjustment.

Thus, for example, if a patient threatens harm to himself or others, his behavior would produce a criticality factor that would impel staff to increase greatly the amount of treatment they judge to be needed. This extra impetus to intense treatment is eliminated quickly when the patient's performance returns to a level commensurate with the staff's standard of functioning.

Figure 4-13.

The "criticality factor" may be viewed as the staff's response to what is defined as a psychiatric crisis or emergency.

> Crisis is manifested in many ways, most often via anger accompanied by varying degrees of aggressive behavior, severe anxiety accompanied by weeping, running, temporary states of confusion, and suicide attempts. Emergencies occur when an individual is faced with a situation beyond his particular adaptive capacity at a particular time. . . . In general, any situation or condition that is stressful may precipitate an emergency state in patients or in normal persons who are already bearing the maximum anxiety that they can effectively handle.[33]

Confronted with a patient in such a state, the staff is motivated by the "criticality factor" to intensify the planned intervention.

History of Functioning is the basis for the second standard of performance, alluded to earlier, against which the staff measures the patient's current status. Unlike the first fixed and general standard, however, this one is specific to the particular patient, and originates in a knowledge of the course of his functioning over a long period of time. "In evaluating . . . deviations, the physician . . . must also remember that in some respects everyone is unique. For these aspects, the patient himself furnishes the standard of reference."[34]

As a professional group, staff has access to the "history" of the patient's illness. On the basis of this long-term trend, it formulates a clinical prognosis of the patient's performance potential, against which his actual functioning can be evaluated at any given point. This staff standard, like the patient's own standard of functioning, is derived from observations of the patient's behavior. Since it is supported by a broader and more objective view of the situation, however, it is more durable—that is, less susceptible to fluctuations in response to short-term changes in the patient's functioning—than is the patient's standard for himself. This perspective is suggested by figure 4-14.

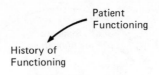

Figure 4-14.

This distinction between patient and staff standards is made explicit by Stevenson and Sheppe in their article on "The Psychiatric Examination".

> The physician should try to compare the patient's present condition with his premorbid level of function. Only in this way can he accurately evaluate the patient's mental state. Sometimes the patient himself can reliably contribute information about his "base line." However, the physician rarely knows the patient's dependability in this regard, at least initially, and so should check the subject's statements with those of others who have known him closely . . . [for] valuable information about the extent of deviation from his usual personality.[35]

Assessed Need for Treatment, shown in figure 4-15, reflects the staff's assessment of the improvement in performance that may be reasonably expected in the patient's response to treatment. A knowledge of the history of his illness—its duration and its course—provides a standard for the patient's optimal level of functioning. The difference between that potential and his present level of functioning defines the magnitude of the individual's need for psychiatric help at a given time.

A textbook in clinical psychiatry describes this variable clearly:

> Our study of the *past personality* and *constitutional background* will tell us a good deal about the extent to which the man has dropped from his previous norm, and the extent of restitution we can hope to obtain. The

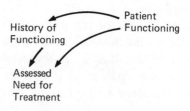

Figure 4-15.

Figure 4-16.

psychogenic factor will have its principal importance in being the one aspect, in this case, in which we can hope for help from our therapeutic efforts. Lastly, purely individual aspects of the case—the fact, for instance, that the man has earned his living throughout his entire life as a painter in the building trade working on high ladders, and now has a phobia for heights—will have to be taken into account in treatment and disposal.[36]

Resources Apportioned refers to the investment in treatment that staff is willing to make for a specific patient. Two of the determinants of the magnitude of this investment are indicated in figure 4-16. The most potent of the two is the assessment of the patient's need for treatment, that is, the amount of help deemed necessary to restore his performance to its "average" level within a reasonable period of time. If the "criticality" factor becomes operative, staff will greatly increase the resources apportioned to treatment (as represented, for example, by hospitalization). Once the criticality dimension is overcome, however, the extra resources engendered by it will be quickly reduced.

The resources allocated to a patient's care depend on more than a statement of his need.[37] As seen below, they are also influenced by the beliefs of staff about the efficacy of the treatment they are rendering, and by their perception of the patient's collaboration in the treatment process.

Staff's Expectations of Treatment Efficacy, which is derived from its training and experience, is indicated in figure 4-17. Although two professionals may judge a patient very similarly in terms of his present clinical condition and his consequent need for help, they will prescribe different treatment programs for him if one of them believes that each treatment unit is enormously effective and the other believes it is only minimally so. To achieve the same clinical goal within the same period of time, the former allocates fewer treatment resources to his case than the latter. At first encounter, this formulation appears contrary to our expectation that a therapist who be-

Figure 4-17.

lieves treatment is more potent will prescribe more of it than the therapist who believes it is less so. The real process, however, is counterintuitive. Assume, for example, that the clinical assessment of a patient reveals a discrepancy between his actual and potential functioning to the magnitude of X, and a goal is set to eliminate that discrepancy within a fixed period of time. One therapist believes that each unit of treatment is moderately effective (let us say capable of restoring $1/X$ of the gap) and plans Y units of treatment to meet the goal; the other attributes twice the power to each unit of treatment (capable of restoring $2/X$ of the gap), and therefore plans only half the number of treatment units ($Y/2$) to achieve the same goal within the same period.

Effect of Patient's Treatment-Seeking Behavior is greatest in the initial phase of the treatment relationship when the staff is made aware of the patient's efforts to get care. Once the program has been engaged by the patient's efforts, additional effort achieves sharply diminished returns, as reflected in figure 4-18. Thus, although some additional effort to get care, for example, a telephone call, may result in an earlier appointment, once the patient is in treatment the

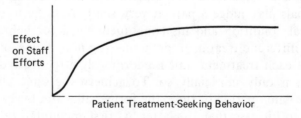

Figure 4-18.

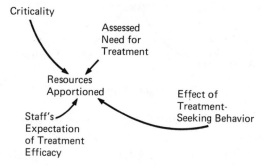

Figure 4-19.

staff is highly autonomous in regulating the intensity of care and does not permit the patient to dictate to it.

On the other hand, this "patient effect" variable builds into the model formal recognition of the fact that staff takes account of the patient's cooperation in treatment: the patient who refuses to cooperate ultimately has a discouraging effect on staff, and causes it to diminish the resources apportioned to his treatment (figure 4-19).

That this effect does indeed occur is confirmed by the admonition to guard against it in a standard text on clinical psychiatry.

> Often the therapist is dismayed by observing that he seems to mean nothing to his patient; despite his efforts as psychiatrist, physician, and well-intentioned, kindly human being, his patient turns from him, or worse yet, does not seem to be aware of him. In brief, the therapist often suffers from a lack of confirmatory feedback from his patient and may attempt to wring from him some indication that treatment has significance and that there is value in what is being done. All people want to be assured, on occasion, that they and their efforts are valued, but the therapist cannot rely consistently on his patient for such reassurance. When he does not find it, he should not withdraw from the situation; rather, he must continue with confidence that a human relationship, however obscure its form may appear to be, has meaning and can offer hope and a way to useful change.[38]

Treatment, shown in figure 4-20, refers to any services rendered by program staff to the patient for the improvement or restoration of his level of functioning. As noted elsewhere, the services are conceptualized here as homogeneous in terms of their potential effect on the patient's health, but varying along a continuum of intensity, so

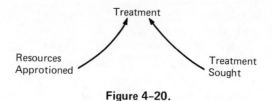

Figure 4-20.

that hospitalization, for example, is more intense treatment than out-patient treatment.

For treatment to occur, two conditions are necessary: the patient must seek help and the program staff must allocate resources to serving him.

Treatment must of necessity terminate if either of these conditions is absent. When it comes to a halt—because the patient ceases to seek or accept help while the staff is still offering resources to him on the basis of its assessment of his need—a situation exists that is commonly labeled a "treatment drop-out".

The causal structure identified here was translated into the mathematical equations of DYNAMO in order to conduct the simulation experiments reported in the next chapter. The technically oriented reader will find an annotated listing of these equations in Appendix A. The nontechnical reader will not be hampered in understanding the simulation results of Chapter Five which depend primarily upon comprehension of the conceptual relationships we have just reviewed.

NOTES TO CHAPTER FOUR

1. Length of therapist-patient acquaintance was found to be a contributing factor in correlations between log number of interviews and success of therapy, but was in itself less highly correlated with outcome. D.S. Cartwright, R.J. Robertson, D.W. Fiske, and W.L. Kirtner, "Length of Therapy in Relation to Outcome and Change in Personal Integration". *Journal of Consulting Psychology*, 1961, p. 25, 84-88.

2. S.L. Garfield and M. Kurz, "Evaluation of treatment and related procedures in 1,216 cases referred to a mental hygiene clinic". *Psychiatric Quarterly*, 1952, 26:414-24.

S.L. Garfield and D.C. Affleck, "An appraisal of duration of stay in outpatient psychotherapy". *Journal of Nervous and Mental Disease*, 1959, 129:492-98.

J.K. Myers and F. Auld, Jr., "Some variables related to outcome of psychotherapy". *Journal of Clinical Psychology*, 1955, 11:51-54.

J. Meltzoff and M. Kornreich, *Research in Psychotherapy,* Atherton Press, New York, 1970, pp. 346-47.

M.R. Bartlett, "A six-month follow-up of the effects of personal adjustment counseling of veterans".. *Journal of Consulting Psychology,* 1950, 14:393-94.

D.M. McNair, M. Lori, A. Young, I. Roth, and R. Boyd, "A three-year follow-up of psychotherapy patients". *Journal of Consulting Psychology,* 1964, 20: 258-64.

3. L.S. Rogers, "Drop-out rates and results of psychotherapy in government aided mental hygiene clinics". *Journal of Clinical Psychology,* 1960, 16:89-92.

See also, as cited in Meltzoff and Kornreich, *op. cit.,* pp. 352-53, E. Dorfman, "Personality outcomes of client-centered child therapy". *Psychology Monographs,* 1958, 72, whole No. 456.

G. Heilbrunn, "Results with psychoanalytic therapy and professional commitment". *American Journal of Psychotherapy,* 1966, 20:89-99.

4. Paul Errera, B. McKee, C. Smith, and R. Gruber, "Length of Psychotherapy: Studies done in a university community psychiatric clinic". *Archives of General Psychiatry,* 1967, 17:454-58.

5. William Reid and Anne Shyne, *Brief and Extended Casework,* New York, Columbia University Press, 1969.

6. R. Feldman, M. Lorr and S.B. Russell, "A mental hygiene clinic case survey", *Journal of Clinical Psychology,* 1958, 14:245-50. These authors are uncertain as to the meaning of this finding and suggest it may reflect the drop-out of improved patients from the samples at the end of the first year, so that the remaining cases seem to show a decline in improvement.

D. Rosenthal, J. Frank, "Fate of psychiatric clinic outpatients assigned to psychotherapy". *Journal of Nervous & Mental Disease,* 1958, 127:330-43.

7. D.S. Cartwright, "Success in psychotherapy as a function of certain actuarial variables". *Journal of Consulting Psychology,* 1955, 19:357-363.

8. Meltzoff and Kornreich, p. 26.

9. H. Himmelweit, "Level of Aspiration". *Dictionary of the Social Sciences,* ed. by J. Gould and W. L. Kolb, New York, The Free Press of Glencoe, 1964. p. 387.

10. Jerome D. Frank, "Recent Studies of the Level of Aspiration". *Psychological Bulletin,* 38 (1941), 218-226.

11. For example, B.C. Muthayya, "Relationship between level of aspiration, performance and future performance". *Psychology Studies,* Mysore 6(1) 41-46.

N.T. Feather and M.R. Saville, "Effects of amount of prior success and failure on expectations of success and subsequent task performance". *Journal of Personality and Social Psychology,* 1967, 5 (20:226-332).

12. H. Himmelweit.

13. This is discussed in Chapter Five.

14. Helen Peak, "Attitude and motivation", in M.R. Jones (Ed.), *Nebraska*

Symposium on Motivation, 1955, Lincoln: University of Nebraska Press, pp. 149-89. Cited in Cofer, C.N. and Appley, M.H., *Motivation: Theory & Research,* New York, John Wiley & Sons, Inc., 1964, p. 387.

15. P. Lichtenberg, R. Kohrman, H. MacGregor, *Motivation for Child Psychiatry,* New York, Russell & Russell, 1960, p. 7.

16. Meltzoff and Kornreich, p. 258.

17. Edward G. Ludwig and Geoffrey Gibson, "Self perception of sickness and the seeking of medical care". *Journal of Health and Social Behavior,* 1959, 10(2):125-33.

18. E. Dengrove and S. Kutash, "Why patients discontinue treatment in a mental hygiene clinic". *American Journal of Psychotherapy,* 1950, 4, p. 465.

19. Meltzoff and Kornreich, p. 254.

20. J.H. Borghi, "Premature termination of psychotherapy and patient-therapist expectations". *American Journal of Psychotherapy,* 1968, 22, 460-73. R. Hoehn-Saric, J.D.Frank, S.D. Imber, E.H. Nash, A.R. Stone and C.C. Battle, "Systematic preparation of patients for psychotherapy". *Journal of Psychiatric Research,* 1964, 2:267-81.

21. L. Ripple and E. Alexander, "Motivation, capacity and opportunity as related to use of casework service". *Social Service Review,* 1956, 30, 38.

22. R.W. Heine and H. Trosman, "Initial expectations of the doctor-patient interaction as a factor in continuance in psychotherapy". *Psychiatry,* 1960, 23:275.

23. Ezra Slotland, *The Psychology of Hope,* San Francisco, Jossey-Bass, 1969.

24. J.D. Frank, L.H. Gliedman, S.D. Imber, E.H. Nash, Jr., and A.R. Stone, "Why patients leave psychotherapy". *AMA Archives of Neurological Psychiatry,* 1957, 77:283.

25. R.S. Lipman, K. Rickels, E. Uhlenhuth, L. Park, and S. Fisher, "Neurotics who fail to take their drugs". *British Journal of Psychiatry,* 1956, 3 (480), 1043-49.

26. D. Mechanic, "The Concept of Illness Behavior". *Journal of Chronic Diseases,* 1962, 15, 189-94.

27. Charles Kadushin, *Why People Go to Psychiatrists,* New York, Atherton Press, 1969.

28. E.E. Levitt, H.R. Beiser, and R.E. Robertson, "A follow-up evaluation of cases treated at a community child guidance clinic". *American Journal of Orthopsychiatry,* 1959, 29:337-49. Cited in Meltzoff and Kornreich, p. 358.

29. E.L. Phillips, A. Raiford, V. Rutledge, and J. Burkhardt, "A perplexing clinical problem". *Psychological Reports,* 1967, 20:26.

30. Marton S. Krauge, "Predicting client discontinuance at intake". *Social Casework,* June 1962, 43.

31. Frank et al., p. 294.

32. Bernice T. Eiduson, "Retreat from help". *American Journal of Ortho-psychiatry,* 38, 1968:910-21, p. 918.

33. Jack R. Ewalt, "Other psychiatric emergencies", in Freedman, Kaplan and Kaplan, *op. cit.,* p. 1180.

34. I. Stevenson and W. Sheppe, Jr., "The psychiatric examination". S. Arieti, Ed., *American Handbook of Psychiatry,* New York, Basic Books, Inc., 1959, Vol. 1, p. 217.

35. Ibid.

36. W. Mayer-Gross, E. Slater and M. Roth, *Clinical Psychiatry,* Baltimore, William and Wilkins Co., 1960, pp. 33-34.

37. The availability of resources is an additional and obvious determinant of the allocation decision. The effects of scarcity of resources are not taken into account here because the program in question was a relatively new one in which scarcity was not yet experienced as a significant constraint. See Chapter Three for a discussion of the implications of resource scarcity.

38. Otto Allen Will, Jr., "Psychological treatment of schizophrenia", in Freedman, Kaplan and Kaplan, p. 660.

※ *Chapter 5*

A Computer Analysis of the Patient Drop-out Phenomenon

In the last chapter the general theory allowed us to analyze the conditions that are likely to lead to drop-out. We now fit the model to the conditions encountered in a real-life setting. We draw upon observations made and data gathered mainly at the Sound View-Throgs Neck Community Mental Health Center, a large urban facility in the Bronx, operated by the Albert Einstein College of Medicine, Yeshiva University. The center provides a complex of comprehensive emergency, inpatient, partial hospitalization, outpatient, and rehabilitative services. Since most of the more than 600 community mental health centers and other large psychiatric programs in the United States share similar experiences with patient drop-out, our analyses apply broadly to them, too.

Community mental health centers were legislated into being by the federal government in 1963 with a mandate to provide a range of basic psychiatric services in such a way as to insure continuous and comprehensive mental health care for residents within their own community. They were designed to end the fragmentation of care that occurs when a patient has to deal with numerous, unrelated, and often geographically remote agencies.

One of the charges to centers was to provide care for seriously disabled psychiatric patients. Programs were to be geared to prevent hospitalization, reduce the duration of any needed hospital stay, and maintain patients in the community at their optimal level of functioning. Patients in this category, who are usually diagnosed as

67

psychotic or borderline psychotic, may require multiple treatment experiences during what is often a long-term, recurring condition. Periods of relatively stable functioning alternate with periods of disrupted functioning. Mental health professionals believe that early identification of slippage in functioning and prompt intensive intervention reduce the duration and severity of an acute episode. They advocate that programs maintain contact with patients during periods of recovery and provide them with a broad range of rehabilitation services to reduce any residual disabilities. Drop-out from a treatment program by such patients represents an important challenge to centers.

In our computer-aided exploration of the factors contributing to drop-out, we first report the behavior of the model with a basic set of assumptions. (The mathematical equations of the model are presented and explained in Appendix A.) Next we show the effects of a number of changes representing differences in patient characteristics and treatment responses. In some cases the changes have little effect on the model's behavior. In others, the changes have profound effect on behavior and help to identify factors that contribute importantly to treatment drop-out. Clinically, drop-out indicates leaving treatment while it is still being offered before full recovery occurs. Generally, drop-out occurs early in treatment. The model has two approximations of the real world. First, it takes into account not only when treatment stops, but the level of the patient's recovery at that point. A return to almost a full level of functioning is not considered in the model as a serious drop-out issue. Second, for simulation purposes, the model is run over a five-year period. Although drop-outs in the real world occur at much earlier points in treatment, the model assumes that the forces and counterforces at work in the model are similar to those that produce early drop-out. For some drop-out-inducing factors, remedial efforts have been simulated and their effects shown. Some changes produce uncertain results and suggest new areas for empirical research. Throughout we are concerned with how the *system,* rather than its individual characteristics, produces drop-out, and what may be done to prevent it.

Consider first the case of a successful response by the system to a crisis. The behavior characteristics of such a successful pattern of interaction between program and patient is displayed in figure 5–1. In this simulation, the patient experiences a 33 percent decrease in his level of functioning as the result of a sudden crisis suffered in the

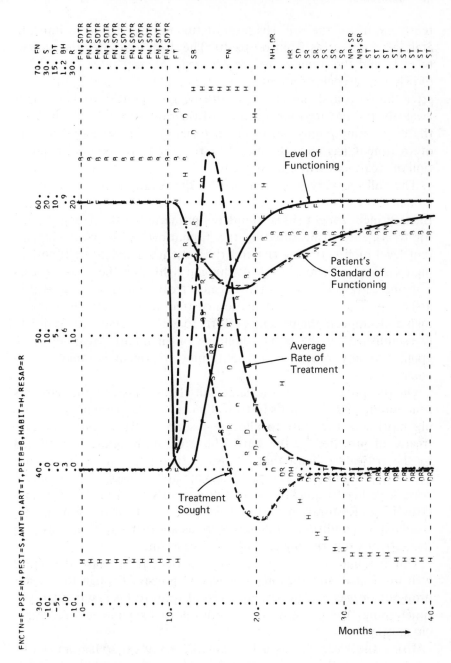

Figure 5–1. Non-Dropout Computer Simulation Run

tenth month of the run. His level of functioning (F) drops immediately after the crisis from 60 to 40. The drop motivates the patient to seek, and the program to provide, care. Average rate of treatment (T) rises to a peak of about twelve treatment units per month soon after the crisis and subsides as health begins to return to its precrisis level. By the twenty-fourth month of the run, fourteen months after the crisis, functioning has returned to its original level and the rate of treatment has gone to zero. This represents a successful completion of treatment without drop-out.

The full recovery was produced by the feedback structure of the model shown earlier in figure 4-1 (page 42). On the patient side, the treatment sought (S) is stimulated primarily by the patient's need for treatment, as measured by the discomfort gap between the current level of functioning (F) and the patient's standard of functioning (N). The large magnitude of this gap right after the crisis initiates a strong care-seeking response. Because treatment is so successful in a short period, patient anticipation of treatment benefit (B) remains high and supports the patient's efforts to get care. Habit (H) is quickly established by the rapid beginning of an intense treatment program, and any resistance to continuing treatment is rapidly overcome.

On the program side, the large initial gap between the patient's functioning and the staff's historical record of the patient's functioning motivates the staff to allocate resources (R) so as to increase treatment provided by the staff. This program response is amplified by the criticality factor that intensifies treatment for lower absolute values of functioning. The rapid seeking and provision of treatment work together to quickly return the patient's functioning to its precrisis level. Restoration of this level acts to return the system to a steady-state condition until such time as another significant drop in the patient's functioning perturbs it once again.

Our baseline run is a success in that the patient was sufficiently well motivated and the program was responsive enough to prevent drop-out or waste. The patient reversed fully to his precrisis level of functioning. We are now in a position to examine less favorable circumstances.

Using the basic run as a benchmark, many other factors can be examined and their importance in causing drop-out can be determined. On the patient side, the investigation will focus upon three elements: (1) patient's standard of functioning; (2) benefit expected (and a combination of patient's standard of functioning and benefit expected); and (3) habit. Three program variables will also be considered: (1) treatment timetable; (2) expectation of treatment efficacy; and (3) the role of criticality.

PATIENT CHARACTERISTICS

Unstable Patient's Standard of Functioning

By the stability of a standard of functioning, we mean the readiness with which the standard changes in response to new levels of health or functioning. What is the effect of an unstable standard of functioning on the treatment system? A person with an unstable standard is little influenced by his previous level of functioning after a crisis, and is unlikely to strive to regain that level. A person with a very stable standard is likely to maintain that standard long after he had suffered a loss of functioning, even though this persistence may require him to endure considerable discomfort.

The baseline run assumed that a lengthy time was required for the patient's standard of functioning to reflect accumulated changes in his actual functioning. Specifically we assumed that a patient's standard would drift toward acceptance of the actual accumulated change in functioning over a period of about one year.

In the run depicted in figure 5-2, this time constant was reduced to only three months. One would expect that a greatly reduced time required to adjust standard of functioning would greatly increase the likelihood of drop-out. This was not the case. Under this experimental condition the patient's level of functioning (F) reaches 55, or 92 percent of the precrisis level of 60. No significant waste occurs, as the patient was able to maintain a standard of functioning sufficient to support an adequate degree of recovery. Recovery occurs rapidly and health returns to a higher value before the standard (N) has had much opportunity to deteriorate.

Apparently, the patient's initial expectation of benefit was strong enough to sustain his efforts to get care. Since the treatment response was adequate, the patient was able to enter treatment and to sustain a belief that the process was beneficial.

Indifference Toward Benefit Expected

The patient's anticipation of treatment benefit represents his estimate of the improvement in health that can be gained from treat-

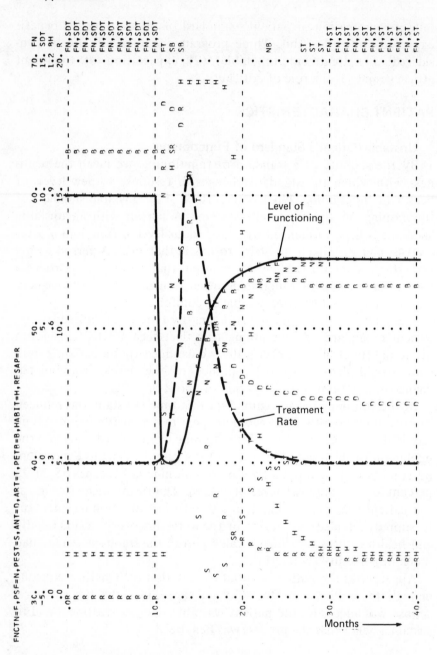

Figure 5-2. Unstable Standard of Functioning

ment. The patient's initial anticipations result from previous personal experiences with the program, impressions of program effectiveness based on the experience of others, and knowledge, if any, of the field of mental health care. These anticipations change depending on changes in health and treatment intensity. If the patient is undergoing an intense program of treatment, he is more likely to attribute changes in health to treatment rather than to social and chemical forces. As changes in level of functioning are attributed to treatment, patient anticipations change, and anticipation of benefit expected is reinforced.

If the patient's expectation of benefit from treatment (or anticipation, or hope) is a critical variable, weakening its influence in the model would be expected to result in less complete recovery than in the baseline run. To test this hypothesis the function that describes the influence of benefit expected upon patient's efforts to get care (or "treatment sought") was changed so as to make the patient's behavior indifferent to the benefit expected.

Figure 5-3 shows the behavior of the system when confronted with a patient whose tendency to seek care is impervious to his expectations of benefit. Again, the illness pattern simulated is of a crisis nature. The results show that the patient's indifference toward expected benefits has only a minor effect on the behavior of the system. The level of functioning recovers to a value of 55 rather than 60 as in the base run. Again, the rapid recovery due to treatment leaves little time for the patient's skepticism to outweigh his discomfort and cause him to drop out. These results are contrary to expectation, since a 92 percent recovery was achieved by the patient in this run. We can say that the patient took reasonably full advantage of the program resources put at his disposal.

The post hoc explanation for this result is that the discomfort experienced by the patient as a result of the discrepancy between functioning and standard of functioning was sustained long enough to cause the patient and program to develop a self-perpetuating relationship (assisted by the habit effect), strong enough to sustain itself despite counterpressure created by declining patient belief in treatment efficacy.

If this explanation is correct, then altered model behavior would stem from weakened effect of "benefit expected" only if it were accompanied by instability of patient standard of functioning. This latter experimental manipulation would cause a more rapid reduction

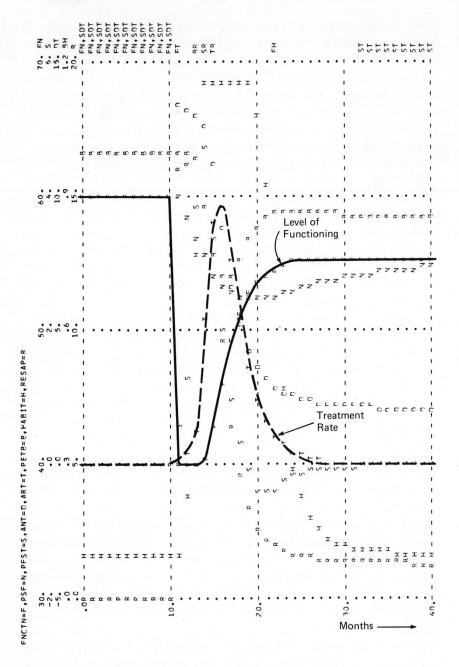

Figure 5-3. Skepticism in Benefit Expected

of the discomfort that is the primary force moving the patient to seek and use the program. The patient would become resigned to a lower level of performance and remove himself from an unpromising relationship before significant benefit could be derived from it.

Combination of Unstable Standard of Functioning and Indifference Toward Benefit Expected

A simulation run was tried with a patient in crisis with both an unstable standard and indifference toward the benefit of treatment. The results are shown in figure 5–4. Clearly, the combination of these detrimental characteristics is sufficient to reduce this patient's efforts to get care long before much of the lost functioning has been recovered. The final level of functioning (F) in this run is 44, as compared to 60 in the crisis baseline run. In this case, his attitude toward anticipation of benefit (B) causes the patient to seek a smaller amount of treatment (S) than is required by his discomfort. Treatment starts off at a lower intensity and the functioning level begins to rise very slowly. In the run with unstable standard alone, the intense treatment rate permitted by the importance the patient attributes to the possibility of treatment success raised the functioning substantially before the falling standard eliminated the discomfort gap and caused the patient to stop seeking help. However, the slow growth in treatment intensity due to patient indifference keeps health at a low level for a long enough time to allow a large decrease in the (unstable) standard. The drop in the standard wipes out the discomfort gap, eliminating the patient's felt need for treatment and causing drop-out when functioning is still far below its precrisis level. The health "deficit" (initial level of functioning minus final equilibrium level) left at the end of the run is greater than the sum of the deficits left in the runs with unstable standard or indifferent anticipation alone.

While each of the detrimental factors alone was insufficient to produce drop-out, the combination of the two crippled the system of staff-patient interaction and caused an early drop-out. This is typical of nonlinear dynamic systems in which combinations of factors can act synergistically to produce disproportionate behavioral changes.

What sort of person is most likely to experience the joint unstable standard and indifference toward anticipated benefits? Considering the standard issue first, clearly the more susceptible is one whose be-

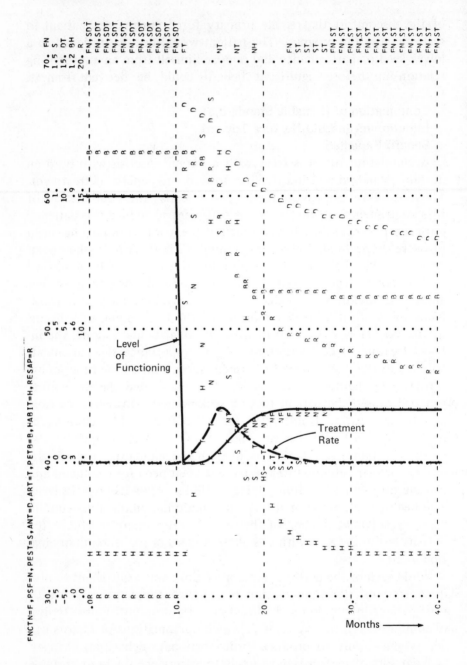

Figure 5-4. Unstable Standard of Functioning and Skepticism in Benefit Expected

havior is responsive less to abstract, symbolic, enduring standards of conduct than to here-and-now reality. The middle class, as described by a generation of sociologists, is dominated by the former, not the latter, which more nearly resembles the many recent portraits of the lower-class agency client. The lower-class patient defines himself in terms of current needs and current performance rather than in terms of aspirations and ideals.

The connection to cultural anthropology is also clear. Kluckhohn's[1] concept of cultural value orientation is dominated by considerations of the psychology of time in terms of the significance for various cultures of present, past, and future, as well as the way in which it regulates the nature of present behavior. The American middle-class family, for example, is characterized by Kluckhohn as oriented toward "doing" as opposed to "being" or "becoming", and toward "the future" rather than "past" or "present".

This seems roughly equivalent to the formulation that such a family is invested in setting standards of performance and acting in such a way as to achieve them.

Another indirect but striking parallel is found in clinical neurology. The frequent observation that white-collar workers complain about deficits following recovery from head injury that are invisible to manual laborers may have as much to do with cultural and class differences as it does with the differential demands of their jobs. The lower-class patient would tend over a period of several months to redefine his personal standards in terms of recent reduced performance, while the middle-class patient would struggle and endure discomfort to preserve his self-image at its original level.

The same reasoning would apply to differential class responses to rising as well as falling performance levels; thus the surprise of many middle-class social-service managers at the speed with which paraprofessionals demand compensation and recognition commensurate with newly acquired levels of work competence. The worker adjusts his standard quickly to accommodate the higher performance, while the manager's evaluation of the worker changes more slowly, since it is influenced to a significantly greater degree by his observation of older behavior.

This argument applies with equal force to the other central concept encountered in the model, especially if we keep in mind that the symptomatic simulation involved a change not in the amount of anticipated benefit or hope but in the degree to which hope is assumed to affect behavior. The sources cited clearly support the view that the behavior of the middle-class person is regulated to a greater extent by hopes, ideals, and fantasies; the lower-class person being more affected by "reality", that is, immediate demands and rewards. While it may be true that the lower-class client fantasizes less and hopes less than the middle-class client, it appears even more likely that for him such activities may be regarded more nearly as pastimes than determiners of behavior. A person with little hope is capable of imagining a better condition, but despairs at being able to achieve it.

Decreasing the Effect of Habit

Habit represents the degree to which a patient is involved in the treatment process. As a unitary factor, a high habitual commitment to the program implies that the patient has major involvement in treatment and openness to increasing the rate of treatment. Low level of habit implies little involvement in treatment and probably resistance to increasing the rate of treatment. The effect on the performance of the system of this element, however, doesn't seem to be substantial. In runs wherein the habit factor was made more unfavorable compared to the baseline run, few differences were generated in the performance of the system.

PROGRAM CHARACTERISTICS

A Delay in Treatment Timetable

We assume that program staff are reasonably accurate in assessing the patient's deficit and in estimating and offering the total amount of care required to return him to his premorbid condition. The main avenue of fallibility open to staff is the rate at which the needed care is provided. In our model the staff regulates this rate through several explicit or implicit assessments and decisions. First, an estimate is made based upon history-taking and observation of ongoing behavior or the level of recovery likely to be achieved and sustained by this patient; second, by comparing his present level of functioning with the level of recovery expected, an accurate projection is made of the amount of treatment effort that will be required to achieve this recovery goal; third, a treatment plan is devised based upon these considerations, including as well a timetable for achievement of this result. In the baseline run, this time constant was set at six months: staff makes treatment available for the patient at whatever intensity is required to attempt to close the gap between performance and expected recovery state in six months. It follows, then, that the shorter the timetable the greater the treatment intensity required to close the gap within the time period; the longer the time schedule the less the treatment intensity required. If patients were infinitely patient, this time constant would be unimportant. The appropriate amount of treatment spread over any period, however long, would result in eventual full recovery. In reality a patient's involvement in the treatment process is subject to the influence of a number of variables, including the discomfort he experiences, the benefit he feels he is deriving from it, the expectation he has of his own potential recovery, and the intensity of his relationship with program staff. At very low rates of treatment intensity, these variables would stabilize his performance at a lower-than-optimum recovery level, causing him to leave treatment long before the full plan is executed. Our simulation experiments show that the tendency for the interaction system to break down and produce drop-out varies directly with the projected length of time for recovery.

An experimental run (not shown) was conducted using one full year rather than six months as the time constant regulating the rate at which treatment is made available by the program. This variation has only limited effect upon recovery. The patient still makes adequate use of the resources offered, recovering to 54 units or 90 percent of his premorbid condition. Extending the timetable goal to twenty-four months, however, leads to a further decrease in the performance of the program-patient interaction system, with a final health value of 50 units. An extremely long timetable goal of sixty months leads to a further (but not proportionate) drop in level of functioning to 46 units (figure 5-5).

System performance for the crisis case undergoes a moderate decrease over that of the run with the twenty-four-month goal. In this case, the patient is already taking advantage of most of the care that is offered. The decrease in system performance merely reflects the lower treatment intensity offered by the staff.

This large a decrease came about because the treatment rate in the sixty-month run takes longer to grow to the point where it can counteract the deterioration of standard of functioning. A delay in the growth of treatment rate is serious, because the continual deterioration in health goes on for that much longer and results in a significantly lower final value of the health level. The decrease in

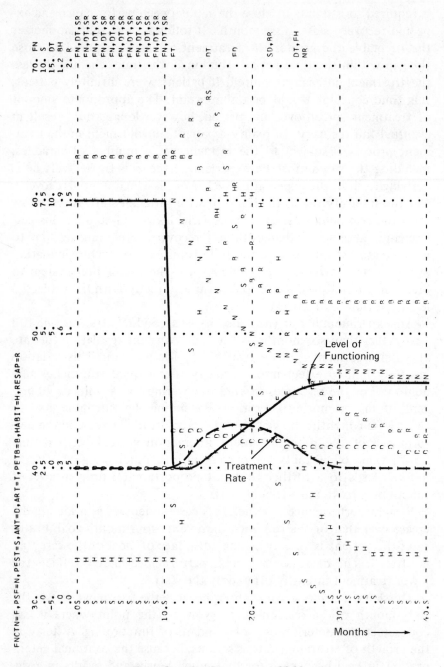

Figure 5-5. Extended Time Goal for Recovery to 60 Months

system performance merely reflects the weak program response by the staff.

What are the implications of this set of runs? One is that responding more slowly to a crisis will not have a great effect on system behavior as long as the delay is not too long. These shorter delays are realistic representations of the effect of overloads in operating programs. Recovery time as long as sixty months more realistically represents a situation in which treatment resources are extremely scarce and a patient must wait a very long time before receiving treatment at all.

Exaggerated Expectation of Treatment Effectiveness

Misjudgment of treatment efficacy can have an effect similar to that of a long delay time. In the run of figure 5-6, the staff's estimate of efficacy is assumed to be four times the actual efficacy of treatment, prompting the staff to give too weak a schedule of treatment. As a result, the level of functioning (F) reaches only about 51 units by the end of the run. As in the runs with long recovery timetables, the patient's standard of functioning (N) and anticipation of treatment benefit (B) both decrease rapidly, while health (F) is rising slowly. This result implies that research is needed on the degree of treatment efficacy when dealing with various forms of mental illness. It also implies a need for careful monitoring of the progress of patients in treatment. This needs to be coupled with action to prevent drop-out in patients making slow progress.

Criticality Factor

Recall that the criticality factor served to amplify the treatment intensity offered by the staff when the patient's health level is at a low enough value (on an absolute scale) to indicate potential danger to the patient and those around him. For lower values of functioning, the treatment intensity is multiplied by a factor of up to 3. As it turns out, though, the criticality factor does not play so important a role. This is shown in figure 5-7, which is the result of a simulation run with the effect of the criticality factor eliminated (i.e., set equal to one for all values of health). The final value of the health level is about 58 rather than 60, as in the base run, representing an insignificant change. In the case of more severe crises, extending over a longer period of time, the criticality factor might be more important.

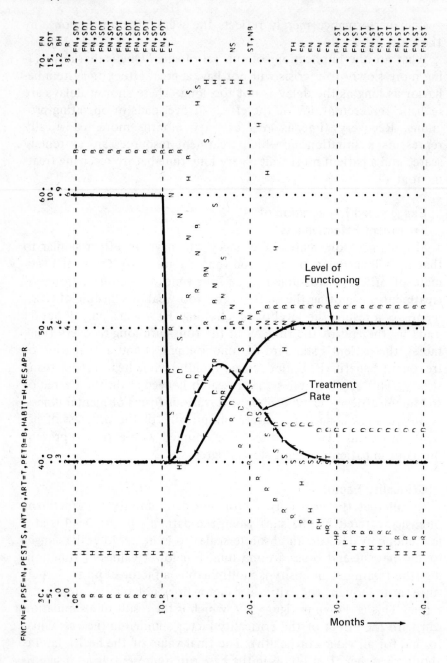

Figure 5–6. Exaggerated Estimate of Treatment Efficacy

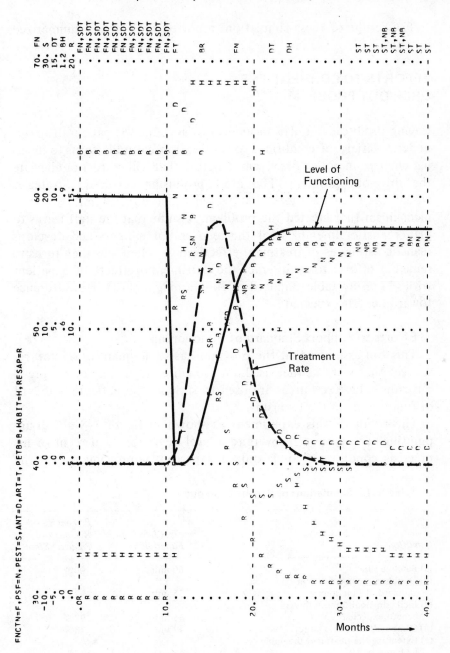

Figure 5–7. Elimination of Criticality Factor

The results of these simulations reported thus far are summarized in table 5-1.

EFFORTS TO CORRECT THE DROP-OUT PROBLEM

Having produced simulation models to account for patient drop-out under a variety of conditions, our attention naturally turns to devising changes in policy or system structure that will correct or alleviate the drop-out problem. The most promising corrective strategies would seem to be those that would most directly influence the mechanism that created the problem. Assume that the staff learns to plan realistic timetables for the recovery of patients and develops realistic estimates of treatment effectiveness. The focus then turns to remedial efforts to counteract the detrimental effects of a patient with (1) an unstable standard of functioning and (2) an indifference toward benefit expected.

Efforts to Support Standard of Functioning

This run assumed that the program has some quantity of staff resources that were neither used nor accounted for in any of the previous runs. These resources are used to support the patient's standard of functioning in the two runs.

The result of this experiment as shown in figure 5-8 are disappointing. The patient recovers to a level of 46, or 77 percent of his precrisis condition. This is only a 4 percent improvement over the

Table 5-1. Simulations of Patient Drop-out

Condition	Final Level of Functioning	Percentage of Recovery to Preacute State
(a) Baseline run	60 units	100%
(b) Doubling the instability of the standard of functioning	55 units	92%
(c) Increasing indifference toward benefit expected	55 units	92%
(d) Combination of (b) and (c)	44 units	73%
(e) Extending the treatment timetable by factor of 10	46 units	77%
(f) Quadrupling the estimate for treatment effectiveness	51 units	85%
(g) Eliminating the criticality factor	58 units	97%

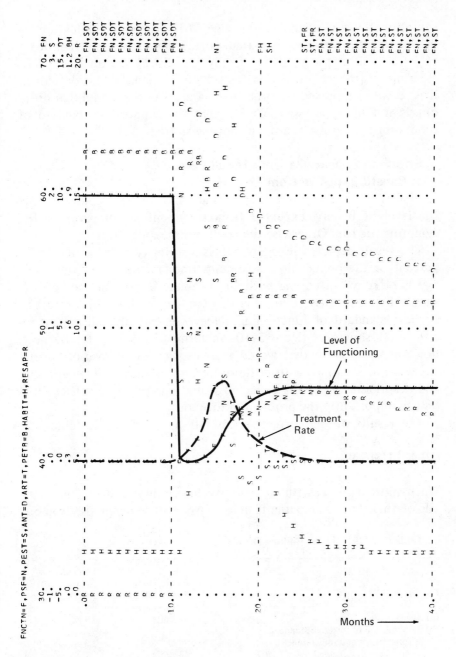

Figure 5-8. Support of Patient's Standard of Functioning (in Patient With Characteristics of Unstable Standard of Functioning and Skepticism in Benefit Expected).

symptomatic run (figure 5–4, page 76). Further examination of model structure reveals that a supported standard has a significant effect only after the patient is firmly established in a treatment relationship. Moreover, once this treatment relationship has developed it is so well supported by other mechanisms in the model that drop-out is not likely anyway. We see that the support of standard of functioning is, by itself, not a promising strategy.

Efforts to Enhance Patient's Initial Level of Benefit Expected from Treatment

In this simulation, staff resources are allocated to rapidly double the level of benefit expected from treatment as compared to the symptomatic run. Otherwise the conditions are identical.

The result depicted in figure 5–9 is a recovery to 54 units, or 90 percent of the premorbid adjustment. Implementation of this strategy is effective in coping with the problem of patient drop-out. It should be noted that combining this strategy with ongoing effort to support standard of functioning achieves essentially full patient recovery, as shown in figure 5–10. In terms of relative effectiveness, however, a program that would increase the initial level of benefit expected in a patient with both an unstable standard of functioning and skepticism in benefit expected would appear to be sufficient to reduce importantly the problem of drop-out.

The results of the corrective simulations are shown in table 5–2.

CONCLUSIONS

When most patients with chronic psychiatric illness spent long periods of their lives as inpatients in large psychiatric hospitals, drop-out

Table 5–2. Efforts to Reduce Drop-out

Condition	Final Level of Functioning	Percentage of Recovery to Preacute State
(a) Baseline run	60 units	100%
(b) Combination of unstable standard of functioning and indifference toward benefit expected	44 units	73%
(c) Support of standard of functioning	46 units	77%
(d) Doubling initial benefit expected	54 units	90%
(e) Combination of (c) and (d)	59 units	98%

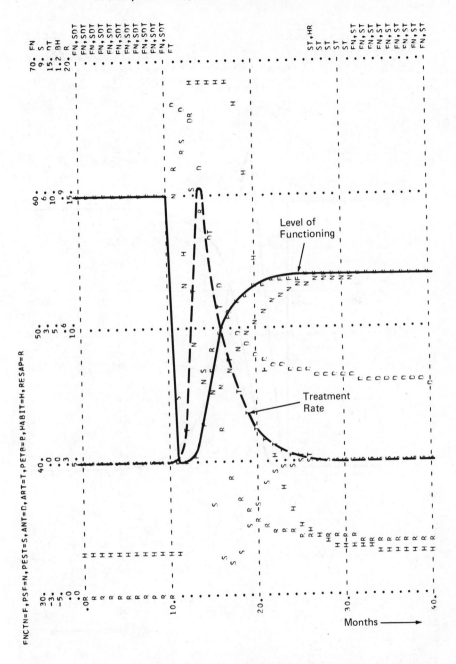

Figure 5-9. Support of Initial Benefit Expected (in Patient With Characteristics of Unstable Standard of Functioning and Skepticism in Benefit Expected)

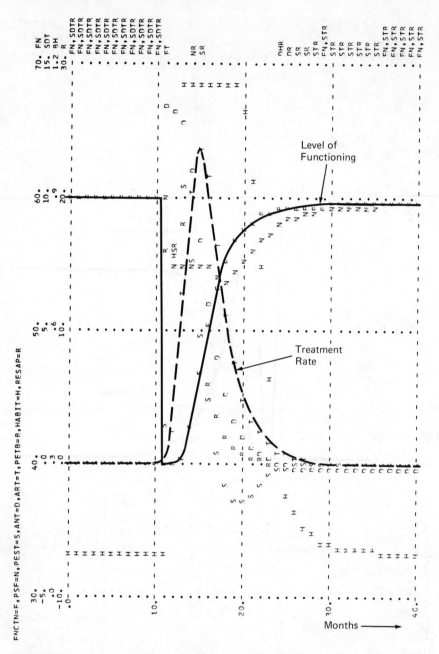

Figure 5-10. Support of Patient's Standard of Functioning and Initial Anticipation of Benefit Expected (in Patient With Characteristics of Unstable Standard of Functioning and Skepticism in Benefit Expected)

from treatment was not as pressing an issue as it is today, as the patients were captive in the treatment system. The current emphasis on the care of such patients in the community highlights the importance of maintaining continuity of the interaction between a mental health program and its patients. Customarily, studies of medical care (and, indeed, of human services in general) conclude that the remedy for less than optimal delivery of care lies in increasing the resources allocated for the purpose. While we do not dispute that recommendation, the application of the system dynamics approach has uncovered a causal structure of the care-delivery system that suggests that treatment drop-out by patients suffering chronic psychiatric disability is not solely a function of scarcity of resources, but, in the case studied, of the interaction of an unstable standard of functioning and indifference toward the benefits expected from treatment. We suggest that a program use some of its resources to raise and maintain the level of anticipation of benefit or hope in such patients to stabilize the treatment system and reduce drop-out.

Ours is not the first suggestion that patient expectations play a critical role in continuity of treatment. What our analysis does offer, however, is an understanding of why these expectations are important, i.e., how they operate to produce the problem situation. The recommendations it offers are, consequently, less intuitive and more specifically geared to the actual causes of the problem, with a greater likelihood of achieving desired results.

The patient's forecast of the benefit he expects to experience in treatment stems from an act of anticipation present at the onset of treatment and developed during treatment by a continuing appraisal of the impact on his level of performance of the treatment received thus far. These formulations, whether correct or incorrect, appear significantly to affect the patient's participation in the treatment system. The patient approaches the treatment process with an initial set of beliefs about the help he may receive from it. Some of these beliefs originate in his social class and cultural milieu and in the basic personality traits of the patient—his optimism and suggestibility— and, as such, are not readily subject to influence. Other beliefs, stemming from prevalent attitudes about the nature of psychiatric illness and its treatment and from prior experience he or others in his social network have had with care-giving systems, are more readily subject to influence. The patient's assessment of how his functioning has changed in response to treatment is also potentially subject to influence.

Let us look at a number of strategies that could be employed on an experimental basis and, if successful, could be incorporated into the standard procedures of a mental health program.

First, a mental health program could attempt to educate the citizens and referral sources in its community in the nature of mental illness and in the availability and efficacy of its treatment programs.

Second, the program could identify those patients with chronic psychiatric disability who do seek help but who are most vulnerable to drop-out from treatment and, as such, require interventions beyond the usual measures of promoting and maintaining a therapeutic alliance. Following the findings of the simulation experiments, staff would administer interviews, attitude questionnaires, and other tests that could uncover those patients who enter treatment with both little hope of treatment benefit and with unstable standards of functioning or who develop these two conditions during the process of treatment. Special remedial efforts could be employed with this group.

Third, the program could make sure it has hired staff who have a genuine interest and concern in treating patients with chronic psychiatric disability, especially those patients from the lower social class who most often constitute the group vulnerable to treatment drop-out. The staff should be well trained in the methods most appropriate for treating patients with chronic disability, and should be encouraged to have confidence in their treatment theories and methods.

Fourth, the early phase of treatment could be marked by an intake process that is especially responsive to the acute needs of the patients and their families. The therapist, patient, and his family, where appropriate, could discuss their expectations of treatment benefit in order to get this critical issue into the open, where it could be more readily subject to influence. The patient and his family, where appropriate, could participate maximally in discussing the treatment goals and the planned treatment procedure and the relationships between the two. The value of the planned treatment regime could be enhanced through educational measures; for example, orientation interviews and reading and audiovisual material. The patient and his family, where appropriate, could participate in group discussions about treatment benefit with other patients who are at various stages of recovery from illness, and their families, to gain group support for a new value system.

And fifth, the staff could reinforce expressions of hope during the treatment process, highlight patient gains and their contiguity to treatment input (within the context of understanding the psycho-dynamics of the patient's pathology), and be sensitive to drops in the level of benefit expected which might require repeated "injections of hope", using the interventions noted above.

NOTES TO CHAPTER FIVE

1. Florence Kluckhohn, "Dominant and variant value-orientations". C. Kluckhohn and H. Murray (Eds.), *Personality in Nature, Society and Culture,* 2nd edition, New York, Alfred A. Knopf, 1953.

Chapter 6

The Structure of Student-Teacher
Interaction in the Elementary Classroom

We now apply the general theory to a problem in the field of education. A review of the literature on academic performance indicates that one key in-school factor is the amount and quality of the teacher-student interaction. The most important out-of-school factor affecting student performance seems to be the family. Here we examine the interdependence of the variables affecting these factors as they in turn affect student performance. This chapter presents the general plan and justification for the teacher-student interaction model developed here. The appropriate literature is cited to justify the model design.

Figure 6–1 pictures the core of our model. The diagram is here presented in its simplest form to emphasize the perspective from which the base model was developed.

Figure 6–1 indicates that the academic performance of a student affects the amount of help he seeks. The child's request for help influences the amount of time a teacher allocates to him. This in turn determines the real help the teacher gives him, which in turn affects his performance. If a student's performance falls, he seeks more help, which causes the teacher to allocate more of her time to him, which provides him with more help, thus improving his performance and causing him to seek *less* help; and so forth. (This of course assumes that the student's goals do not fall in the meantime—an assumption that will be reviewed later.)

The full base model of teacher-student interaction is presented in

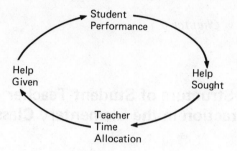

Figure 6-1. Educational System Overview

figure 6-2. The model can be divided into two parts: the teacher's side and the student's side. However, it must be recognized that this division is made only as a means of organizing the following discussion. The two sides of the model have important overlapping variables. In addition, each aspect is part of the total system and therefore the action in one area clearly has impact on the other area.

THE STUDENT

Student Goals

A student comes to school at the beginning of the year with a preset but approximate notion as to what he would like to attain academically. Since the year has not yet started, his immediate goals are initially no different from his longer-term aspirations. As the education process gets under way, the student begins to sense and reflect upon his actual performance. The student judges himself in relation to his other classmates and absorbs the information about his performance that is conveyed by the teacher. As this process continues, the student gradually begins to believe that his actual performance represents what he will be able to attain. He slowly surrenders, confirms, or raises his prior aspirations, and becomes more realistic about his goals, that is, adjusts them to his recent performance level.

The literature clearly supports this description of student goal setting. We assume that self-concept or self-esteem generally determines the student's goals. That is, if a student's academic self-concept or self-esteem is high, his goals will be proportionately high.

LaBenne and Greene say that self-concept is "the person's total appraisal of his appearance, background and origins, abilities and resources, attitudes and feelings which culminate as a directing force

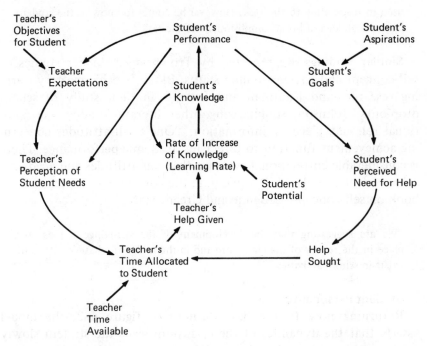

Figure 6-2. Systems Diagram of Student-Teacher Interaction as it Affects Classroom Performance

in behavior."[1] Coopersmith defines self-esteem as "The evaluation which the individual makes and customarily maintains with regard to himself: it expresses as attitude of approval or disapproval and indicates the extent to which the individual believes himself to be capable, significant, successful, and worthy."[2]

Bloom, in his work, distinguishes between the explicit curriculum —reading, math, social studies, science—and the implicit curriculum, "the curriculum which teaches each student who he is in relation to others."[3] In explaining further this implicit curriculum, Bloom states: "There are few school hours, during which the student is not judging himself against the standards set by himself, the teacher, or peers and his family."[4] He goes on:

The student may judge his own success on the task by inferring whether the teacher approves or disapproves of him and his work. The student may also infer how well he accomplished the task by the degree of confidence he has in the work he did, the questions he answered, or the procedures he used in responding to the task. However he comes to know it, the student has a rough idea of his accomplishment of the task.[5]

Similar findings are reported by Trowbridge,[6] in her studies of self-concept and socioeconomic status, Block,[7] in his mastery-learning research, and Kaufman and Lewis,[8] in their study of school drop-outs. Johnson, summarizing other literature, adds one additional relevant piece of information: "One's self-attitudes concerning achievement function to direct his academic performance. There is considerable correlational evidence that self-attitudes and academic achievement are related."[9] Finally, in the concluding chapter of their book on self-concept, LaBenne and Greene state,

> "We are suggesting that the development of the self-concept does take place in the reality of the classroom and in the midst of whatever dynamic exists in school activities."[10]

Student Personality

Returning now to the base diagram of figure 6-2, the model asserts that the dynamics of the classroom leads the student slowly to change his goals so that they are closer to his current performance. Even though his goals may be shifting, the student tends to get disappointed when his performance fails to live up to his present objectives. Sometimes he recognizes that he is in need of extra help if he is to attain his goals. The enthusiastic child makes a concerted attempt to get extra help from the teacher. If the student is unenthusiastic or turned off, he makes little or no effort to get extra help.

The little literature found in the area of student perseverance confirms the model assumptions just described. "Of all the mastery learning variables, perseverance is the one about which there are the least data."[11] Barton, Dielman, and Cattell, in their study to identify a personality factor capable of predicting school achievement, report that the "personality factor 'conscientiousness' and I.Q. predicted achievement in all areas (sixth and seventh grade social studies, science, math, and reading)."[12]

Combs, investigating children with reading difficulties, describes a personality type that might be considered the opposite to conscientious and achieving.

> Such a child is likely to avoid reading and thus the very experience which

might change his concept of self is bypasssed. Worse still, the child who believes himself unable to read, confronted with the necessity for reading, is more likely than not to do badly. The external evaluation of his teachers and fellow pupils, as well as his own observations of his performance, all provide proof to the child of how right he was in the first place! The possession of a particular concept of self tends to produce behavior that corroborates the self-concept with which the behavior originated.[13]

LaBenne and Greene make the same observation in their book. Brophy and Good comment on both personality types.

> Relaxed and active students who frequently initiate contact with teachers will get more attention and are more likely to correct any misconceptions that teachers may have about them. In contrast, quiet, withdrawn students who avoid teachers and do not say much when questioned leave the teachers more room for error in judging them.[14]

At this point in the model, the student-teacher interaction begins to affect the student.

Teacher Help

The model diagram conveys that the student's efforts to get more help from the teacher affect how much attention the teacher gives him. If the teacher finds a very enthusiastic and concerned student, she may give him more help than she feels he needs. However, if the child makes no effort at all to clarify his misunderstandings and shows no interest in learning, the teacher may be discouraged or even turned off, and may therefore end up giving this student *less* help than she actually feels he needs.

If the teacher gives a child extra help, and this help is effective, the child's ability to absorb knowledge is increased. As the child improves his ability to learn, his body of knowledge grows. Additional follow-up help the teacher might give this child will then have a greater payoff, because the teacher will be working with a child with greater understanding and knowledge.

Several researchers have described this kind of phenomenon. Brophy and Good discuss a study of theirs where they

> had first-grade teachers rank their students according to expected achievement. Three high and three low boys, and three high and three low girls

were then observed in each class. Clear teacher expectations were found. The teachers were more likely to stay with highs [students the teachers expected to achieve well], after they failed to answer an initial question (by repeating the question, giving a clue, or asking another question). In contrast, they tended to end the interaction by giving the answer or calling on someone else in parallel situations with lows. Differences in teacher feedback reactions were also noted. Teachers failed to give feedback to highs in only 3 percent of their response opportunities, while the figure for lows was 15 percent. In addition, highs were more likely to be praised when they answered correctly and less likely to be criticized when they answered incorrectly or failed to respond. These differences were observed even though highs made more correct responses and had fewer failures than lows.[15]

Rosenthal and Jacobson[16] and Kester and Letchworth[17] report almost identical findings to Brophy and Good.

Olsen, reporting on a compensatory education program that in effect provided for more teacher time for precollege students, states, "Analysis of the data showed that the compensatory education did have a positive social-psychological effect on the academic self-concept of the students."[18] Sears, reporting her study in which individualized help was given to children, states that "individualized teaching appears to be especially effective with those children with a relatively positive self-concept to start with."[19]

Student's Learning Rates

Carroll, in his "model of school learning", espouses the theory that anyone, provided he has the aptitude, can master a learning task if he is given enough time by the teacher and if he is willing to spend the time necessary for mastery. Carroll identifies two other variables important to learning.

These two variables are: (1) the quality of instruction and (2) the student's ability to understand and profit from instruction. The author assumes that these variables interact, and, indeed, there is considerable research evidence that they can and do. For example, students who have a high ability to understand and profit from instruction are little affected by variations in quality of instruction, while students with low ability to understand instruction are much more affected by variations in quality. Ability to understand and profit from instruction is probably associated with verbal intelligence and reasoning ability. Thus, students with high verbal intelligence can learn pretty well even with a poor program of instruction.[20]

Thus, the variables Carroll considers in his "model of school learning" are similar to those in our model of student performance.

Student Intelligence

The model embodies Carroll's assumption that the child's learning rate is affected by his innate potential. This is described in the model in terms of I.Q., the most easily understood and best scale available at present for measuring innate potential. The child with a high I.Q. has a fast learning rate. However, of two children with the same I.Q., the child with more knowledge on the subject learns faster because level of knowledge also affects learning rate.

The literature clearly supports the significant correlation between I.Q. and achievement. In a study to measure retention of social studies concepts among elementary school children, Arnoff reports, "Among the main findings of the study were: . . . at all grade levels the number of concepts learned and retained was directly related to mental age."[21] Baker, Schutz, and Hinze,[22] Kirsh,[23] and Klansmeier[24], among many others, all report similar findings.

Thus the base model reflects three factors affecting learning rate: innate potential, level of knowledge of the student, and extra help given by the teacher. In addition, the impact of family background on school performance is considered later in a separate section.

The level of knowledge and understanding of a child manifests itself in the daily performance of that child. A child with a high level of understanding and knowledge does better work in school than a child with a low level of knowledge and understanding.

This completes the feedback loop of variables on the student's side of the student-teacher interaction. In review, during the course of a school year, a child adjusts his goals so they are in line with his performance. The gap between how well a child is performing and how he would like to perform determines the amount of teacher help the child thinks he needs. This in turn influences the amount of help the student seeks, which affects the amount of time and help the teacher gives the student. This help, combined with the student's innate potential and current store of knowledge, influences his rate of learning. Learning rate increases as the student's knowledge base increases.

This knowledge accumulation will then determine the student's performance.

THE TEACHER

Teacher's Expectations

The teacher's side of the model parallels to some extent the student side. A teacher's objectives for a particular student are often set at the very beginning of the school year, based on information obtained from the student's record as well as from other faculty members. As Johnson sums up:

> Expectations of teachers are affected in many overt and covert ways in a school. The things one hears from other teachers, the records of the student, the opinions of the counselor, the previous academic performance of the student, all affect a teacher's expectations about how a student will behave.[25]

Some authors criticize this practice. LaBenne and Greene feel:

> One of the most damaging and vicious practices in our public schools today is the tendency on the part of some teachers to make judgments about a student on the basis of his cumulative record, without ever having seen the student.[26]

Wellington and Wellington,[27] Good and Dembo,[28] and Bloom agree with LaBenne and Greene. Bloom goes a step further:

> These expectations are transmitted to the pupils through school grading policies and practices and through the methods and materials of instruction. Students quickly learn to act in accordance with them, and final sorting through the grading process approximates the teacher's original expectations. A pernicious self-fulfilling prophecy has been created. . . . Such a system fixes the academic goals of teachers and students. It reduces teacher's aspirations and students' desires for further learning.[29]

Initially, the teacher's expectations for a student are the same as her objectives. She has not yet received additional information that would lead her to expect otherwise. As the teacher becomes familiar with a student's classroom work, she gradually changes her expectations for that student so that they correspond more closely to the level of the student's actual recent performance. The process of a teacher setting her expectations for a student is therefore modeled in a manner similar to the process of a student setting his own goals.

Teacher's Help

As the teacher recognizes that a difference exists between the level of work a student can do, and the level of work he is in fact doing, she makes an effort to give him extra help. The base model assumes that the teacher allots extra time to a student based primarily on her evaluation of that particular student's needs. The amount of time is limited by the amount of extra-help time a teacher can find during a school week. Given the typical tightness of a teacher's schedule, the amount of time a teacher spends with a student who does not seek help will no doubt be less than the teacher feels he needs. If the student occasionally asks for help, the teacher might be motivated to give him what she feels he needs. The student who is constantly looking for extra help might sometimes pressure the teacher into giving him more time than she really feels he needs. However, beyond some definite saturation point further pressure for attention and special consideration will have negative effects on the teacher. Christopher Jenks comments on this when he says, "The athlete is a good example. If you're 4 percent behind, a 5 percent increase is important, and if you're 60 percent behind, it's hardly worth talking about."[30]

The importance of the teacher's decision to give help is further highlighted in the report of the President's Commission on School Finance: "Despite diligent searches and widespread opinion to the contrary, the Commission finds no research evidence that demonstrates improved student achievement resulting from decreasing pupil-teacher ratio."[31]

The teacher side of the model and the student side now overlap. As the teacher gives the student more individual attention she increases his learning rate and therefore his base of knowledge, which is reflected in better performance by the student. The student's increased knowledge then also makes the teacher's help more effective.

As the student's performance improves, the teacher gradually feels the student's needs are less and therefore gives him less extra help. Eventually this could cause a slow-down in the student's learning rate. The resulting gradual change in his rate of performance may cause the student to cease to meet the teacher's expectations. As this happens the teacher then reassesses the student's needs, once again allocating more time to him.

As they have been described, each of the two main modeled feedback loops can lead to cyclic fluctuations in student performance, accompanied by fluctuations also in student goals and teacher objectives, in help-seeking and help-giving, and in student rate of learning. The student and teacher are clearly shown as affecting each other, with student performance being the joint product.

Each modeled loop also reflects the processes whereby goals or objectives shift to accommodate short-term performance. Through these changes over time either the student or the teacher or both can turn off the help-seeking/help-giving interchange that so critically influences the dynamics of performance.

The literature reviewed here indicates that our basemodel is in harmony with the available education research. Appendix B explains how the model is translated into computer language.

NOTES TO CHAPTER SIX

1. Wallace LaBenne and Bert Greene, *Educational Implications of Self-Concept Theory,* Pacific Palisades, Calif., Goodyear Publishing Company, Inc., 1969, p. 10.

2. S. Coopersmith, *The Antecedents of Self-Esteem,* San Francisco, W.H. Freeman and Company, 1967, pp. 4–5.

3. Benjamin S. Bloom, "Affective Consequences of School Achievement", in James H. Block, *Mastery Learning: Theory and Practice,* New York, Holt, Rinehart and Winston, Inc., 1971, p. 14.

4. Ibid.

5. Ibid., p. 16.

6. Norma Trowbridge, "Self-Concept and Socio-Economic Status in Elementary School Children". *American Educational Research Journal,* 1972, 9, 525–37.

7. James H. Block, *Mastery Learning: Theory and Practice,* New York, Holt, Rinehart and Winston, Inc., 1971.

8. Jacob Kaufman and Morgan Lewis, *The School Environment and Programs for Dropouts,* University Park, Pa., The Pennsylvania State University Institute for Human Resources, 1968.

9. David W. Johnson, *The Social Psychology of Education,* New York, Holt, Rinehart and Winston, Inc., 1970, p. 88.

10. LaBenne and Greene, p. 121.

11. Block, p. 94.

12. K. Barton, T.E. Dielman, and R. Cattell, "Personality and I.Q. Measures as Predictors of School Achievement". *Journal of Educational Psychology,* 1972, 63, 398.

13. A.W. Combs, "Intelligence from a Perceptual Point of View". *Journal of Abnormal and Social Psychology*, 1952, 47, 669-70.

14. Jere E. Brophy and Thomas L. Good, "Teacher Expectations: Beyond the Pygmalion Controversy". *Phi Delta Kappan*, 1972, 54, 277.

16. Robert Rosenthal and Lenore Jacobson, *Pygmalion in the Classroom*, New York, Holt, Rinehart and Winston, 1968.

17. Scott Kester and George Letchworth, "Teacher Expectations and Their Effects on Achievement and Attitudes of Secondary School Students". *The Journal of Educational Research*, 1972, 66, 51-55.

18. Henry Olsen, "Compensatory Education and Academic Self-Concept". *Phi Delta Kappan*, 1973, 54, 351.

19. Pauline Sears, *Effective Reinforcement for Achievement Behaviors in Disadvantaged Children: The First Year*, Stanford University, Stanford, Stanford Center for Research and Development in Teaching, 1972 (EDO67 442).

20. John B. Carroll, "Problems of Measurement Related to the Concept of Learning for Mastery", in Block, p. 33.

21. Melvin Arnoff, "An Investigation of Factors Related to the Ability of Children in Grades Two, Three and Four to Comprehend Concepts of Government with an Elementary Social Studies Course on Government", in Richard Gross and Leonardo de la Cruz, *Social Studies Dissertations 1953-1960*, ERIC Clearinghouse for Social Studies/Social Science Education, Boulder, Colo., 1971 (EDO54 999), 202.

22. Robert Baker, Richard Schutz, and Richard Hinze, "The Influence of Mental Ability on Achievement when Socio-economic Status is Controlled". *Journal of Experimental Education*, 1961, 30, 255-58.

23. Bernard Kirsh, "An Evaluation of Levels of Cognitive Learning in a Unit of Fifth Grade Social Studies", unpublished doctoral dissertation, University of Southern California, 1967.

24. Herbert Klansmeier, "The Effects of I.Q. Level and Sex on Divergent Thinking of Seventh Grade Pupils of Low, Average and High I.Q." *The Journal of Educational Research*, 1965, 58, 300-302.

25. Johnson, p. 151.

26. LaBenne and Greene, p. 30.

27. Jean and Burleigh Wellington, "Should Teachers See Student Records?", in H.F. Clarizio, R. Craig, and W. Mehrens (eds.), *Contemporary Issues in Educational Psychology*, Boston, Allyn and Bacon, Inc., 1970.

28. Thomas L. Good and Myron H. Dembo, "Teacher Expectations: Self-Report Data". *School Review*, 1973, 81, 247-53.

29. Bloom, p. 94.

30. Donald Robinson, "An Interview with Christopher Jenks". *Phi Delta Kappan*, 1972, 256.

31. Ian Templeton, *Class Size. Educational Review Series Number 8*, Oregon University, Eugene, ERIC Clearinghouse on Education Management, 1972 (EDO66 779), 1.

Chapter 7

A Computer Analysis of Student Performance

We now present and discuss a variety of computer simulations of student performance. We look first at the direct influences between student and teacher within the classroom, and then with the aid of an englarged model turn our attention to the influence exerted by the home environment.

IN THE CLASSROOM

The Average Student

The first set of runs simulates an average student (I.Q. 110) with moderate aspirations and a teacher expecting average work.

In the first run, shown in figure 7-1, the student initially seeks thirty minutes of extra help per week. (Help Wanted, W, equals 0.5 hours per week initially on the graph.) But the teacher, perceiving no gap in her expectations (E) for the student, feels little pressure to provide help. Consequently, she gives the student very little help (H). The maximum this student receives is about .15 of an hour, 9 minutes per week of extra help. Because of the small amount of extra help, this student's performance (P in the figure) climbs very slowly from 75 toward, but not reaching, 76. Because his performance basically does not change, his goals (G), which started at 80, drop down by the end of the year to meet his performance. As his goals drop, he seeks even less than his initial desire of thirty minutes per week. Because neither student nor teacher perceives a need for help (N is

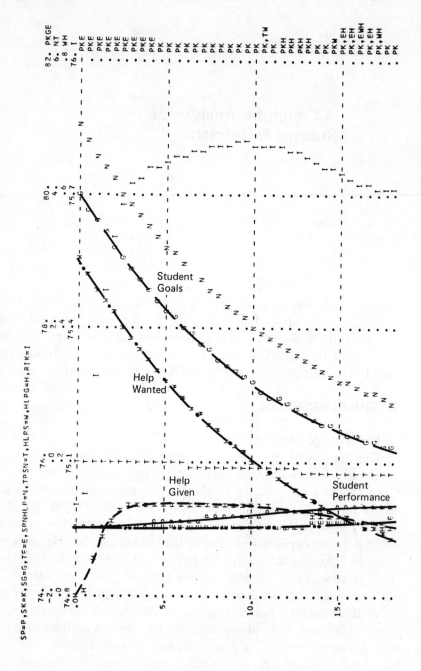

Figure 7-1. Base Test: Student Performance Model

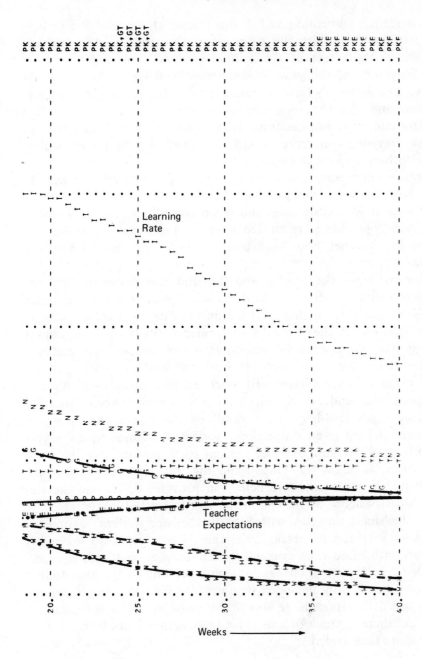

the student's perception and T the teacher's), the amount of help he receives drops virtually to nothing. The student's learning rate (I) shows the effect of the small amount of assistance he gets at the beginning of the year by going merely from 75 to 75.8 at its peak. This boost in learning rate accounts for the slight change in performance that the student does achieve.

This computer run illustrates what happens to the average student when everyone concerned is basically satisfied with things as they are. Nothing very much changes.

In the run reported in figure 7-2, three constants were changed to see what the effect would be on this student. The Time for Changing Student Knowledge was shortened from 25 weeks to 4 weeks, Teacher Objectives were shifted from 75 to 80 and the amount of Time the Teacher Had Available was doubled (from 10 hours to 20 hours/week).

Because both the teacher and the student initially believed the student could do better work, the teacher gives the student an extra half-hour per week of help (H) within the first five weeks of school. This help boosts the student's performance (P) from 75 to almost 78 by the ninth week of school. However, because the student's performance does not reach 80, both the student's goals (G) and the teacher's expectations (E) start drifting downward. As this happens, the student (N) and teacher (T) each perceive that the student needs less help. As a result of the closing goal gap, the amount of help given drops down to almost nothing by the seventeenth week. Because extra help is cut back, performance, by week seventeen, is below 77. Once again the teacher perceives that the student needs a little more help, and provides it, causing the student's performance by the end of the year to level off at 76.

In this simulation run, with both teacher and student starting out the year with the impression that the student could do somewhat better, with more time available to the teacher, and with less time needed for effecting a change in cumulative knowledge, the student performance is only increased by one point. The doubling of teacher time had little effect. Note also that if both student and teacher do not feel there is much of a need for help, help will not be given even with more time available.

A third simulation retained the changes made for the previous run and added two additional changes. Time for changing teacher expectations and time for changing student goals were both set so that teacher and student objectives were held essentially constant at 80 for the year. As figure 7-3 reveals, modification did have some impact on student performance, which went from 75 initially to 78 at the end of the year, peaking at over 79 for weeks 10-14. This increase was due to the boost provided by about 40 minutes of extra help per week in the early part of the year. The computer run seems to show that when both teacher and student have constantly held but moderate goals for an average child, this child can make reasonable gains during a school year with some extra help.

The Underachiever

The next set of runs simulate an underachieving student. First, the student's I.Q. was set equal to 130, with his historic performance low, at 75, and his aspirations also low, at 80, but the teacher's objectives are set high, at 95. Teacher's time available was set back to 10 hours per week, and time for change in student knowledge was also returned to 25 weeks.

The results of this simulation are shown in figure 7-4. Because the student perceives only a 5-point gap between his performance and his goals, he seeks only one half-hour of extra help per week. However, the teacher perceives a 20-point gap between performance and expectations. This situation results in the student getting, at peak, over forty minutes of help per week, about the same as the amount of help received in the previous set of runs (figure 7-3), when the teacher perceived only a 5-point gap. The student's low goals contribute to discouraging the teacher from giving as much extra assistance as she might like. Furthermore, the teacher's own perception tends to discourage her, given the large and frustrating gap in student performance that she senses. Because the resulting amount of help the student receives is fairly small, his performance rises very slowly, causing the teacher's expectations to drop fairly rapidly (down from 95 to about 77 by the middle of the year). Then, as both the teacher's expectations and the student's goals fall, the amount of extra help goes to only five minutes per week by midyear. Nevertheless, because the student's I.Q. is high, and learning rate increases, his performance increases to over 77 by the end of the year.

The second simulation of underachievement reverses the above situation, setting student aspirations at 95 and teacher objectives at 80, with historic performance at 75. As figure 7-5 shows, the student initially seeks 2½ hours per week of help, but, at most, receives only

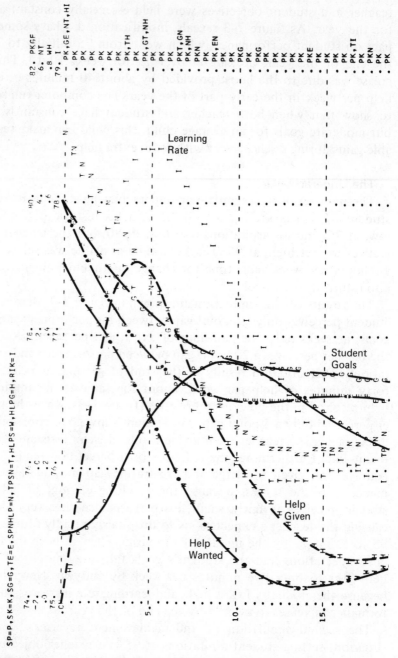

Figure 7–2. Increased Teacher Time and Objectives, Shortened Time to Affect Knowledge

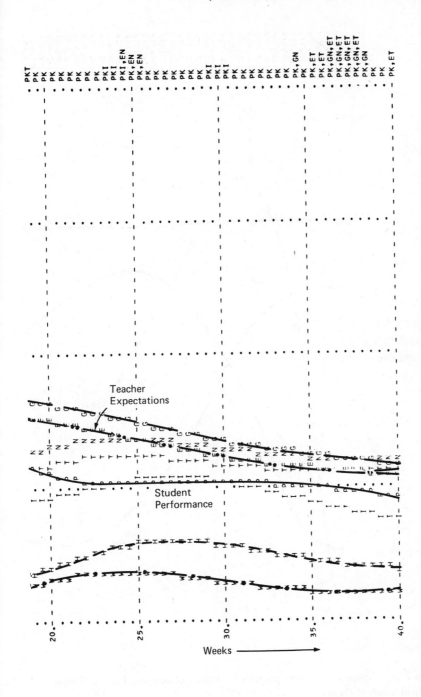

Teacher Expectations

Student Performance

Weeks ⟶

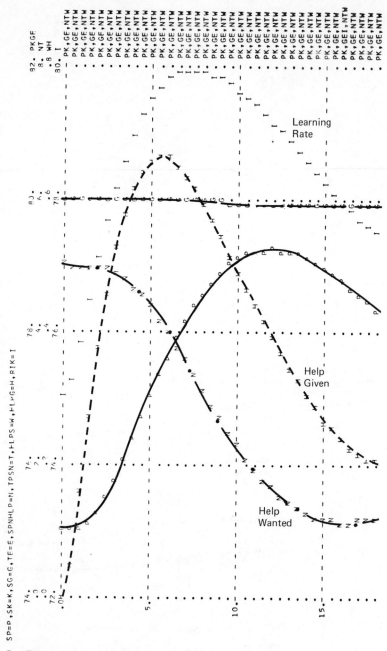

Figure 7–3. Figure 7.2 Conditions Plus Essentially Constant Teacher Expectations and Student Goals

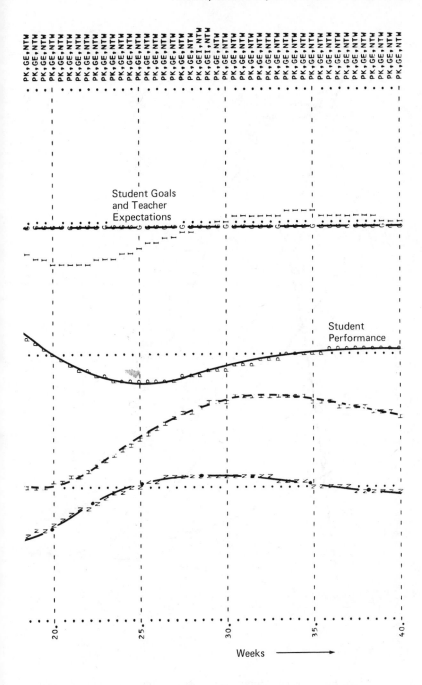

Student Goals
and Teacher
Expectations

Student
Performance

Weeks ⟶

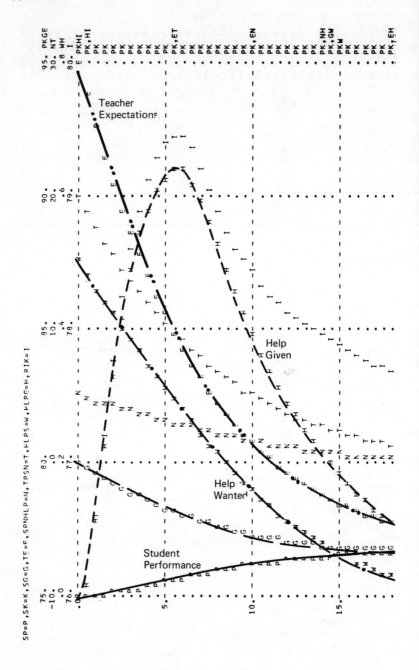

Figure 7–4.   Underachiever—Low Student Aspirations, High Teacher Objectives

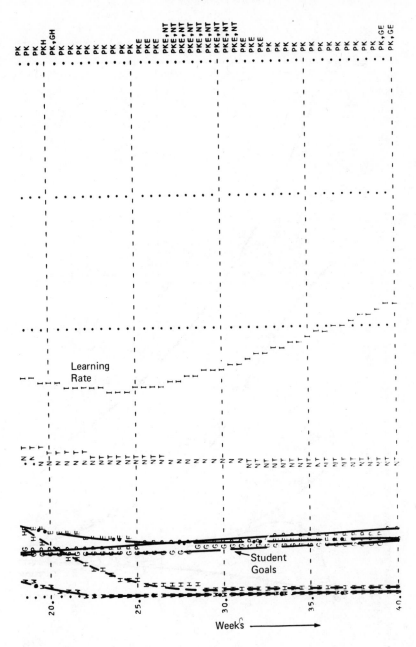

Learning
Rate

Student
Goals

Weeks ⟶

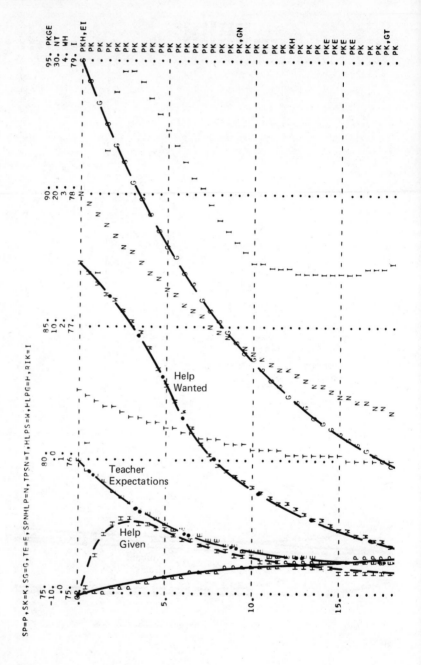

Figure 7-5. Underachiever—High Student Aspirations, Low Teacher Objectives

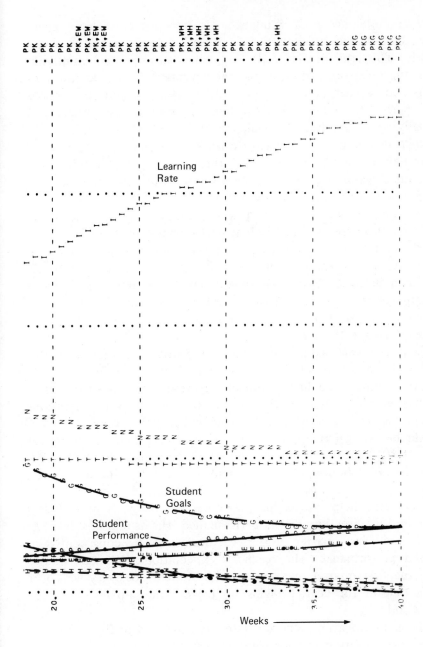

Learning Rate

Student Goals

Student Performance

Weeks ⟶

thirty minutes per week. Student goals drop just as teacher expectations had in the previous run, because his performance rises very slowly. This student also ends the year with about a 2-point gain.

In the third simulation of underachievement, both student aspirations and teacher objectives are initially set at 95 with historic student performance at 75. As indicated in figure 7-6, the student again initially seeks 2½ hours of help per week. This time, because the teacher also perceives his need, by week 6 he gets almost 2 hours of extra help per week. From week 3 through week 9, he receives over an hour a week of extra help. Because of all this the student's performance climbs fairly rapidly and consistently. Student goals and teacher expectations come down as they did in the previous runs, but this time, because of good student performance, by the last quarter of the year they have started to rise again. By the end of the year, the student has made a 7-point gain, his performance up to about 82. This run indicates that if a student has the potential, and this is recognized by both teacher and student, therefore producing the assistance the student needs, serious underachievement can be corrected in two or three years.

Two runs were conducted with the model changed slightly to make the teacher directly responsive to student desires for help. This situation simulates a little more closely that which is theorized to occur in an open classroom. This time our underachiever's aspirations were set at 95, indicating that the student recognizes the fact that he should be doing much better work. The teacher's objectives are set only at 80. Because he perceives a gap of 20 points, the student initially seeks 2½ hours per week of help, as figure 7-7 shows. By week 5 he is getting almost 2 hours from his assumed-to-be responsive teacher. This help boosts his performance. His goals nevertheless drop in the direction of his performance. His aspirations turn up again in the last quarter of the year because of his consistently increased performance. The teacher's expectations also start to rise after the first quarter of the year. This student does very well over the course of the year, bringing his performance up to 84 by the year's end.

Another simulation, whose results are displayed in figure 7-8, reverses the situation, setting student aspirations at 80 and teacher objectives at 95. Here the underachieving student seeks only 30 minutes per week initially, because of the small gap between his performance (75) and his goals. Given the assumed responsive teacher, the student gets almost that much help by the fifth week of school. As the student's goals come even closer to his performance, he seeks and gets even less help. The teacher's expectations for this student drop off sharply. By the end of the year this student has made only about a 2-point gain in performance. For this student, the year was virtually wasted. These two runs illustrate the usefulness of the open classroom for some students, allowing them to work and be helped to their potential; as well as its disadvantage for other students who need closer attention by the teacher and might not receive it.

AT-HOME INFLUENCES

A parental sector has been added to the base model to enable analysis of parental influence on student performance. The literature indicates wide agreement that parents and family do affect a student's academic achievement. Exactly how parents help or hinder their children in their school work is not yet clear. As Jenks said in a recent interview:

> So you know it isn't just a function of schooling and I don't think we have any real evidence one way or the other about the relative importance of the school and the home. I have a biased way of thinking that homes are important, but I certainly don't have any evidence on this particular score.[1]

Buchan, in a review of educational accountability, concludes that schools alone cannot possibly be held accountable for the total student performance. "What conclusions may be drawn from this expanded perspective of educational accountability? The first would be a clarification of the new role of the parent as a full partner in the educational process."[2]

Parental Sector
The computer runs made with the parent sector added to the base model are an attempt to understand more about the effect parents have on their children's performance. Figure 7-9 shows the relationship of the parental sector to the base model. Student performance and student goals are the overlapping variables.

All parents have some general academic aspirations for their chil-

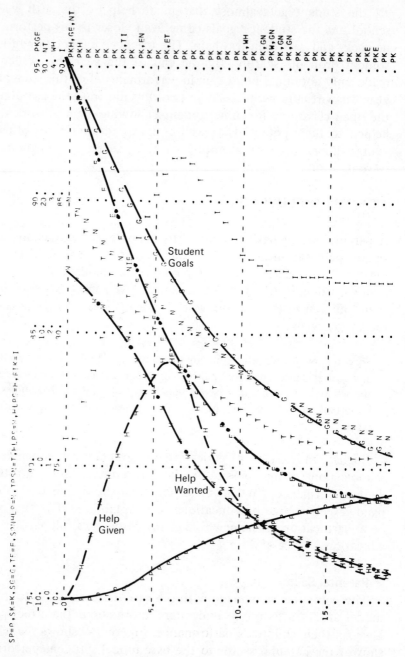

Figure 7-6. Underachiever—High Student Aspirations, High Teacher Objectives

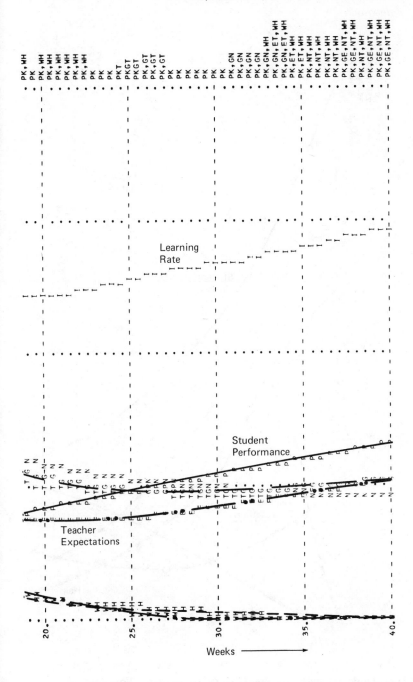

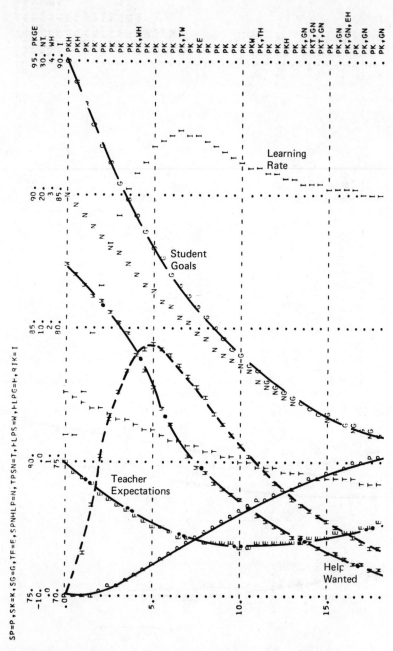

Figure 7-7. Underachiever—Teacher Directly Responsive to Student, High Student Aspirations, Low Teacher Objectives

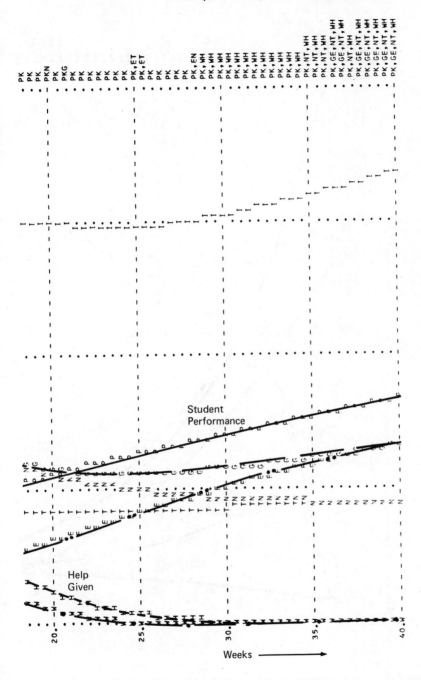

Student
Performance

Help
Given

Weeks ⟶

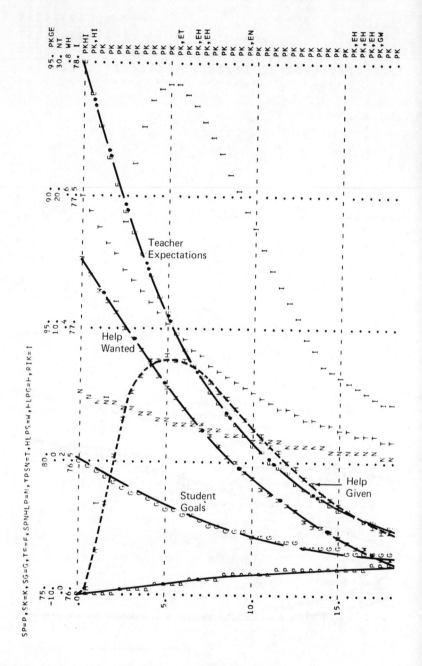

Figure 7-8. Underachiever—Teacher Directly Responsive to Student, Low Student Aspirations, High Teacher Objectives

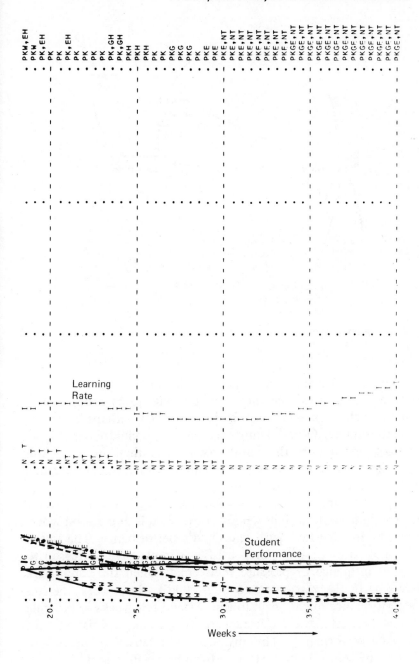

Learning
Rate

Student
Performance

Weeks ⟶

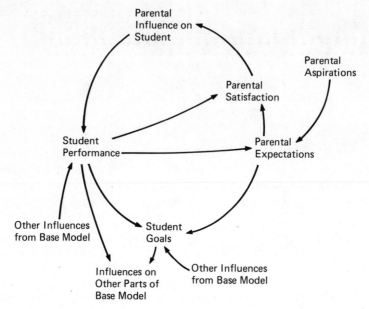

Figure 7-9. Parental Sector

dren, undoubtedly influenced in part by the family's socioeconomic level. Some families assume their children will go to college, some assume their children will finish high school and perhaps go on for vocational training. Other families assume their children will leave school to help support the family as soon as they are able. Still others desire to have their children remain in school, but are resigned to the likelihood that they will not do so.

If a family assumes its children will go to college, then the parents expect the child to do well in school. If the child is doing good work, the parents are satisfied with the child's performance. The initial model formulation assumes that satisfied parents have no reason to attempt to influence or pressure their child. When the parents are not being particularly attentive to their child's school work, the student's performance might begin to slip. After a few weeks of bringing home poor reports, the modeled parents become dissatisfied with their child's performance. This dissatisfaction causes the parents to attempt to influence their child to perform better in school.

Often this increased attention will suffice to cause the child to work harder in school. Once the child's work improves, the parents reduce their pressure. This type of family may maintain a balanced system throughout the child's schooling.

However, sometimes a student's performance drops because the work is in fact too hard or the teacher-student interaction is not functioning properly. If the student's performance continues to drop, the parents will eventually modify their expectations for their child. Parental expectations, though, are assumed to drop more slowly than either the student's goals or the teacher's expectations, for the parents usually have a far greater emotional stake in their child's achievement and have less immediate access to information about his classroom behavior.

The literature generally supports the description just presented. In summarizing the findings of the Coleman Report, Welsh states:

> What is fed into the schools in the way of teachers, books, buildings, and other resources have much less effect on achievement levels than the students' family background and the social environment of the student body. In other words, the schools bring little influence to bear on a child's achievement that is independent of his background and general social context.[3]

In reviewing the literature and in studies of their own, Kaufman,[4] Levine,[5] and Trowbridge[6] all found a high correlation between parental pressure to achieve in school and school achievement. Bloom[7] and Brembeck[8] both feel that consistency of values between home and school is crucial. Bloom sums up these ideas by saying:

> When the parents' educational aspirations for their children are high, they will reward achievement and punish lack of achievement. Under such conditions, the reward and punishment system of the school is paralleled by the reward and punishment system of the home. For such children the effective consequences of school achievement should be far greater than when the home has a different basis for reward and punishment than does the school.[9]

Finally, Pringle, summarizing her findings from her study of 103 underachievers, concludes: "The emotional and cultural climate of the family, parental interest and ambition, standards of expected achievement both at home and at school, can foster or limit, or seriously impair, intellectual development."[10]

Simulations of Parental Influence

Figure 7-10 shows the results of a run using the enlarged model. Parental expectations appear as X on the time plot. In this run an average child (I.Q. 110) begins the year performing at about the 74 percent level. Because of his previous average performance, both the student and his parents have moderate (80 percent) goals for this pupil's achievement. The teacher, as in the initial base run depicted in figure 7-1, has assessed the child as average and has set her expectations at 75. The parental influence on student performance is seen to have a slight negative influence when compared to figure 7-1. Because the parents' expectations for their child are moderate, they are satisfied with their child's average performance. As a result, the parents do not encourage their child to improve his school work and the child's performance begins to slip. The child asks for and gets some help from the teacher, but not very much because of the teacher's own expectation level.

By the end of the year, in this base run with parental influence added, the child's performance is slightly higher than it was at the beginning of the year. In the earlier base run without parental influence the child had also made a slight improvement in his performance. The parents' expectations have also slowly dropped to 77 percent, more in line with this year's performance.

Additional runs were made with this enlarged model to parallel the simulations shown in figures 7-2 and 7-3. A similar effect was evident. The parents' complacency with their child's performance caused his performance to be a bit lower than the original model without parental influence.

Parental influence is added to the simulation of underachievement in the runs shown in figures 7-11 and 7-12. Both runs simulate a child with an I.Q. of 130 and a school record of 75 percent performance level. At the beginning of the year the teacher assesses this child as an underachiever and initially sets high (95 percentile) expectations for the child. However, the student alone (figure 7-11) and with his parents (figure 7-12) base their goals and expectations on past performance and set their hopes moderately (80). As the year progresses, the student's performance climbs steadily, based on the help the teacher gives. The student performs at about the same level with and without parental influence until about week 18. At this point the parents finally acknowledge the fact that their child's performance has improved, and rather quickly raise their expectations. Because of the increased parental interest and attention, the child's performance increases more rapidly and ends considerably higher in figure 7–12 then in figure 7–11. These two runs indicate the positive influence parents can have on their children when they are responsive to the situation.

The simulation depicted in figure 7–13 is another situation similar to figure 7–12 in all respects except the time it takes the student to absorb new knowledge. In figure 7–12 the time was set at 4 weeks. In figure 7–13 the time was set at 25 weeks. This second child might be one who has been an underachiever for several years. He has therefore fallen further and further behind on his skill and knowledge accumulation. This accumulated deficiency causes the child to absorb new information much more slowly than someone who has had difficulty in school for a shorter time. As a result of this background, the help the teacher gives this child produces little improvement in his performance. The teacher becomes discouraged, her expectations slowly become more realistic, and the help she is willing to give this child decreases. Because this child's performance rises slowly, the student's goals and the parents' expectations slowly drift downward into line with actual student performance.

Another situation is simulated in figure 7–14. In this run, the under-achieving student is given a turned-off teacher and high-pressuring parents. The child begins the year performing at the 85 percent level because of the history of parental pressure. His knowledge base, however, is only at 75 percent, because he has been placed in the slow learning group in sschool. Because of continual pressure from his parents, the child raises his performance almost to the 95 level by the end of the year. The teacher's expectations rise steadily during the year, but because they are always below the performance level of the student she provides almost no extra help. His knowledge base therefore does not reflect his performance level. If this teacher passes on higher expectations for this child, his next year's teacher might fill in some of the gaps in his knowledge that probably will show up in initial achievement testing. This run illustrates the situation where the parents refuse to accept the school's assessment of their child, continue a close involvement with his schooling, and "prove" to the teacher that their child can do the work.

One final run was made to test the opposite situation—a similar child, but a turned-on teacher with turned-off parents. Figure 7–15 shows that this child begins the year performing at the 65 percent

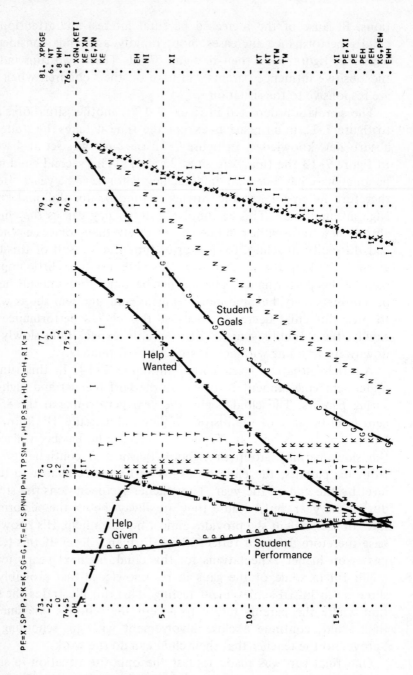

Figure 7-10. Parental Sector Test Run

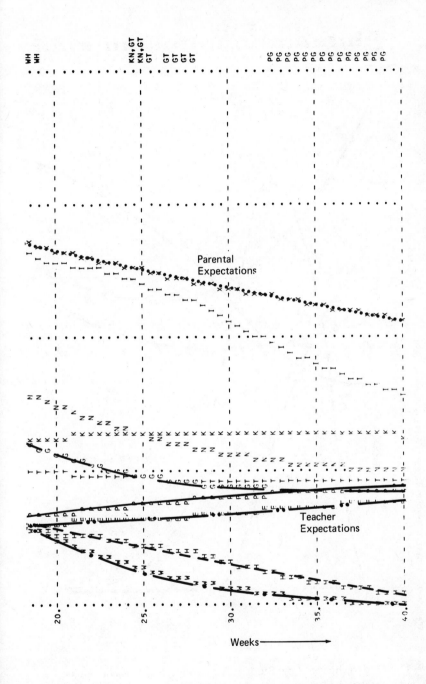

Parental Expectations

Teacher Expectations

Weeks⟶

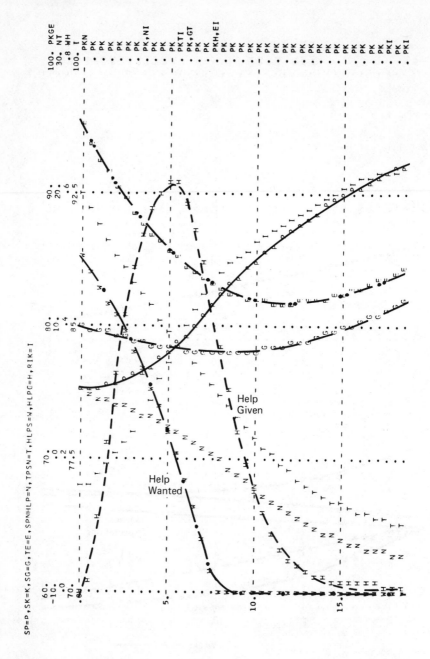

Figure 7-11.   Underachiever—Low Student Aspirations, High Teacher Objectives, Rapid Knowledge Absorption, No Parental Influence

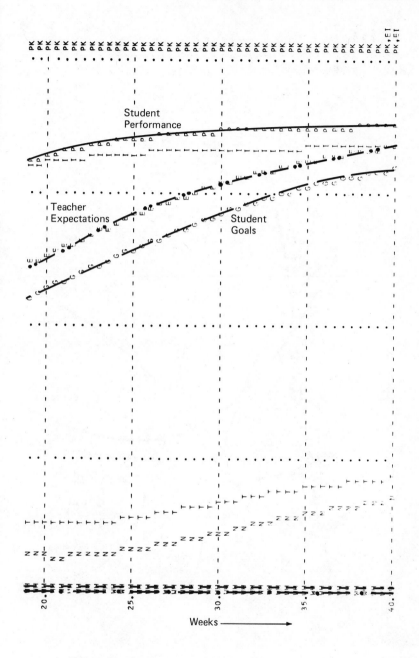

Weeks ⟶

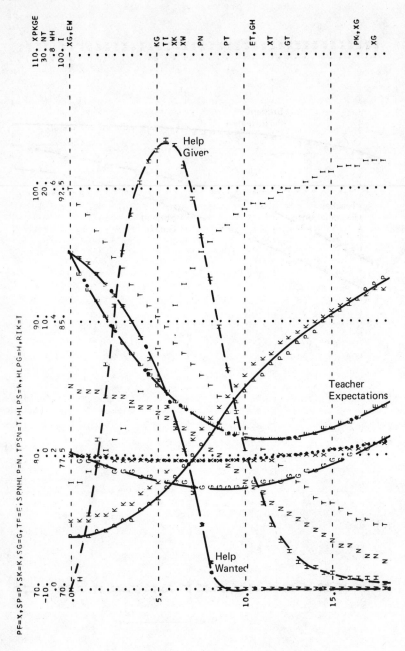

Figure 7-12.   Underachiever—Low Student and Parent Aspirations, High
Teacher Objectives, Rapid Knowledge Absorption, Parental Influence

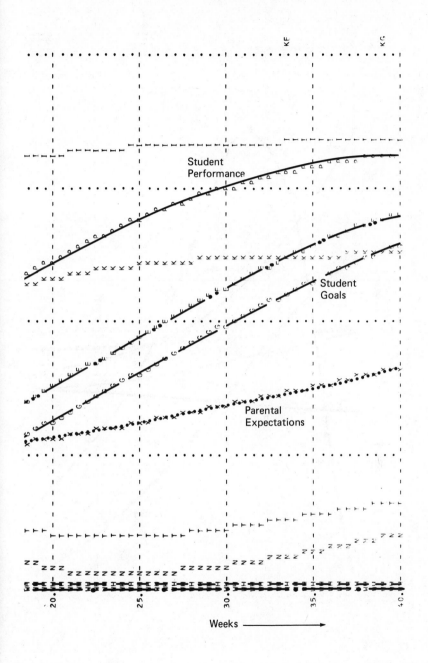

Weeks ⟶

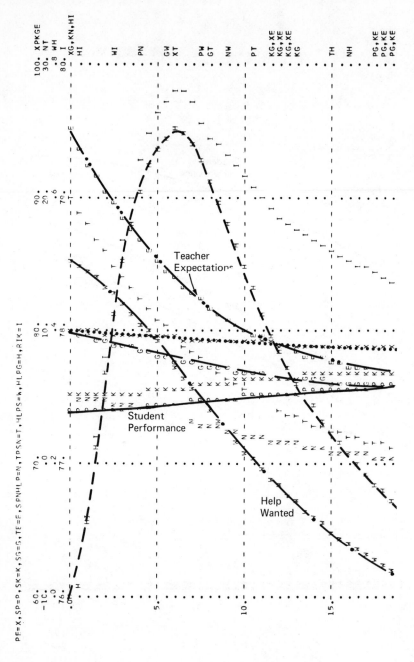

Figure 7-13.   Figure 7-12 With Longer Knowledge Absorption

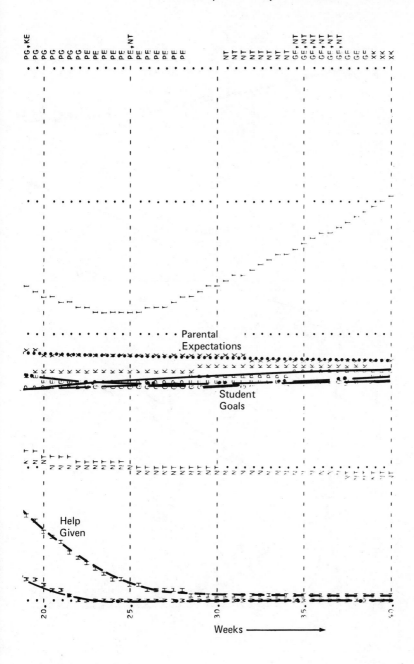

Parental
Expectations

Student
Goals

Help
Given

Weeks ⟶

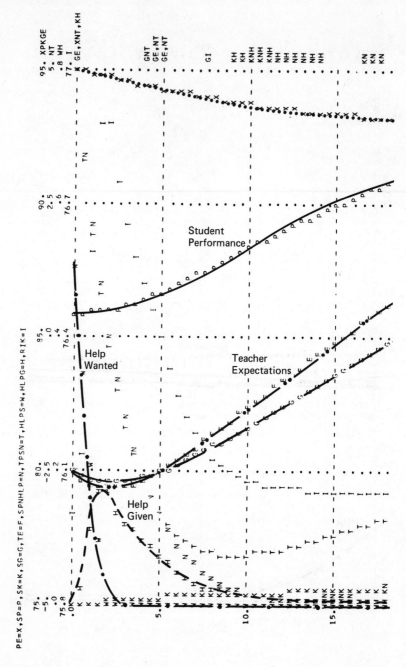

Figure 7-14. Underachiever—Turned-Off Teacher, Turned-On (High-Pressuring) Parents

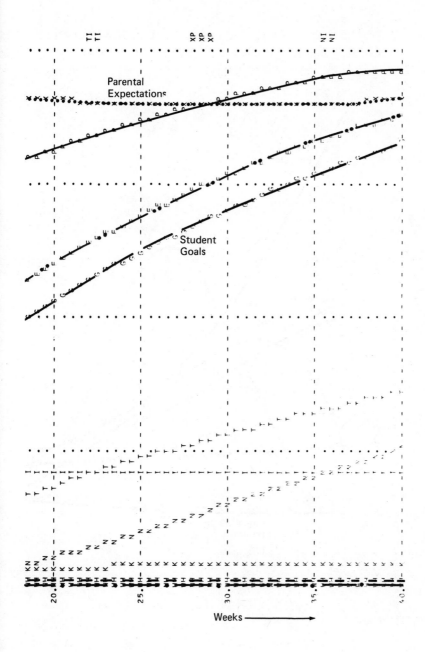

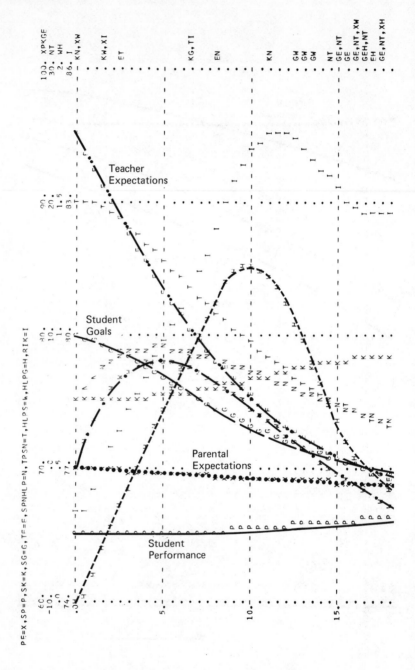

Figure 7-15.   Underachiever—Turned-On Teacher, Turned-Off Parents

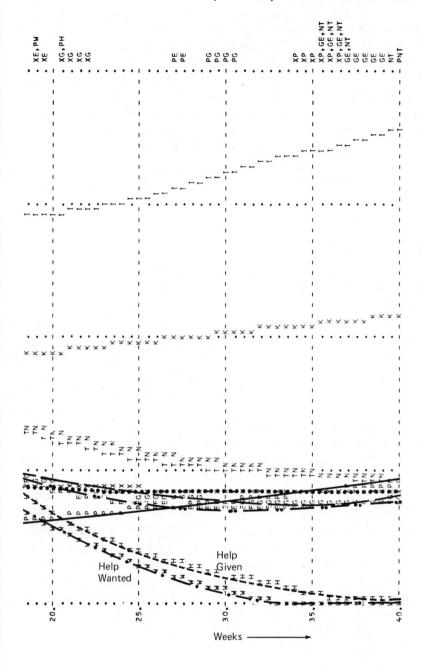

Weeks ⟶

level because of his parents' discouraging attitude throughout his schooling. However, the teacher recognizes this child as an under-achiever and gives him as much as 1¼ hours of extra help per week. Because the parents are uninterested and negative toward school, the child is unresponsive to the teacher's help. In spite of himself, his knowledge base and rate of learning do rise, but not enough to reflect significantly in his performance. As the year goes on, the teacher's expectations drift more into line with the student's current performance, and she therefore gives him less and less help. During the course of the year, the child's performance goes up a few points, reflecting his increased knowledge as a result of the teacher's initial help.

CONCLUSIONS

These computer simulations of student performance in an elementary classroom point out the importance of three elements: student goals, teacher expectations, and the amount of extra help given. When both student and teacher recognize that a problem exists and work together to overcome it, great gains can be made by the student. However, when either party fails to recognize a problem, much less is accomplished toward correcting the problem. The importance of teacher expectations has been shown in the studies by Rosenthal and Jacobson[11] and Brophy and Good.[12] The education research literature does not, however, indicate substantial empirical results in the area of student goals, or in the situation of combined student and teacher goals. An experiment in which student goals as well as teacher expectations were the jointly manipulated subjects of the study would not only test the findings of the simulation results but would importantly extend the empirical boundaries of classroom research.

Teachers often blame pressure on their time for poor pupil performance. These runs indicate that time (or class size) is not all that important. Table 7-1, summarizing eight computer simulations (performed with a 130 I.Q. student), indicates that the doubling of teacher time is not the sensitive variable. However, raising both teacher expectations and student goals does cause a significant increase in student performance.

The enlarged model of figure 7-16 suggests other areas that might influence student performance. Parents not only influence students directly by encouraging or discouraging performance and the setting

Table 7-1. Effect of Doubling Teacher Time Available for Extra Help on Student Performance

		Student Performance	
Teacher Expectations	*Student Goals*	*Teacher Time 10 Hours/Week*	*Teacher Time 20 Hours/Week*
75	80	75.5	76.2
75	95	76	77
95	80	76.8	78
95	95	82	84.8

of objectives, but also indirectly by applying pressure (or not applying pressure) to both the principal and the teacher. The other children in the classroom are also a source of performance pressure for the student, and might also be added to the modeled equations structure.

Moreover, the enlarged model indicates the possible addition of an evaluation process by both the teacher and the student, to assess and then affect the help given. As the teacher gives help to the student, this increases his learning rate, causing the teacher to feel that her help has been effective. As she evaluates her help positively, the model indicates that this encourages her to give more time, and then more help to the student. If the teacher encounters a reverse effect, wherein help given is not enough to increase noticeably a child's learning rate, this would probably cause the teacher to evaluate her help negatively, and therefore decrease it. A perverse implication of this changed assumption is the possible outcome that the teacher will spend most time with those who respond best to her, leaving the worst students falling farther behind and harder to reach.

On the student's side of the suggested model expansion, if he feels the help he is getting has enabled him to learn more easily, he will positively evaluate the help and attempt to influence the teacher to give him still more. The opposite effect can also take place here, with the student getting turned off by what he feels is ineffective help. The enlarged model therefore suggests other areas that obviously affect the dynamics of student performance.

NOTES TO CHAPTER SEVEN

1. Donald Robinson, "An Interview with Christopher Jenks". *Phi Delta Kappan,* 1972, 256.

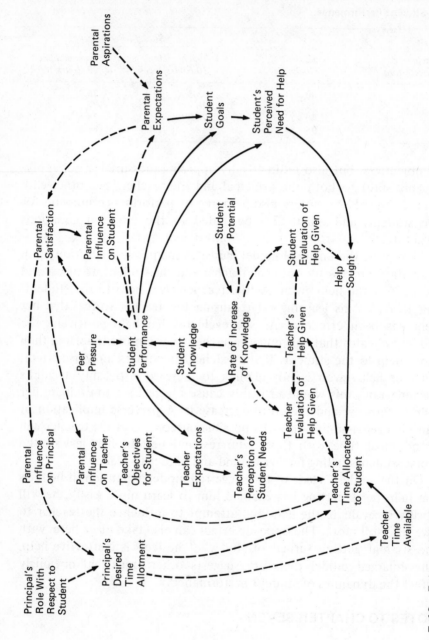

Figure 7-16. Enlarged Model

2. William J. Buchan, "Educational Accountability: The Parents' Role". *Education,* 1972, 93, 22.

3. James F. Welsh, "The Coleman Report", in H.F. Clarigio, R. Craig, and W. Mehrens (eds.), *Contemporary Issues in Educational Psychology,* Boston, Allyn and Bacon, Inc., 1970, p. 676.

4. Jacob Kaufman and Morgan Lewis, *The School Environment and Programs for Dropouts.* University Park, Pa., The Pennsylvania State University Institute for Human Resources, 1968.

5. Daniel Levine, et al., "The Home Environment of Students in a High Achieving Inner-City Parochial School and a Nearby Public School". *Sociology of Education,* 1972, 45, 435–45.

6. Norma Trowbridge, "Self-Concept and Socio-economic Status in Elementary School Children". *American Educational Research Journal,* 1972, 9, 525–37.

7. Benjamin S. Bloom, "Affective Consequences of School Achievement", in James H. Block, *Mastery Learning: Theory and Practice,* New York, Holt, Rinehart and Winston, Inc., 1971.

8. Cole A. Brembeck, *Social Foundations of Education,* New York, John Wiley and Sons, Inc., 1966.

9. Bloom, p. 25.

10. M.L.K. Pringle, *Able Misfits,* London, Longman Group Limited, 1970, p. 96.

11. Robert Rosenthal and Lenore Jacobson, *Pygmalion in the Classroom,* New York, Holt, Rinehart and Winston, Inc., 1968.

12. Jere E. Brophy and Thomas L. Good, "Teacher Expectations: Beyond the Pygmalion Controversy". *Phi Delta Kappan,* 1972, 54, 276–77.

Chapter 8

A Framework for Projecting Dental Care Supply and Demand

Our general theory provides a framework useful for planning human services, in this case dental health services, to meet future needs. In this chapter we examine the present and anticipated requirements for dental care and the resources that are expected to be available to meet them. In the process we consider the impact of the utilization of dental auxiliaries and the greater availability of insurance on the future quality and quantity of care.

Figure 8-1 shows an overview of the dental care system. It is portrayed as essentially similar to the general theory depicted earlier in figure 2-5 (page 22). The dotted lines indicate linkages that have little importance for the particular analysis of the dental system that we report. At any moment in time a given population of a city, state, region, or nation has a level of need for dental services, determined by its oral health relative to its standard. For part of the population this standard includes a concern for prevention of dental problems. Thus a population's perceived "need" for dental services is the sum of symptomatic requirements (e.g. toothaches, loose teeth) and preventive requests. This need manifests itself in service-seeking behavior, which is augmented or diminished by the population's expectation of benefit. Benefits expected rise or fall depending upon the population's experience with its providers. In particular the patient population's perceived accessibility of dental care (e.g., how soon an appointment can be arranged, how much initiative the den-

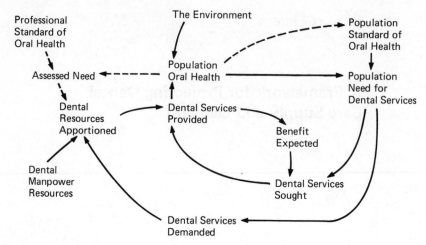

Figure 8-1. Dental Care Supply-and-Demand System

tist takes to encourage the patient to return) importantly influences the benefits that are expected. The strength of demand for services creates workload pressure on the delivery system, affecting the total quantity as well as the type of dental care provided. These busyness ramifications arise in many ways throughout the model. The amount and type of services provided affect the population's oral health.

In carrying out the analysis of this system, we extend the application of the general theory of human service delivery in two important directions. First, we focus upon the provision of physical health care, in this case dental services, rather than services directed at enhancing personal growth or adaptation. Second, we attend to the overall interactions between consumers and providers at the national level, in contrast to our earlier orientation toward the individual client relating to a program.

In undertaking this extension of our basic theory we wish to highlight here some differences between the dental care system model and, for example, the mental health system as described in Chapter Four.

1. The concept of preventive patient behavior needs inclusion, not just a response to perceived need for treatment. To be sure, some preventive mental health activities are also undertaken, and preventive physical health activities are being increasingly urged. But in the dental system preventively oriented behavior by consumer and provider are sufficiently real that they are given explicit representation

in the model, in addition to symptomatically oriented demand and supply.

2. Provider influences upon patient treatment-seeking behavior must be represented, rather than merely including provider response to patient-initiated treatment episodes. In reality the same phenomenon has been dealt with in relation to embodiment of habit and benefit-expected influences in the mental health model. But the dental model is explicit in calculating provider busyness, and in inputing its effects upon provider orientation toward patient education, toward encouragement of patient preventive attitude, and toward encouragement of comprehensive patient dental care.

3. Focus upon a real national health manpower planning problem, in contrast with the generic client-program models of chapters Four and Six requires: (a) utilization of a realistic data base for derivation of model parameters and initial conditions; (b) inclusion of exogenous changes affecting dental care supply, both in terms of projected changes in the number of dentists practicing and in terms of likely changes in the use of dental auxiliaries and in their contribution to overall productivity; and (c) recognition of exogenous economic influences upon patient care-seeking behavior that must be considered in assessing patient willingness to enter orthodontic or complete treatment and in projecting the possible impact of extensive dental insurance coverage.

RATIONALE UNDERLYING THE DENTAL MODEL

Patterns in which care is sought and delivered are essential determinants of demands on dental resources and, ultimately, of the level of oral health in a population. Patient motivations play a major role in establishing care-seeking patterns. Motivation for seeking care is affected by prior experience with the care system, perception of susceptibility to dental disease, attitudes toward dentists, and their social class.[1,2,3,4,5] In addition, several aspects of the dentist's behavior influence the way in which patients seek, and actually receive, care.[6]

Certain researchers have already developed models of interaction between dental practices and patients, taking an economic view of the process as a market for dental visits.[7] While the economic variables that have been stressed are important, they do not represent a complete picture. For example, visits are not entirely suitable as a measure of output and tend to distort conclusions about dental productivity or manpower requirements. Visits are nonuniform in objectives, results, and resources used. A 1971 survey by the American Dental Association (ADA) indicated that 48 percent of all dentists had visits of 30 minutes or less, while 25 percent had visits of an hour or longer, a range that was due to differences in the type of practice and size of the cities in which practices were located.[8]

The interval between visits is another attribute of nonuniformity. The 1965 ADA needs study found, for example, that patients with a six-to-eleven-month interval between visits required an average of 1.75 fillings, while those with an interval between visits of more than three years needed 5.09 fillings. Similarly, those with the shorter interval were found to require .07 extractions due to decay and to have 1.47 teeth missing, while those who had not seen a dentist for the longer interval needed 1.37 extractions due to decay and had 6.9 teeth missing.[9]

Perhaps most important, different patterns of visits result in different effects on a patient's oral health. Several visits at short intervals involving prophylaxis and treatment of minor problems are likely to do more to maintain oral health (and prevent or delay future care needs) than the same number of visits coming after several years with no care. The latter pattern can, at best, temporarily halt deterioration. Most dental visits deal with the effects of deterioration rather than prevention. A 1968 analysis found that over two-thirds of dental visits by people in its sample were for restorative services.[10]

Demand for Treatment

In developing a demand segment for the model, we asked, "Why do people seek treatment?" Observation of the dental care system and study of the dental health literature indicate division of the patient population into two groups which display different care-seeking patterns, preventive and symptomatic. The preventive-symptomatic distinction was first made by Hochbaum[11] and Kegeles,[12,13] who assert that a person who takes preventive health action, as opposed to being driven by symptoms, is brought to a state of "readiness to act" by three considerations: (1) he is susceptible to some disease; (2) the disease is potentially serious in its effects on him; and (3) a course of action to overcome the disease is both available to him and effective. Preventive dental behavior was further investigated and tested by Metz,[14] O'Shea,[15] and Tash.[16] Some people are committed to the maintenance of their natural teeth by means of periodic check-ups and treatment, while others seek treatment on a symptomatic basis, i.e., only when something troubles them, such as toothache, bleeding gums, or a loose tooth. Of course, dental behavior follows a continuous spectrum between these two extremes, but for our attempt to create an initial dental system framework the two-way split seems sufficient.

Information regarding the size of the two groups was obtained from surveys. One recent report, referred to earlier, indicated that only one-third of the respondents last visited a dentist for preventive rather than restorative care. This same survey obtained data regarding time since last visiting the dentist, as presented in table 8-1.[17] The results of a survey dealing with length of time since last initiating treatment are presented in table 8-2.[18] If we assume that patients who initiate treatment at intervals of less than a year are preventively oriented and the others symptomatically oriented, the resulting rough estimate is that between 35 to 50 percent of the

Table 8-1. Distribution of Time Since Last Visit

Time Since Last Visit to a Dentist	*Percentage of Respondents*
Within the last year	48%
Between 1 and 2 years ago	16
Between 2 and 3 years ago	7
Between 3 and 5 years ago	7
Between 5 and 10 years ago	8
10 or more years ago	13
Have never been	1

Table 8-2. Distribution of Time Since Last Treatment Initiation

Length of Time Since Last Initiating Treatment	*Percentage of Respondents*
Less than 6 months	15.9%
6 to 11 months	37.0
1 year	15.1
1.5 years	7.0
2 years	8.8
3 years	4.3
More than 3 years	7.6

population is preventively oriented and that from 50 to 65 percent of the population is symptomatically oriented.

Treatment Demands of Preventive Patients. The number of preventively oriented patients per month who initiate a preventive visit is a function of the interval between preventive visits as well as the size of the preventive population. From data describing length of time since last initiating treatment, we estimate that the current interval is approximately twelve months[19], i.e., one-twelfth of the preventive group is currently initiating treatment each month. This number may be used in conjunction with the current average care needs to estimate the demand of preventive patients. However, the average arrival rate may be influenced by factors such as changes in insurance coverage, introduction of dental education programs, average wait for an appointment, and dentist use of reminders. In order to include these effects in the model, we assume that a six-month interval between preventive visits prevails when all of these factors have their most positive influence. Factors relating to insurance coverage, education, and dental busyness (as it affects average wait for appointment and dentist use of reminders) are assumed to cause the interval to vary upward as they depart from their most positive values. Figures 8-2 and 8-3 show the effects of insurance coverage and dental education on the preventive patient arrival rate (thereby also affecting the interval between preventive visits).

The tables assume that 20 percent of the population are covered currently by some form of dental insurance and perhaps 50 percent have adequate knowledge of the requirements for good oral health.[20] The effect of these assumptions when combined with the relation-

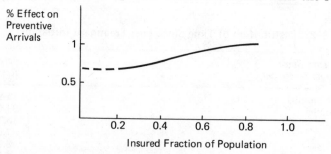

Figure 8-2. Insurance Effect on Preventive Patient Arrival Rate (Effect of Reducing Rate for Less-Than-Ideal Condition)

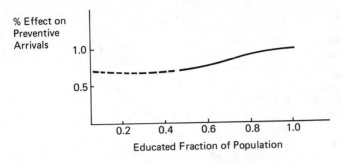

Figure 8-3. Education Effect on Preventive Patient Arrival Rate (Effect of Reducing Rate for Less-Than-Ideal Condition)

ships shown in fugures 8-2 and 8-3 is to yield an arrival rate of preventive patients that is half what it would be under the most positive insurance and education conditions. This, in turn, implies an interval between preventive visits of twelve months (i.e. half the arrival rate with the same number of preventive patients would mean that twice as long an interval occurs between their visits).

To complete the specification of preventive treatment demand, the average total time required to treat each arriving patient must be determined. This total time is comprised of three aspects: prophylaxis, examination and treatment planning, and treatment time for the average care needs. Prophylaxis has been found to represent an average of 17 minutes of treatment by one source and examination and treatment planning found to represent 10 minutes.[21] Treatment time depends on the average care needs and the treatment time required for each. Figure 8-4 indicates the variation in fillings required, teeth affected by periodontal disease, and extractions required as a function of time since last initiating treatment.[22] From these graphs and the average arrival interval, a reasonable estimate of the oral health needs of arriving preventive patients may be made. Based on the data that fillings require ten minutes of workload and extractions require nine minutes, a partial answer for treatment minutes demanded by preventive patients may be obtained. A complete answer may be obtained upon consideration of periodontal and orthodontic treatment requirements. While other treatment needs are added to the dental practices workload at the time treatment is initiated, these two types of care are dealt with differently because their demands on dental resources are spread out over time. Orthodontic treatment is represented as requiring 15 minutes of

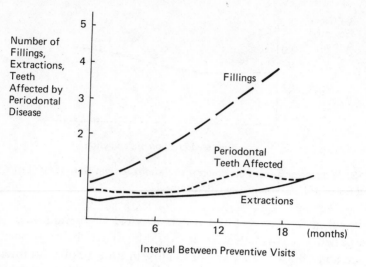

Figure 8-4. Dental Needs of Preventive Patients

workload per month for 36 months. Periodontal treatment for preventive patients requires 30 minutes of workload per month for two months. These treatment sessions are applied to the demand of succeeding months rather than the entire block being applied to the month in which treatment is initiated. The total minutes of treatment demand for preventive patients is then the sum of the minutes required for prophylaxis, examination and treatment planning, fillings, extractions, and periodontal and orthodontic treatment.

Figure 8-5 illustrates the generation of demand by preventive patients and indicates the impact of several variables on this demand.

Treatment Demands of Symptomatic Patients. The arrival of a symptomatic patient is motivated not by a general desire for good oral health but by a problem, e.g., a toothache, bleeding gums, or a loose tooth.[23] Hence the arrival rate is dependent upon the presence of a symptom and subsequent care-seeking behavior. Data dealing with the issues are presented in table 8-3, and may be used for the calculation of a monthly symptomatic arrival rate.[24] For example, 20 percent of this survey's respondents had a toothache in the year previous to the survey and 75 percent of them had sought care. Thus, approximately 15 percent of the total population had visited the dentist that year due to a toothache symptom. A monthly rate is then approximately 1.25 percent of the symptomatic population.

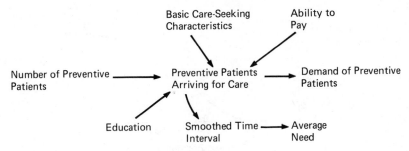

Figure 8–5. Treatment Demand of Preventive Patients

Similar calculations may be made for the other symptoms, and a total symptomatic arrival rate determined.

In modeling symptomatic arrivals we assume that the proportion with a condition who make a visit are influenced by an income factor, an education factor, and a dental busyness factor. For example, if payment is not a problem, then more people with a particular symptom will present themselves for treatment. For decay or periodontal symptoms, the data indicate that the average number of patients who made a visit was 58 percent. Ability to pay might raise this percentage by 45 percent at its most positive value and dental education might raise it by 10 percent—resulting in approximately 90 percent of those patients with symptoms seeking care. These factors are illustrated in figures 8–6 and 8–7.

For symptomatic patients who decide to seek care three treatment outcomes are assumed possible:

1. Treatment of offending symptom only, with the patient immediately returning to the pool of potential care-seeking symptomatic patients;

Table 8–3. Distribution of Dental Conditions and the Proportion of Persons with Conditions Who Made a Dental Visit

Condition	Proportion with Condition	Proportion with Condition Who Made a Visit
Toothache	20%	75%
Sore or bleeding gums	8	45
Loose permanent tooth	5	61
Pain in tooth when drinking hot or cold liquid	14	54
Crooked teeth	7	32

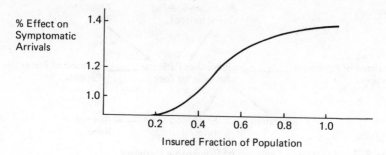

Figure 8-6. Insurance Effect on Symptomatic Patients Seeking Care

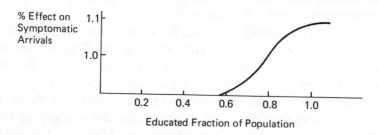

Figure 8-7. Education Effect on Symptomatic Patients Seeking Care

2. Treatment of all dental needs followed by a period in which additional symptoms are unlikely, and gradual return to potential care-seeking pool as a result of new dental problems that develop; and

3. Treatment of all dental needs and the patient becoming preventively oriented.

The split is illustrated in the diagram of figure 8-8.

The model embodies the assumption that the treatment desired by most symptomatic patients is simply administration of palliative medication and/or extraction of the offending tooth. These patients would then be susceptible immediately to additional symptoms, because many of their dental care needs would not have been cared for. However, some of the arriving symptomatic patients may be convinced by the dentist to have all of their dental needs treated, not just the symptom motivating the visit. This fraction accepting complete treatment is determined to a large extent by the proactivity of the dentist in suggesting and recommending complete treatment. (This proactivity, in turn, depends to a certain extent on the busy-

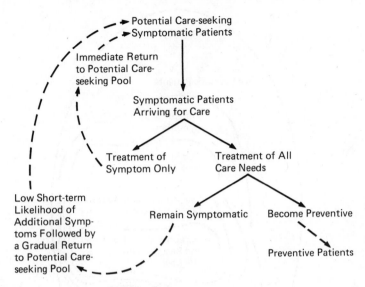

Figure 8-8. Symptomatic Patient Flow

ness of the dentist.) The fraction accepting complete care is also assumed to be affected by the symptomatic patient's ability to pay for extensive dental work. Those patients accepting complete care are assumed to have very low treatment needs after their sequence of visits. However, we do assume that in several years they will again begin to have treatment needs resembling the average symptomatic patient, because new dental problems will develop. The size of the symptomatic patient group potentially seeking care is assumed to be diminished by the number of symptomatic patients recently receiving complete care. This potential care-seeking pool has the symptoms and care-seeking behavior presented in table 8-3. The model also assumes that symptomatic patients will not adopt a preventive orientation without first getting care for their complete set of needs. Figure 8-9 aids in describing the segmentation of the symptomatic patient group by treatment outcome; each additional inner loop represents in a sense another hurdle toward gaining effective preventive orientation.

To determine the minutes of treatment, we must identify (1) the split between symptomatic and complete care treatment, and (2) the needs of both groups. Patients receiving care only for the symptom that motivated them to seek care are assumed to require on average a single extraction (of the offending tooth), as well as the time for

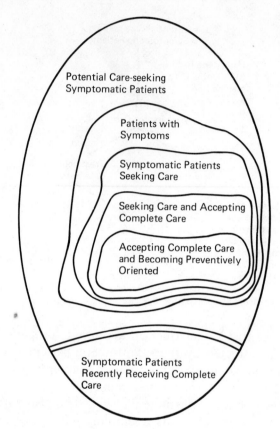

Figure 8–9. Symptomatic Patient Group

examination and treatment planning. Thus, some patients will require no extractions, while others will require more than one. The
model also assumes that the fraction accepting complete care is affected by dentist proactivity, which in turn reflects his busyness, and
by the ability of the patient to pay. That fraction is currently estimated at 20 percent; if payment were not an issue, it is estimated to
increase to 50 percent. Evidence for that large an impact of ability
to pay can be seen in data from a University of Chicago study, displayed in table 8–4.[25]

The "time since last visit data" indicate that the average interval
between symptomatic patients initiating treatment for complete care
is at least three years. For this length of time, according to the ADA
Needs Survey, the typical patient accepting complete care will require five fillings, two extractions, eight months of periodontal treat-

Table 8-4.   Mean Expenditures as a Function of the Ability to Pay a Large
Dental Bill

Ability to Pay a Large Dental Bill	Mean Expenditures for People with Symptoms in the Past Year
Not much trouble	$40
Very difficult	$32
Not able to pay	$15

ment, and endodontic treatment at the rate of 0.07 teeth per patient.[26]   In addition, 5 percent of those accepting complete care are
assumed to need orthodontic treatment. However, because of the ex-
pense and treatment time required, the number actually entering
orthodontic treatment is determined by an ability-to-pay factor and
a busyness factor. Currently only about 10 percent of arriving
symptomatic patients are believed to accept orthodontic treatment,
but overall insurance coverage would mean an increase toward 100
percent. Based on other data we also assume that each patient entering orthodontic treatment requires 0.5 extractions. Combination of
these needs with the minutes required for each procedure or monthly
requirement for orthodontic or periodontal treatment yields the
monthly minutes of demand initiated by symptomatic patients.

Delivery of Treatment

The procedure for estimating the monthly demand for dental care
(in minutes), based on a preventive-symptomatic breakdown of the
patient population, has already been described. A similar quantity
must be determined for the amount of treatment that can actually
be delivered in a month. This quantity is determined by combining:
(1) the number of dentists available; (2) the amount of time (measured in minutes) spent treating patients per dentist; and (3) any
productivity increase due to the use of auxiliary personnel. More
specifically, the productivity of a practice in delivery treatment is
basically dependent upon the dentist time required to perform
various treatment procedures. These time requirements are a function of the number and type of auxiliary personnel in the practice
and the procedures in which the auxiliaries may assist. Thus, by
knowing the number and type of various treatment services demanded, the procedures on which auxiliaries may assist, the number of auxiliaries, and the time savings introduced by specific auxil-

iaries, the treatment delivered in a month by an average practice may be calculated. However, for simplification we adopt a more straight-forward model of productivity, based on data such as that provided in table 8–5.[27] By taking the base number (i.e., dentist working alone) as normal productivity, the figures may be converted to a productivity amplification factor, as illustrated in figure 8–10. Multi-plying the number of minutes worked by a dentist by the produc-tivity amplification factor yields the effective minutes of dental care that can be delivered.

Figure 8–11 illustrates the structure of the system regarding de-mand and treatment supply.

Table 8–5. Number of Visits as a Function of Auxiliaries

Number of Auxiliaries	Mean Number of Visits
0	2355
1	3015
2	3946
3	4409
4 or more	6170

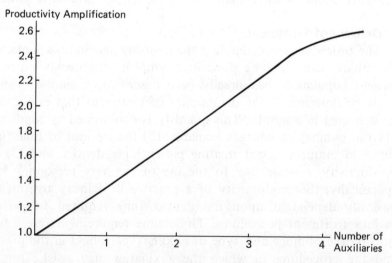

Figure 8–10. Auxiliary Productivity Amplification Factor (Yields Number of Minutes of Treatment That Can Be Delivered in a Month When Multiplied by the Number of Minutes Worked by a Dentist)

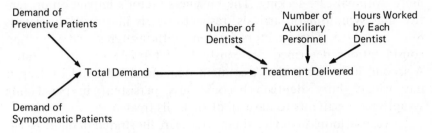

Figure 8-11. Structure of Treatment Delivered

Dental Busyness and the Impact of Supply on Demand

As described in the previous section, the maximum amount of treatment that can be delivered in a month is determined by the number of dentists and the average number of auxiliaries employed per dentist. This figure may be considered to reflect the capacity of the dental system. If the treatment initiated in a month exceeds the maximum treatment that can be delivered, the amount actually delivered is equal to that maximum. In those months in which demand exceeds the treatment capacity, a backlog of treatment demand builds up, i.e., the practice has more business than it can handle in a month. This backlog is built up by the rate at which patients initiate treatment requests each month and is diminished by the rate at which treatment is delivered.

The concept of treatment backlog provides one technique for quantitatively addressing the issue of dental busyness. The reader is reminded that the concept of busyness, as used here, is different from the self-perceived notion of busyness used in the ADA Practice Surveys. Specifically, dividing the current backlog by the treatment delivery rate produces an estimate of the number of months it would take a dental practice to eliminate its backlog at its current rate of delivering treatment. Alternatively, this represents the number of months a patient would have to wait for an appointment. This quantity is proposed as an indication of busyness.

As this number grows larger and larger, it can affect demand in several ways. First, the rate of initiating treatment can drop because both preventive and symptomatic patients experience increasing difficulty in seeing a dentist. The preventive arrival rate would probably be more sensitive to this effect, since their behavior reflects more optional care-seeking. The busyness factor's impact on preventive and symptomatic arrivals, respectively, is illustrated in figures 8–12 and 8–13. These factors combine with insurance and education considerations described previously to determine the arrival rates. A second influence is that treatment demanded will tend to drop if increasingly busy dentists become less persistent in persuading symptomatic patients to have all of their ills treated.

The causal loops involving these effects are illustrated in figure 8–14. Figure 8–14 shows that as busyness grows, several stabilizing effects involving dentist and patient behavior tend to arise and reduce the backlog and the busyness level. An additional stabilizing effect that may arise is the hiring of auxiliary personnel by the dentist so as to increase the treatment delivery rate and reduce the backlog to a reasonable level.

In addition to affecting the arrival rates and the acceptance of complete care, dental busyness can also affect patient decisions regarding preventive-symptomatic behavior. Symptomatic patients who accept treatment of all their dental needs may be convinced to

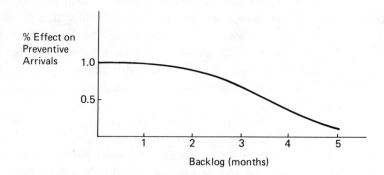

Figure 8–12. Busyness Factor for Preventive Arrivals

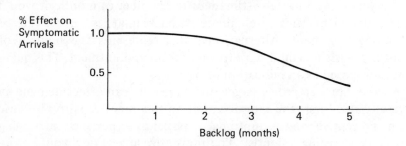

Figure 8–13. Busyness Factor for Symptomatic Arrivals

adopt a preventive orientation if their dentist has devoted sufficient time to patient education. However, as busyness grows, the dentist has less time for patient education. Patients also encounter more difficulties in arranging to see the dentist. Both of these factors work to reduce the number of symptomatic patients who might join the preventive group. The percentage of those patients accepting complete care who become preventively oriented is assumed in figure 8–15 to be a function of busyness.

Preventive patients can also be affected by a large busyness level because of increased difficulty in seeing the dentist. If the difficulty becomes great enough, certain preventive patients may become symptomatic in their attitude toward dental health, with a damaging effect on their oral health as a result. The percentage of preventive patients regressing to join the symptomatic group is related to busyness in figure 8–16.

Movement of patients between the two groups serves as another

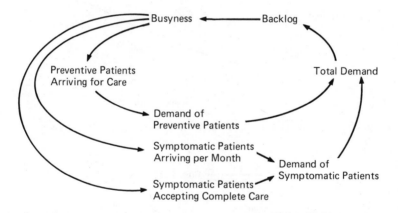

Figure 8-14. Causal Loops Relating Patient Behavior to Demand/Busyness

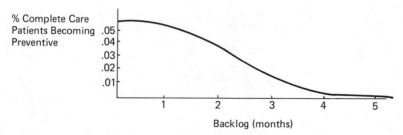

Figure 8-15. Busyness Factor Effect on Symptomatic Becoming Preventive

mechanism for stabilizing workload and reducing busyness. The causal loops in which this mechanism are embedded are displayed in figure 8–17.

The causal loops shown in both figures 8–14 and 8–17 work to bring the workloads of dental practices in line with the practices' ability to deliver treatment. The presence of these loops has important implications for the oral health of a patient population. Major changes in the supply of or demand for dental care (possibly due to some manpower or health insurance program) have a direct impact on busyness and gradually affect the preventive-symptomatic distribution of patients in each group. The ultimate effect of adjustments made by these causal loops is to increase or decrease oral health. Simulations presented in the next chapter affirm the importance of these causal loops and the role of the workload and busyness variables.

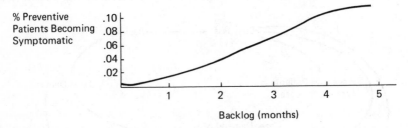

Figure 8–16. Busyness Factor on Preventive Becoming Symptomatic

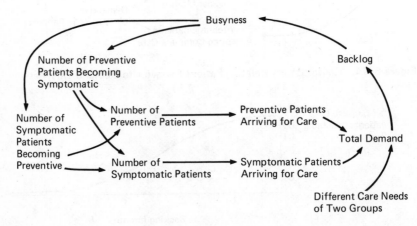

Figure 8–17. Causal Loops Relating Demand to Preventive-Symptomatic Shifts

NOTES TO CHAPTER EIGHT

1. N.D. Richards. "Utilization of Dental Services", in N.D. Richards and L.K. Cohen. *Social Sciences and Dentistry: A Critical Bibliography*, pp. 209-40.

2. R. Tash, R. O'Shea, and L.K. Cohen. "Testing a Preventive-Symptomatic Theory of Dental Health Behavior". *American Journal of Public Health*, March 1969, pp. 514-21.

3. S. Stephen Kegeles. "Why People Seek Dental Care: A Review of Present Knowledge". *American Journal of Public Health*, September 1961, pp. 1306-11.

4. S. Stephen Kegeles. "Some Motives for Seeking Preventive Dental Care". *Journal of the American Dental Association*, July 1963, pp. 90-98.

5. S. Stephen Kegeles. "Why People Seek Dental Care: A Test of a Conceptual Formulation". *Journal of Health and Human Behavior*, 1963, no. 3, pp. 166-73.

6. Robert M. O'Shea. "Characteristics of Dental Practice", in Richards and Cohen, pp. 157-58.

7. Paul J. Feldstein. "An Econometric Model of the Dental Sector", University of Michigan, School of Public Health, September 1973.

8. American Dental Association, *The 1971 Survey of Dental Practice*, p. 37.

9. American Dental Association, *Survey of Needs for Dental Care*, 1965, pp. 19-20.

10. A 1968 survey by the National Opinion Research Center reported in L.K. Cohen and A.E. Fusillo. "Utilization of Professional Care as Reported by U.S. Adults". *Journal of Public Health Dentistry*, Spring 1971, p. 141.

11. Godfrey M. Hochbaum. "Some Principles of Health Behavior". *Proceedings 1959 Biennial Conference of the State and Territorial Directors with the Public Health Service and the Children's Bureau*, PHS Publication 698, 1959.

12. S. Stephen Kegeles. "An Interpretation of Some Behavioral Principles in Relation to Acceptance of Dental Care". *Proceedings 1959 Biennial Conference of the State and Territorial Directors with the Public Health Service and the Children's Bureau*, PHS Publication 698, 1959.

13. For additional arguments by Kegeles, see also references 3, 4, and 5 above.

14. A.S. Metz, and L.G. Richards. "Children's Preventive Visits to the Dentist: The Relative Importance of Socio-Economic Factors and Parents' Preventive Visits". *Journal of American College of Dentists*, 34:204-212, October 1967.

15. R.M. O'Shea and S.B. Gray, "Dental Patients' Attitudes and Behavior Concerning Prevention". *Pub. Health Reports 83*, May 1968.

16. Tash, O'Shea, and Cohen.

17. Cohen and Fusillo, p. 141.

18. *ADA 1965*, p. 6.

19. Ibid.

20. Kegeles, 1963 (b), p. 170.

21. Indian Health Services, Dental Services Branch, *Dental Resources Criteria and Program Requirements for the Indian Health Service,* p. 4-a.

22. *ADA 1965,* pp. 19–20.

23. Kegeles, 1963 (b), p. 166.

24. J.F. Newman and O.W. Anderson. *Patterns of Dental Service Utilization in the United States: A Nationwide Social Survey,* Center for Health Administration Studies, University of Chicago, Research Series 30, 1971, p. 84.

25. Ibid., p. 61.

26. *ADA 1971,* pp. 19–20.

27. American Dental Association, *Dentistry in National Health Programs,* 1971.

Chapter 9

A Computer Analysis of Dental Manpower Requirements

This chapter reports computer explorations with the model described in the previous chapter. The simulations were designed to address two primary issues: (1) The performance of the dental health system subject to different projections of dental resources; and (2) the impact of increased insurance coverage on system behavior and performance. (Appendix C contains a complete listing of the computer model.)

ADDITIONAL INPUTS FOR THE SIMULATIONS

In order to assess the performance of the dental care system and to investigate the impact of changes in demand and supply on performance, measures of dental health and projections of future dentist supply are required for the model. Typical measures that are frequently collected in surveys are the number of missing and decayed teeth. However, the number of missing teeth is a measure of a long-term impact of care. It reflects care-seeking behavior and the treatment obtained by a patient over a lifetime. Changes in demand and supply only affect the number of missing teeth in the population after a long period of time has passed. Since the time span of interest for our projections is ten to twenty years, we decided to make the primary measure of oral health decay oriented so as to reflect short-term changes. However, rather than using "number of decayed teeth", a more detailed measure is used, "number of fillings required". This is used because a single tooth may require multiple fillings, and because data exist that permit determination of current values of this measure for symptomatic and preventive patients. It is calculated by focusing on the oral health needs of preventive and symptomatic patients taken from our definitions of the two groups and the findings of the ADA's Survey of Dental Needs. Thus, the average number of fillings required for (1) preventive patients (obtained from the relationship shown in figure 8–4), (2) symptomatic patients (5 fillings/patient), and (3) symptomatic patients recently receiving complete care (3 fillings/patient) was used to indicate the performance of the dental care system in the time span of interest. This measure reflects several critical aspects of dental health system performance: (1) the check-up interval of preventive patients, (2) the number of symptomatic patients accepting complete care, and (3) the proportional split of the population between the preventive and symptomatic patient groups.

Treatment supply is determined by the number of dentists and their productivity. Since employing auxiliaries is the primary means of augmenting productivity, changes in supply can be brought about by an increase in either the number of dentists or the number of auxiliaries. In the model analyses three alternative estimates of the national dental service supply are used. The first estimate employs a conservative projection of dentists and an average of 1.5 auxiliaries per dentist. The dentist projection is based on the historical growth rate of dentists from 1950 to 1970, and forecasts a dental population of 126,000 in 1990.[1] The second supply estimate is based on a somewhat optimistic A.D.A. forecast, including all currently planned dental school expansions, which generates a 1990 dental population estimate of 144,650.[2] A third supply forecast is based again on the more conservative dentist projection, but the average number of auxiliaries per dentist is assumed to increase linearly from 1.5 to 2.5 in the first five years of the computer simulation run. These alternative forecasts are used in the model to illustrate system behavior under varying plausible assumptions.

In regard to the demand side, the symptomatic and preventive populations in all the simulations are assumed to grow at the rate corresponding to the Series D population projections of the 1970 U.S. Census.[3]

ALTERNATE PROJECTIONS OF
TREATMENT SUPPLY

Table 9-1 displays the results of computer simulations based on these three sets of supply projections. Conditions prevailing at the beginning and end of each simulation are shown. Significant differences exist among the three simulations.

The first simulation assumed a population growing only slightly faster than the available supply of dentists. The most evident effect of the assumptions is an increase of the dental busyness measure from 1.35 months of backlog to 1.41 months. The slight increase in dental busyness had inconsequential impact on the nature of care delivered and the state of the population's oral health (as measured by the per capita need for fillings). The number of fillings needed stayed approximately fixed (increasing from 3.76 to 3.79) over the ten-year period. A slight decrease in the fraction of symptomatic patients accepting complete care, a change in the interval between visits of preventive patients, and other slight adjustments keep the dental busyness measure from rising any further. Most other variables also remain near their initial values at the end of the ten-year simulated time period. Numbers of preventive and symptomatic patients initiating treatment during a month both increase somewhat during the simulation as the result of overall growth in population from 1970 to 1980. The proportional split between the preventive and symptomatic populations does not change.

The second simulation, with an optimistic forecast of dentist supply, shows the dental care system performing somewhat better. This run assumed that supply of care grows more rapidly than the total patient population. This led to a decline in dental busyness over the course of the simulation from a waiting time of 1.35 months to 1.05 months. As a consequence several causal loops came into play to adjust treatment-seeking behavior and to keep dental busyness from declining any further. Of major importance was a shift in the relative proportion of patients seeking and receiving preventive care as opposed to symptomatic care. The number of patients per month initiating preventive care increased markedly, from 6.1 million in 1970 to 8.3 million in 1980. This increase is due in part to a decrease in the interval between preventive visits due to reduced busyness of dental practices. Reduced busyness manifests itself in greater pro-

Table 9-1. Simulation Results Forecasting the Provision of Oral Health Under Alternative Projections of Treatment Supply

	Proportion of Population in:		Number of Patients Initiating Treatment per Month (millions)		Dental Busy-ness (Months of Backlog)	Average Number of Fillings Needed per Capita	Fraction of Symptomatic Patients Accepting Complete Care
	Preventive Group	Symptomatic Group	Preventive Group	Symptomatic Group			
Initial conditions (January 1970)	.33	.67	6.1	5.3	1.35	3.76	.55
Ten-year projections: (January 1980)							
1. "Conservative" dentist projection	.33	.67	6.8	6.1	1.41	3.79	.54
2. "Optimistic" dentist projection	.38	.62	8.3	5.7	1.05	3.63	.59
3. "Conservative" dentist projection with increasing numbers of auxiliaries	.44	.56	9.0	5.0	.85	3.48	.65

activity on the part of dentists who encourage patients to accept care through devices such as reminders, and by advance scheduling of preventive visits when patients have completed treatment for their current needs.

Though relatively fewer symptomatic patients arrive for care each month, a somewhat larger fraction of those patients (59 percent vs. 55 percent) accept treatment for their complete set of care needs. The increase in acceptance of complete treatment is, again, due to the decrease in busyness, causing dentists to encourage symptomatic patients more strongly to accept complete treatment. Completely treated patients are unlikely to develop new symptoms quickly, thus further reducing the pool of symptomatic patients who may arrive for care.

As a result of the increase in the preventive population, more frequent preventive visits, and greater acceptance of complete care by symptomatic patients who seek care, the dental care system in the second simulation (with the more optimistic projection of dentist supply) is able to produce somewhat better oral health in terms of the numbers of fillings needed by the average patient.

The third simulation in this group results in even better performance. By the end of that ten-year computer projection, the number of fillings needed by the average patient has declined to 3.48, as a result of the care received by the patient population. Improvements in care and oral health in this simulation were due to the assumed growth of availability of dental care at a more rapid rate than the growth in total patient population. Though the conservative projection for the number of dentists was used in this simulation, auxiliary personnel were assumed to increase from 1.5 to 2.5 per dentist over the first five years of the simulation. Productivity increases made possible by the increased use of auxiliaries is the source of greater availability of dental care.

Effects of growth of care availability in excess of population growth are very apparent in the dental busyness measure. Over the course of the simulation, the average practice's appointment backlog declined from 1.35 times its monthly capacity to .85 times capacity as its productivity and output increased. The availability of "excess" capacity allowed shifts to take place in patient care-seeking behavior as patients found easier access to care, and dental practices had an incentive to encourage modes of care-seeking behavior that make more intensive use of dental resources. The most striking shift is the flow of patients from the symptomatic to the preventive category, resulting in 44 percent of the patients being in the preventive groups at the end of the simulation and 56 percent in the symptomatic. This shift is primarily responsible for the decrease in arrivals for care by symptomatic patients and increase in preventive patient arrivals. Moreover, those patients remaining symptomatic showed a greater tendency (.65, compared with .55 initially) to accept complete treatment for their care needs. These shifts in care-seeking behavior are, together, responsible for the improvement in the number of fillings needed per capita (the surrogate oral health measure) seen over the course of this simulation and in comparison to the other two simulations.

Given the underlying premise of the model, that the availability of dental care affects the manner in which it is sought and provided, these simulations have shown that making higher levels of dental manpower available can produce better oral health in a patient population. Improvement in oral health is accomplished not merely by producing more visits, but by permitting and encouraging shifts in patterns of care.

INCREASED INSURANCE COVERAGE

Provision of any dental benefits under a national health insurance program can obviously be expected to have a significant impact on the delivery of dental care. One would hope that increased expenditures for dental care under the insurance program would yield a proportionate improvement in the nation's oral health. But is this necessarily so? The three simulations presented in this section suggest that the opposite may be true if a concerted effort is not made simultaneously to increase levels of dental manpower and the availability of dental care.

In the first two of these simulations, the fraction of the population with dental insurance coverage is assumed to increase immediately from 20 percent to 60 percent at the end of the first year of the simulation. In the first of these, "conservative" growth in the dentist population is assumed based on the 1950–70 trend while the second assumes a more "optimistic" growth rate for the number of dentists. Both assumed that there are 1.5 auxiliary personnel for each dentist over the course of the simulations. The third simulation assumes both a gradual increase in insurance coverage (going from 20 percent to 60 percent over a four-year period, beginning at the end of the first year rather than immediately) and a gradual increase in the number of auxiliaries (from 1.5 per dentist to 2.5 per dentist over the first five years of the simulation). The third simulation also assumes that the "conservative" projection for the number of dentists will hold true. All three simulations have the same rate of population growth as that assumed for the three simulations already discussed. The results of these simulations are presented in table 9-2, revealing significant differences among the three simulated scenarios.

The conditions at the end of the first simulation indicate the potential for disaster when insurance benefits are suddenly instituted without commensurate increase in dental manpower. Though spending on dental care has presumably undergone a substantial increase to finance the assumed insurance coverage, oral health measured in terms of the per capita need for fillings has worsened over the simulation and reached a lower level (i.e., higher number of fillings needed) than that reached in the simulation with the conservative dentist projection and no increase in insurance coverage.

Several shifts had to take place to produce this worsening in oral health. Initially, the inception of broader insurance coverage created a surge of demand. The simulations indicate that an additional 1.5 million preventive patients and 1.8 million symptomatic patients initiated treatment in the first month the new benefits were available. 60 percent of the symptomatic patients arriving in that month accepted complete care (compared to 55 percent prior to the increase in coverage). This surge in demand due to the lowering of financial barriers caused the workload of the average dental practice to increase substantially. Eight months after the new benefits had gone into effect, dental practices had busyness levels (backlogs) equal to over three times the amount of care they could provide in a month. The high busyness level impacted the care-seeking behavior of both types of patients. Substantial reductions occurred in the rates at which preventive and symptomatic patients initiated treatment because dental practices were overloaded with work from patients whose treatment needs had already been identified. Patients initiating treatment endured long waits for care. In the eighth month after benefits begin, only 5.4 million preventive patients and 4.8 million symptomatic patients initiated treatment, while only 42 percent of the symptomatic patients chose to accept complete care. At the same time, the preventive-symptomatic mix also began to change

Table 9-2.   Simulation Results Forecasting the Provision of Oral Health Under Increased Insurance Coverage

	Proportion of Population in:		Number of Patients Initiating Treatment per Month (millions)		Dental Busyness (Months of Backlog)	Average Number of Fillings Needed per Capita	Fraction of Symptomatic Patients Accepting Complete Care
	Preventive Group	Symptomatic Group	Preventive Group	Symptomatic Group			
Initial conditions (January 1970)	.33	.67	6.1	5.3	1.35	3.76	.55
Ten-year projections: (January 1980)							
1. "Conservative" dentist projection, immediate increase in insurance	.21	.79	3.9	7.6	2.46	4.04	.47
2. "Optimistic" dentist projection, immediate increase in insurance	.23	.77	4.7	7.6	2.21	3.93	.52
3. "Conservative" dentist projection, gradual increase in insurance and auxiliary personnel	.40	.60	9.8	6.0	1.46	3.41	.66

as a result of decreased dental practice motivation to maintain preventive behavior by their patients due to their heavy workload. This shift caused a further decrease in the number of preventive patients initiating treatment.

The depressing picture presented at the end of the simulation is reflected in table 9–2. Symptomatic patients are receiving care for needs that have been neglected. A large fraction of those symptomatic patients do not even get complete care for their needs, because dental practices are so heavily overloaded. A much smaller number of preventive patients initiate care each month at the end of this simulation than at the end of the simulation (shown in table 9–1) with the conservative dentist projection and no change in insurance. Though dental busyness is at a level below the peak reached after benefits began, it is high enough to maintain a symptomatic-dominated care-seeking pattern. With all of these adverse shifts in care-seeking behavior, oral health can only decline, as is evident in the higher number of fillings required in the patient population.

The second simulation shows results that are only marginally better. Additional dentists provided by the optimistic forecast have little effect. Busyness is somewhat lower at the end of the simulation and the number of fillings required per capita is slightly lowered, though much higher than in the simulation with optimistic dental forecast and no change in insurance coverage. A few more patients are preventively oriented, and they initiate treatment more frequently. A larger fraction of symptomatic patients (52 percent) who initiate treatment accept complete care for their needs. On the whole, though, this represents a poor (really negative) return on a large investment in better oral health.

The third simulation suggests hope for improvement or oral health through insurance programs if insurance coverage is introduced gradually and is combined with an increase in resources. The number of fillings required per capita after ten years reflects the best oral health achieved in any of the simulations. Though the busyness level is somewhat higher at the end of the run than at the end of the same simulation without a change in insurance coverage, it is not high enough to counteract the stimulus that insurance benefits have on all aspects of care-seeking behavior. The system is dominated by preventive care-seeking, with 9.8 million patients initiating treatment in the last month of the simulation. Of the patients who continue to seek care on a symptomatic basis, a large fraction (66 percent) accept complete care for their needs.

These favorable results came about because the assumed gradual broadening of insurance coverage kept large backlogs from building up. As backlogs of treatment did accumulate, they were accommodated by the growing capacity of dental practices to provide treatment that resulted from the assumed addition of auxiliary personnel. Improved oral health came about because people were afforded better access to care through the removal of financial barriers, and because that access was kept open by providing additional care delivery resources to match the growing demand.

Though the model described here is a tentative one, the results of these three simulations indicate that, at the very least, careful consideration be given to the impact that dental benefits under a national health insurance program will have on the workloads of dental practices and, ultimately, on care-seeking patterns and oral health.

A PROGRAM OF FURTHER RESEARCH

Chapter Eight presented a simple model for projecting the implications of changes in manpower availability, productivity, and the financing of dental care on oral health. Simulations using the model were described in the preceding sections of this chapter. While the model and its results are suggestive, extensions of the model would provide a more useful framework for projection and program policy analysis. Important additional structural elements could be developed on the basis of data that are not readily available. An expanded model would permit the analysis of important dimensions of policy that were not amenable to analysis with the simplified version presented here.

Additions to Model Structure. The simple model represents the impact of dental treatment on disease in a highly aggregated manner. Dental disease should be represented as a progressive self-worsening process to yield a more accurate picture of the consequences of neglecting treatment (e.g., decayed teeth requiring extraction if not filled within a particular interval). A more complete account might include periodontal disease along with malocclusion. Varieties of dental treatments might be included, such as fillings, extractions, endodontic care, periodontic care, orthodontia, prosthetic replacement, prophylaxis, and examinations and X-rays.

The patient population should be segmented by age to reflect the different care needs of children, adults, and older people. Careful accounting could be done to keep track of the dental problems people carry with them through life. This would be of special use in assessing the value of programs aimed at young people. A more detailed representation might also differentiate among groups within the patient population that exhibit different types of care-seeking behavior. In addition to the preventive and symptomatic groups already identified, we should consider representing symptomatic patients who are especially attentive to care needs once they are identified.

The oral health measures included in the existing model are highly simplified. More sophisticated measures might at least reflect damage already done by dental neglect (e.g. missing teeth by age) and disease that has implications for current and future workload (e.g. periodontal disease). Along with better measures of oral health, other factors affecting oral health should be added, such as toothbrushing and nutrition. Influences on these oral health habits by patient education in the dental office could also be considered.

Economic variables require more complete representation than is present in the current model. This would include a more elaborate picture of the impact of dental benefits under a national health insurance program. Another set of economic variables to be included might be the prices of different dental services and their differential effects on patient behavior.

The supply of dentists requires better representation to reflect such characteristics as the age mix, an important determinant of the dentist population's productivity and its willingness to adopt new practices. Another level of detail that might be added would involve the availability and demand for dental specialists. Representation of specialists could include referral relationships, the specialists' workloads and their relative availability, and the propensity of general practitioners to refer as a function of their own busyness.

More explicit representation is also required for the factors affecting dentists' decisions to expand the capacity of their practices by working longer hours, hiring auxiliaries, or adding operatories. Auxiliaries might also be disaggregated in the model to reflect the impact of different types of auxiliaries on dental productivity.

Data Requirements. Extension of the model in the directions suggested would require much additional data, both to improve the accuracy of the parameters in the existing model and to provide parameter estimates for new structural elements to be added. A possible dimension of such a data-collection effort would be an in-depth examination of the factors affecting both patient and dentist behavior. This effort could look at differences in the nature of care received by patients as a function of such factors as their reason for visiting a dentist (preventive or symptomatic), the busyness of the dentist they see, their own socioeconomic characteristics, and the nature of dental influences on their care-seeking behavior.

Additional data would have to be gathered to determine the potential for tradeoff between dentist and auxiliary time in the provision of each service and the effect of dentists' perceptions of tradeoff possibilities on their decisions to hire auxiliaries. Similarly, data are needed to support inclusion in the model of the effect of busyness (actual and self-perceived) on dentists' decisions to hire auxiliaries, add operatories, or work longer hours.

To get data that are not available from existing sources or ongoing studies, a Delphi process might be used. In such a process, panels of experts in various areas of dental care are asked to estimate the values of parameters for the model. These estimates are then "fed back" to the panels for revision until consensus is reached. Such an approach might be used, for example, to model the possible development and acceptance of new dental technology that would enhance productivity.

Policy Analyses with an Extended Model

The extended version of the model would give a much more accurate picture of the impact on oral health of various strategies to increase the availability of dentists and auxiliary personnel or increase the accessibility of care through insurance programs. With its more detailed representation of the care delivery process, the model could help perform such tasks as determining the best mix (lowest cost, most effective) of personnel to augment the dental work force in achieving a particular oral health goal. The extended structure could also help policymakers determine required numbers of dental specialists and specific types of auxiliaries. The model would also provide a better picture of the impact of dental benefits under national health insurance. Impacts of various proposed benefit packages could be assessed and the value of insurance programs with a special focus, such as young people or low-income groups, could be more clearly ascertained. Large-scale private insurance programs could also be tested, through simulation, for their projected impact on the dental care system.

One trend that might be examined is the increasing prevalence of group practice and prepaid dental plans. This trend can have important implications for productivity. Greater use of prepayment may motivate dental practices to encourage preventive care patterns among their patients, with significant ramifications for oral health. A sufficiently detailed representation of care delivery would also enable the model to be used as a guide for setting dental research priorities. In such an application, the model would reveal the impact of specific improvements in the effectiveness of dental treatment, thereby indicating high-priority research areas.

Clearly, the model's generic nature permits it to be used to simulate any level of the dental delivery system. The model can, for example, simulate individual practices and clinics and yield insights for improving their operations. On a larger scale, the model could be used to simulate the delivery systems of cities, counties, states, and regions, and help estimate the dental manpower needed in those areas to attain particular levels of oral health. Strategies for helping dental scarcity areas and alleviating the effects of maldistribution can be evaluated in this manner.

NOTES TO CHAPTER NINE

1. American Dental Association, *Dentistry in National Health Programs,* 1971.

2. American Dental Assoication, Task Force on National Health Programs, *Dentistry in National Health Programs: Reports of the Special Committees,* 1971, pp. 29-39.

3. Bureau of the Census, *Statistical Abstract of the U.S., 1970.*

Postscript

The general theory of human service delivery in Chapter Two has been put to use, hence to the test, in a number of contexts. First, the two basic loops of our supply-demand formulation were augmented in order to provide a conceptual grasp of the forces that may lead to deterioration in the effectiveness of an agency through its life cycle. In this analysis we reached the uncomfortable conclusion that providing good service may stimulate a demand for more service, resulting ultimately in poor service being delivered.

In Part II we applied the theory to three very different human service systems and in each case used the theory in a somewhat different manner.

In the application to mental health service delivery the theory was used as a device for organizing and evaluating a body of clinical and empirical knowledge. The dynamic viewpoint enabled us to focus on classes of variables that are important in the real world of the practitioner but are often slighted by the statically oriented perspective that underlies much empirical research. Our computer analysis of patient drop-out showed how declining standards of functioning and low levels of patient expectation of benefit contribute to drop-out, which may be avoided by changed patterns of program resource allocation.

Our analyses of student-teacher interaction lead to the conclusion that educational goals shared by both student and teacher are most likely to be fulfilled. In this application a third party, namely the home environment, was added to the program client paradigm.

In applying our theory to the dental health system we looked at a population of health consumers and providers rather than at a "typical" consumer and provider in interaction. Using the theory in this instance as a planning tool, we called attention to the dangers of too rapidly expanding insurance coverage without simultaneously augmenting the pool of dental manpower.

Our intention has been to assess the utility of the general theory by applying it to several different delivery systems and employing it for various practical purposes. Each model presented contains additional potential for elaboration, further extension, and disaggregation. While additional work with the theory is not required for our present purpose, we hope that other workers, researchers as well as practitioners with problems to solve, may have the incentive to carry the analyses further.

We believe that the general theory may also prove useful in the analyses of human service delivery systems beyond those treated here. The theory seems to us to be particularly promising as a means for gaining clarity on the dynamics of service delivery in such areas of societal concern as the criminal justice system and the system of providing economic assistance to those in need.

Technical Appendixes

Appendixes A, B, and C present and discuss the three
detailed simulation models described and used in chapters
Four through Nine of this book. In Appendixes A and B
formal flow diagrams are also presented, and each group of several
equations is discussed in terms of its underlying assumptions and
implications for model behavior.

FLOW DIAGRAM FORMATS

The formal flow diagrams show the structure of a model in a form
that can readily be converted into computer equations. The symbols
used follow the convention shown in Forrester, *Industrial Dynamics*
(Cambridge: M.I.T. Press, 1961). The major symbols used are:

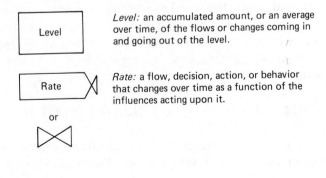

Level: an accumulated amount, or an average
over time, of the flows or changes coming in
and going out of the level.

Rate: a flow, decision, action, or behavior
that changes over time as a function of the
influences acting upon it.

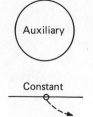

Auxiliary: a combination of information inputs into concepts that are used to reduce the complexity of rate equations.

Constant

Constant: a parameter of a model whose value is assumed to be unchanging throughout a particular computer simulation.

EQUATION FORMATS

The three models presented in this book are represented in the DYNAMO simulation language. DYNAMO was developed at M.I.T. by Alexander L. Pugh III as a tool for carrying out what were then called Industrial Dynamics studies. (Application of the methodology to a broad set of social problems later led to the adoption of System Dynamics as the field's title). DYNAMO has since been extended and improved by Pugh-Roberts Associates, Inc. It is useful to explain DYNAMO's equation formats at this point to help the reader understand the structure of the models and the nature of the assumptions embodied in them. More complete technical information is available in Pugh, *DYNAMO II User's Manual* (Cambridge: M.I.T. Press, 1974).

DYNAMO simulates the behavior of a system over time by computing changes that take place over each time interval and "updating" the status of the system to reflect those changes. The updated system becomes the basis for the set of changes to take place over the next time interval. In DYNAMO's notation, .K refers to the current point in time, .J refers to the previous point in time (one time interval ago) and .L represents the next point in time (one time interval into the future).

Level equations describe the system's state at each point in time. There are two types of levels. One type represents measurable quantities such as the level of patient functioning, student knowledge, or the number of dentists. Equations for this type of levels take the following form:

L   LEVEL.K = LEVEL.J + (DT) (RATEIN.JK–RATEOUT.JK)

This equation form indicates that a level at the current point in time (*.K*) is equal to its value at the previous point in time (*.J*) plus the net change that took place over the past time interval (*.JK*). Net change is the resultant of flows into and out of the level (there may be several in each direction) multiplied by the appropriate time interval (DT) used in the simulation. Levels do not change instantaneously, but are subject to rates of change having this cumulative effect over time.

The second type of level equation represents an average of another quantity that serves as a descriptor of the system's state. One use of this type of level equation is to simulate the delay between the time a condition develops in a system and the time it is perceived by decisionmakers and others. Another use is to average a rate of change, since rates of change cannot be observed at any one point in time and must be measured by the effect they have over time. Examples of such levels are average rate of treatment and teacher's perception of student performance. This type of level equation has the following forms:

L   LEVEL.K = LEVEL.J + (DT) (1/TA) (QUANT.J–LEVEL.J)

or

L   LEVEL.K = LEVEL.J + (DT) (1/TA) (RATE.JK–LEVEL.J)

These forms indicate that a level of this type at the present point in time is equal to the level at the previous point in time adjusted by any change in its value that has taken place over the last time interval. That change is some fraction (1/*TA*) of the difference between the value of the quantity or rate of change being averaged and the previous value of the level, multiplied by the time interval being used. This averaging process is referred to as exponential smoothing. It causes changes in the level to occur gradually at a rate determined by the value of *TA*. In many model equations, this averaging process is represented by the following equivalent shorthand:

LEVEL.K = SMOOTH(QUANT.K, TA)

or

LEVEL.K = SMOOTH(RATE.JK, TA)

Rate equations are based on the state of the system at the current point in time (*.K*) and indicate rates of change that will occur over the next time interval (*.KL*). These equations take the following form:

R   RATE.KL = f(LEVEL.K, AUX.K)

As indicated, rates in the next time period are functions of level and/or auxiliary variable values at the current point in time.

Auxiliary variables provide computational linkages between levels and rates of change. They take the following form:

A   AUX.K = f(LEVEL.K, AUX.K)

Auxiliaries are computed at the current point in time from level and other auxiliary values at the current point in time.

Many of the auxiliary and rate equations in the models are straight-forward algebraic expressions and require no explanation. One equation form that appears throughout the models does require some explanation, however. It is the following:

A(or R)   Y.K = TABHL(YTB, X.K, L, H, I)

This type of equation indicates a functional relationship between an independent (*X*) and dependent variable (*Y*). *L, H,* and *I* describe the low end (*L*), high end (*H*), and interval (*I*) between points in a set of values of the independent variable. *YTB* is an associated set of values of the dependent variable that correspond to each of the values of the *X* variable. Thus,

Y.K = TABHL(YTB, X.K, 0, 5, 1)
YTB = 3, 7, 9, 11, 13, 14

would represent the following functional relationship:

X	0	1	2	3	4	5
Y	3	7	9	11	13	14

DYNAMO interpolates when values of the independent variable fall between these discrete values to yield a pseudo-continuous functional relationship. Values of the independent variable falling below or above the *L–H* range are given the *Y* values at either end of *YTB*. Thus, in the example, an *X* value of 6.5 would be assigned a value of 14, the high-end value on *YTB*.

The DYNAMO processor translates equations of these various types into computer instructions and causes system behavior to be simulated in the stepwise manner described earlier. Computations begin with a set of initial conditions (each level equation must have an initial condition associated with it) and produce rates of change during the first time interval being simulated. System states at the first point in time are then derived from these rates of change and become the basis for computing the next time interval's rates of change. Computations continue in this sequence for the duration of the simulation. DYNAMO's output routines print and plot the values of selected variables over that duration.

Treatment Drop-out Model

Figure A–1 presents a formal flow diagram of the patient sector of the model of treatment drop-out model used to produce the results discussed in Chapter Five. The program sector is presented in figure A–6. The symbols used in these diagrams are explained in the section preceding this appendix.

The equations for the model, presented in the DYNAMO notation also explained in the section preceding this appendix, will be discussed here in an order that seems logical according to the flow diagram.

PATIENT BEHAVIOR

The first equation is:

```
FNCTN.K=FNCTN.J+(DT)(RCFSCF.JK+RCFTR.JK)                    1, L
FNCTN=60                                                    1, N
    FNCTN—level of FuNCTioNing (functioning units)
    RCFSCF—Rate of Change of Functioning due to Social and Chemical Forces
            (functioning units/month)
    RCFTR—Rate of Change of Functioning due to TReatment (functioning
            units/month)
    DT—Delta Time (months)            •
```

The level of the patient's FuNCTioNing is subject to two rates of change, one due to treatment and the other due to social and chemi-

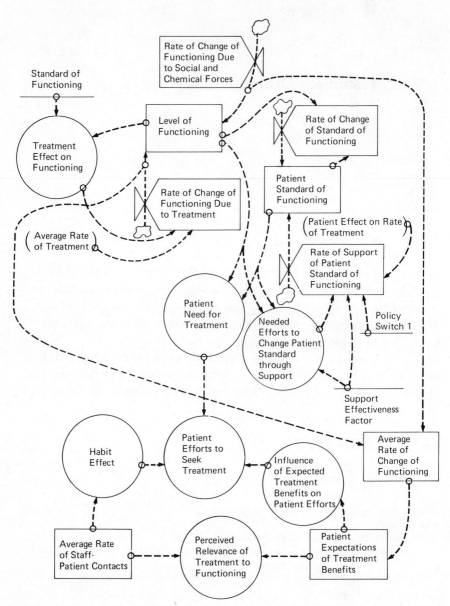

Figure A-1. Formal System Dynamics Flow Diagram of Patient Sector of Model

cal forces independent of the treatment itself. Functioning is para-
meterized along a scale of 0 to 100 and given an initial value of 60,
a value representing some socially acceptable performance. The level
of functioning is an aggregate measure that is not tied to the presence
of a specific symptom. As the functioning level drops below 50, more
actute mental illness is indicated.

The second group of equations is:

```
RCFSCF.KL=PULSE(PH,10,INT)                                        2, R
PH=HT/DT                                                          3, N
HT=-20                                                            4, C
INT=120                                                           5, C
    RCFSCF—Rate of Change of Functioning due to Social and Chemical Forces
        (functioning units/month)
    PULSE—DYNAMO special notation for imPULSE
    PH—Pulse Height (functioning units/month)
    HT—HeighT (functioning units)
    INT—INTerval between pulses (months)
```

The Rate of Change of Functioning due to Social and Chemical
Forces serves as an external stimulus to the model. It represents
forces, both detrimental and positive, that are not under the control
of the staff and independent of treatment. The particular form
shown in the equation above represents a crisis in which the patient
loses PH functioning units at month 10. The HT value of – 20 indicates a decline of 33 percent. INT is set for repeat crises every 120
months or 10 years. Changes in this equation form can be used to
simulate other forms of patient crises. These might include a gradual
degradation of functioning at some constant rate or a cyclical degradation and improvement of functioning peculiar to the chemical
forces of some forms of illness. The equation form shown could
represent a crisis due to the social force of the patient's wife leaving
him or the loss of a close relative.

The next equations are:

```
RCFTR.KL=(ART.K) (TEF.K)                                          6, R
TEF.K=TABHL(TEFTB,SOF-FNCTN.K,0,25,5)                             7, A
TEFTB=.25/.35/.4/.4/.4/.4                                         8, C
SOF=50                                                            9, C
    RCFTR—Rate of Change of Functioning due to TReatment (functioning
        units/month)
    ART—Average Rate of Treatment (treatments/month)
    TEF—Treatment Effect of Functioning (functioning units/treatment)
```

TABHL—DYNAMO special notation for TABle, High-Low
TEFTB—Treatment Effect on Functioning TaBle (functioning units/
    treatment)
SOF—Standard Of Functioning (functioning units)

The Rate of Change of Functioning due to TReatment (in functioning units/month) is the product of the number of treatment units being given per month (Average Rate of Treatment) and the number of functioning units that are gained with each treatment (TEF). TEF is dependent upon the criticality of the patient's condition. If his level of functioning is well below some fixed standard of functioning, it is assumed that treatment will have a much greater effect than when he is at or near this standard. The use of the relationship depicted in the figure A–2 graph will cause the patient to gain .25 functioning units per treatment when his level of functioning is at the standard of 50 and up to .4 units per treatment when his functioning goes below a level of 40 functioning units. A different relationship between treatment and functioning, based on treatment intensity rather than criticality, was developed from a staff survey described in Chapter Four. The survey results suggested that the most realistic form of the relationship would have some small amount of benefit derived for moderate rates of treatment with a much higher rate of treatment required to effect any additional benefit. The initial reported experiments with the model make use of this form.

Equations for the Patient's Standard of Functioning come next:

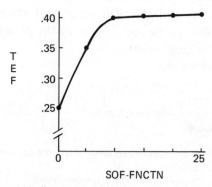

Figure A-2. Treatment Effect on Functioning

```
PSF.K=PSF.J+(DT) (RCF.JK+RSPSF.JK)                                    10, L
PSF=FNCTN                                                             10, N
RCF.KL=(FNCTN.K-PSF.K)/TTCSF                                          11, R
TTCSF=12                                                             12, C
RSPSF.KL=(NECPSS.K) (PERT.K) (SEF) (SW1)                             13, R
NECPSS.K=( (PSF.K-FNCTN.K)/TTCSF)/SEF                                14, A
SEF=2.5                                                              15, C
SW1=0                                                               16, C
```

> PSF—Patient Standard of Functioning (functioning units)
> RCF—Rate of Change of standard of Functioning (functioning units/month)
> RSPSF—Rate of Support of Patient Standard of Functioning (functioning units/month)
> FNCTN—level of FuNCTioNing (functioning units)
> TTCSF—Time To Change Standard of Functioning (months)
> NECPSS—Needed Effort to Change Patient Standard through Support (functioning units/month)
> PERT—Patient Effect on Rate of Treatment (percentile)
> SEF—Support Effectiveness Factor (percentile)
> SW1—policy SWitch 1 (dimensionless)

The Patient's Standard of Functioning is the sum over time of two sets of influences. The first and main contributing Rate of Change of standard of Functioning moves the patient's standard toward a smoothed average of his actual level of functioning. As with the rest of the patient sector, the standard is not only that of the patient, but also the standard used by his family and others around him to judge his behavior. The smoothing delay of 12 months implies that it takes about one year for a patient and his family to become accustomed to a particular level of functioning and to maintain this new standard rather than his original standard. The use of a delayed perception of functioning as a standard rather than some absolute is more realistic because patients and their families must make comparisons between current and recent levels of functioning in order to discern a trend.

The second source of change is the Rate of Support of the Patient Standard of Functioning, a policy option embodied in the model, and controlled by SWitch 1. The option permits the human service agency to allocate efforts directly toward encouraging the patient to maintain or restore his previous standard. This represents an attempt to affect patient beliefs, as opposed to patient behavior directly. The Needed Effort to Change the Patient Standard through Support is dependent upon the gap between the patient's standard and his actual functioning, divided by a factor reflecting the effectiveness of support efforts.

PNT.K=PSF.K−FNCTN.K   17, A
    PNT—Patient Need for Treatment (functioning units)
    PSF—Patient Standard of Functioning (functioning units)
    FNCTN—level of FuNCTioNing (functioning units)

    The Patient Need for Treatment is the difference between the patient's standard and his actual level of functioning. This serves as the patient's (and his family's) perception of the magnitude of his mental health problem. This need indicates a discomfort measure of the acuteness of the problem as perceived by the patient and his family.

PEST.K=(PNT.K) (HABIT.K) (IETBPE.K)   18, A
    PEST—Patient Efforts to Seek Treatment (functioning units desired)
    PNT—Patient Need for Treatment (functioning units)
    HABIT—HABIT effect on treatment seeking (percentile)
    IETBPE—Influence of Expected Treatment Benefits on Patient Efforts
    (percentile)

    Patient Efforts to Seek Treatment has the same units as Patient Need for Treatment (functioning units), and is equal to PNT modified by the effect of two factors. The HABIT effect reflects the hesitancy of the patient to start a program of treatment if he is not currently receiving treatment. In addition to his own hesitancy, the patient must also cope with the difficulty of attracting the attention of the staff. The Influence of Expected Treatment Benefits on Patient Efforts reflects the patient's expectations, based on a set of initial expectations modified by his consideration of changes in health that have taken place (from both treatment and external causes) while treatment is going on. This assumes that the patient credits a large part of his improvement to (or blames worsening on) the treatment he is currently getting, regardless of its cause. Patient Efforts to Seek Treatment expresses the number of functional units for which the patient is seeking treatment. This number will be smaller than his perceived need for treatment when the patient is not currently in treatment or when he anticipates few benefits from treatment because of negative past experiences.

HABIT.K=TABHL(HABTB, ARSPC.K,0,3,.5)   19, A
HABTB=.1/.3/.7/.9/1/1.1/1.15   19, C
    HABIT—HABIT effect on treatment seeking (percentile)
    HABTB—HABit effect TaBle (percentile)
    ARSPC—Average Rate of Staff-Patient Contact (treatments/month)

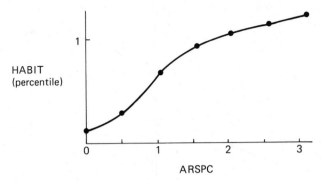

Figure A-3. Habit Effect on Treatment-Seeking

This factor serves to reduce patient efforts to get care for low values of average staff-patient contact rate and has less effect for higher values of ARSPC. This effect assumes that a patient not currently receiving treatment will be reluctant to contact the staff about any new problems that have developed.

```
IETBPE.K=TABHL(IETBTB,PETB.K,L,U,I)                          20, A
IETBTB=.1/.3/.7/.9/1                                          20, C
L=-2                                                          21, C
U=2                                                           22, C
I=1                                                           23, C
```
        IETBPE—Influence of Expected Treatment Benefits on Patient Efforts
            (percentile)
        IETBTB—Influence of Expected Treatment Benefits TaBle (percentile)
        PETB—Patient Expectations of Treatment Benefits (functional units/month)
        L—Lower end of scale (functional units/month)
        U—Upper end of scale (functional units/month)
        I—Increment in scale (functional units/month)

The Influence of Expected Treatment Benefits on Patient Efforts is a function of the Patient's Expectations of Treatment Benefits (some number of functioning units/month of improvement that the patient attributes to care, regardless of its actual cause). For low values of PETB, the patient's efforts to get care will be reduced because he is skeptical that further treatment will be of benefit to him. Higher values of PETB will have the effect, through this function, of causing the patient to seek care for most of the treatment need he perceives. It seems reasonable to assume that a chronic patient will only seek treatment when he has some experience that treatment has helped him in the past. Because the patient may have

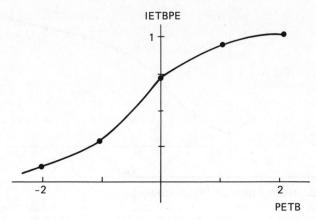

Figure A–4.   Influence of Expected Treatment Benefits on Patient Efforts

difficulty discriminating between changes in his functioning due to
treatment and those due to social and chemical forces, it must be
further assumed that, when he is undergoing a high rate of treatment,
he will attribute any changes in his functioning to the treatment;
conversely, he will fail to attribute any health changes to the treatment when he is undergoing only a low rate of treatment. Lower
and Upper scales as well as scale Increments are set as model parameters for ease of change during simulations.

```
PETB.K=PETB.J+(DT) (PRTF.J/TCETB) (ARCF.J–PETB.J)              24, L
PETB=NPETB                                                     24, N
NPETB=1                                                        25, C
TCETB=24                                                       26, C
        PETB—Patient Expectations of Treatment Benefits (functioning units/
            month)
        PRTF—Perceived Relevance of Treatment to Functioning (percentile)
        TCETB—Time to Change Expected Treatment Benefits (months)
        ARCF—Average Rate of Change of Functioning (functioning units/month)
        NPETB—iNitial Patient Expectations of Treatment Benefits (functioning
            units/month)
```

   Patient Expectations of Treatment Benefits represents the rate
at which the patient expects his health to change during treatment.
He brings with him an initial anticipation of treatment benefit
assumed to be one functioning unit per month. The expected benefit
will change with the patient's experience as treatment progresses. If
the Average Rate of Change of Functioning (due to both causes)
exceeds the patient's expectations, the patient will begin to expect
more benefit from treatment. If, on the other hand, the Average

Rate of Change of Functioning falls below what the patient anticipated, the patient will begin to expect less from treatment and deem it less worthwhile. Changes in the patient's anticipations are slow to take effect, represented initially in the model as a 24-month average delay. The weight that the difference will have in changing the patient's expectations depends on the Perceived Relevance of Treatment to Functioning. This multiplier depends on the Average Rate of Staff-Patient Contact and will take on a small value for low rates of treatment.

```
ARCF.K=SMOOTH(RCFSCF.JK+RCFTR.JK,TTSRCF)                      27, L
ARCF=0                                                        27, N
TTSRCF=3                                                      28, C
    ARCF—Average Rate of Change of Functioning (functioning units/month)
    RCFSCF—Rate of Change of Functioning due to Social and Chemical
        Forces (functioning units/month)
    RCFTR—Rate of Change of Functioning due to TReatment (functioning
        units/month)
    TTSRCF—Time To Smooth Rates of Change of Functioning (months)
```

ARCF is an aggregate Average Rate of Change of Functioning. The use of the aggregate rate allows the patient's inability to discriminate between the two kinds of change to be simulated. ARCF is averaged over a period of 3 months.

```
PRTF.K=TABHL(PRTFTB,ARSPC.K,0,2,.5)                           29, A
PRTFTB=0/.1/.5/.9/1                                          29, C
    PRTF—Perceived Relevance of Treatment to Functioning (percentile)
    PRTFTB—Perceived Relevance of Treatment to Functioning TaBle
        (percentile)
    ARSPC—Average Rate of Staff-Patient Contact (treatments/month)
```

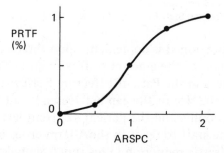

Figure A-5. Perceived Relevance of Treatment to Functioning

This factor relates functioning changes to treatment-seeking. The greater the extent of care the patient is receiving, the greater is his (and his family's) perception that changes in his functioning are attributable to the treatment. The PRTF multiplier also reflects that changes in functioning are seen as irrelevant to treatment when the rate of program contact has been very low or nonexistent.

PROGRAM SECTOR

The formal System Dynamics flow diagram of the program sector of the model follows in figure A–6, the associated equations being described below.

```
RTRT.KL=(RESAP.K) (PERT.K)                                              30, R
     RTRT—Rate of TReaTment (treatments/month)
     RESAP—RESources APportioned (treatments/month)
     PERT—Patient Effect on Rate of Treatment (percentile)
```

The Rate of TReaTment actually provided to the patient is determined by the RESources APportioned by the program and the Patient Effect on the Rate of Treatment. The program's resource allocation is stated in treatments per month and the Patient Effect on the Rate of Treatment is a nondimensional multiplier that causes RTRT to be less than RESAP if Patient Effort to Seek Treatment is low. A unit of treatment represents some amount of care given to the patient. This can take the form of a one-hour session with a psychiatrist or a day spent in a vocational rehabilitation program, some modes of treatment being more intensive than others.

```
RESAP.K=(ANT.K) (CRIT.K) (PESE.K)                                      31, A
     RESAP—RESources APportioned (treatments/month)
     ANT—Assessed Need for Treatment (treatments/month)
     CRIT—CRITicality factor (percentile)
     PESE—Patient Effect on Staff Effort (percentile)
```

RESources APportioned is dependent upon three components: the staff's assessment of the amount of treatment needed, the CRITicality factor, and the Patient Effect on Staff Effort. The first is proportional to the size of the gap between a long-term average of the patient's functioning and the patient's current level of functioning. This causes the staff to react to short-term crises in which the patient suffers a drastic reduction in his functioning level. If a low

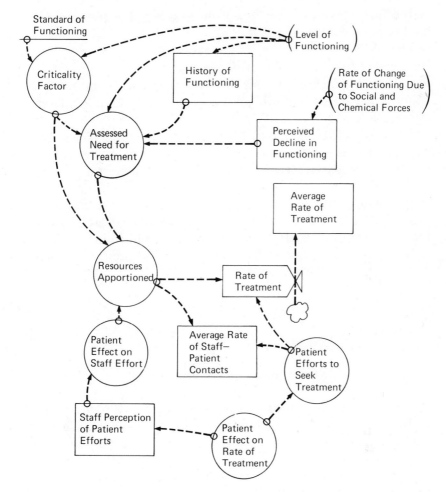

Figure A-6. Flow Diagram of Program Sector of Model

level of functioning persists for a long enough time, this formulation will cause the staff to lower its sights and be satisfied with the patient's maintenance of a lower level of functioning than the one he had before the crisis. The use of a long-term average rather than some absolute standard allows the treatment program to be more closely geared to the individual patient's needs. This essentially means that the staff of a program will be satisfied with a small improvement in a chronically ill patient rather than trying to bring him up to some "normal" level of functioning. Similarly, a patient whose functioning dropped drastically would at first be subject to intensive staff effort. This would decrease if the lower level persisted and the staff became accustomed to it.

The CRITicality factor is, on the other hand, related to the absolute level of functioning and works to increase staff efforts for very low values of functioning. This corresponds to a program staff's concern that the patient is in poor enough condition to harm himself or others.

The Patient Effect on Staff Effort reduces the program staff's willingness to give care when the patient is making little effort of his own to cooperate. Over a period of time, uninterest in treatment shown by the patient (in missing appointments and refusing to cooperate in general) will cause the staff to gradually reduce the amount of effort it is willing to devote to him. The degree to which the staff tolerates low effort shown by the patient would, in an actual situation, depend on the magnitude of the pressure of the staff's current workload.

```
HSF.K=SMOOTH(FNCTN.K,TTPHF)                                        32, L
HSF=FNCTN                                                         32, N
TTPHF=120                                                         33, C
     HSF—HiStory of Functioning (functioning units)
     FNCTN—level of FuNCTioNing (functioning units)
     TTPHF—Time To Perceive History of Functioning (months)
```

The HiStory of Functioning is an averaging over a 10-year period of the patient's level of functioning. This is the long-term average used by the staff to discern trends in the patient's condition.

```
ANT.K=(HSF.K–FNCTN.K)/(SETE*TTEFD)+(PDEC.K/(SETE*TTRFDC))          34, A
AVDEC.K=SMOOTH(RCFSCF.JK,TTSD)                                     35, A
AVDEC=0                                                            35, N
PDEC.K=(PDP)MAX(AVDEC.K,–AVDEC.K)                                  36, A
SETE=.25                                                           37, C
TTEFD=6                                                            38, C
TTRFDC=100                                                         39, C
TTSD=12                                                            40, C
PDP=1                                                              41, C
     ANT—Assessed Need for Treatment (treatments/month)
     HSF—HiStory of Functioning (functioning units)
     FNCTN—FuNCTioNing level (functioning units)
     SETE—Staff Expectations of Treatment Efficacy (functioning units/
          treatment)
     TTEFD—Time To Eliminate Functional Discrepancy (months)
     PDEC—Perceived DECline in functioning (functioning units)
```

TTRFDC—Time To Reduce Functional DisCrepancy (months)
AVDEC—AVerage DECline in functioning (functioning units/month)
RCFSCF—Rate of Change of Functioning due to Social and Chemical
        Forces (functioning units/month)
TTSD—Time To Sense Decline (months)
PDP—Perceived Decline Period (months)

The two components of Assessed Need for Treatment reflect the established discrepancy between long- and short-term levels of functioning and a consideration of the potential for further short-term exogenous decline. The functional gap is divided in each case by the staff's estimate of how much improvement will result from each treatment (SETE) to determine the number of treatments potentially needed. This in turn is divided by the number of months over which the staff hopes to eliminate the discrepancy (TTEFD). Six months was chosen as reasonably representative of this amount of time. The potential further decline in the patient's functioning was taken as a one-month extension of the recent average rate of change of the patient due to exogenous (nontreatment) sources (RCFSCF). A small treatment component was added in light of this potential.

CRIT.K=TABHL(CRTTB,SOF—FNCTN.K,—5,25,5)   42, A
CRTTB=.8/1/1.2/1.5/2/2.5/3   42, C
    CRIT—CRITicality factor (percentile)
    CRTTB—CRiTicality factor TaBle (percentile)
    SOF—Standard Of Functioning (functioning units)
    FNCTN—level of FuNCTioNing (functioning units)

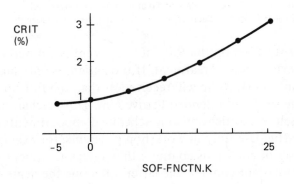

Figure A-7. Criticality Factor

The criticality factor is based on the difference between the standard of health and the patient's actual health level. For large values of this difference, the criticality factor causes a significant increase in the staff's intended efforts. This would correspond to taking special measures to keep a seriously ill patient from harming himself or others.

```
PESE.K=TABHL(PESETB,SPPE.K,0,5,1)                                   43, A
PESETB=.8/.87/.92/.96/.98/1                                        43, C
       PESE—Patient Effect on Staff Effort (percentile)
       PESETB—Patient Effect on Staff Effort TaBle (percentile)
       SPPE—Staff Perception of Patient Efforts (functioning units desired)
```

The Patient's Effect on Staff Effort is a function of a delayed value of the Patient's Efforts to Seek Treatment. It causes the intended staff effort to be decreased when the staff perceives very little effort, shown by the patient, to get care. The use of SPPE represents a delay of 3 months between the time a patient begins to show changed cooperation and the time when this has an effect on the staff's effort.

```
SPPE.K=SMOOTH(PEST.K,TTPPE)                                         44, A
TTPPE=3                                                             45, C
       SPPE—Staff Perception of Patient Efforts (functioning units desired)
       PEST—Patient Efforts to Seek Treatment (functioning units desired)
       TTPPE—Time To Perceive Patient Efforts (months)
PERT.K=TABHL(PERTTB,PEST.K,0,5,1)                                   46, A
PERTTB=0/.1/.4/.7/.9/1                                             46, C
       PERT—Patient Effect on Rate of Treatment (percentile)
       PERTTB—Patient Effect on Rate of Treatment TaBle (percentile)
       PEST—Patient Efforts to Seek Treatment (functioning units desired)
```

The Patient Effect on the Rate of Treatment is a function of Patient Efforts to Seek Treatment. If the patient is only making a small amount of effort, he will receive less than the full amount of care that the staff had intended to give him. This mechanism would manifest itself in a patient missing scheduled appointments and failing to participate fully in workshop programs, for example.

The last set of equations compute the average treatment and the average staff-patient contact, the latter reflecting the degree of harmony between staff allocation of resources for the patient and the patient efforts to utilize these resources.

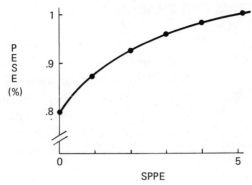

Figure A-8. Patient Effect on Staff Effort

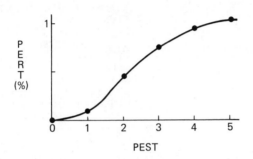

Figure A-9. Patient Effect on Rate of Treatment

```
ART.K=SMOOTH(RTRT.JK,TTATR)                              47, L
ART=0                                                   47, N
TTATR=3                                                 48, C
ARSPC.K=SMOOTH((RESAP.K) (PERT.K), TTATR)               49, L
ARSPC=0                                                 49, N
        ART--Average Rate of Treatment (treatments/month)
        RTRT—Rate of TReaTment (treatments/month)
        TTATR—Time To Average Treatment Rate (months)
        ARSPC—Average Rate of Staff-Patient Contacts (treatments/month)
        RESAP—RESources APportioned (treatments/month)
        PERT—Patient Effect on Rate of Treatment (percentile)
```

The Average Rate of Treatment is simply an exponentially smoothed average of the Rate of TReaTment taken over 3 months. This represents a delay of 3 months before a change in the Rate of TReaTment will affect the Rate of Change of Functioning due to TReatment. Average Rate of Treatment is initially assumed to be 0. The same is true of the Average Rate of Staff-Patient Contacts.

MODEL SETTINGS FOR CHAPTER FIVE SIMULATIONS

For the reader who wishes to use the model in further study of patient-program interactions, this final part of Appendix A lists the model settings that produced the various DYNAMO output graphs shown in Chapter Five. All simulation runs used the previously specified equations 1 through 49, with minor changes in the values of constants (introduced in the DYNAMO rerun mode).

Figure Number	*Model Form Used, Including Changes*
5–1	Treatment Drop-out Base Model
5–2	TTCSF = 3
5–3	L = 0, U = 4
5–4	L = 0, U = 4, TTCSF = 3
5–5	TTEFD = 60
5–6	SETE = 1
5–7	CRTTB = 1/1/1/1/1/1/1
5–8	L = 0, U = 4, TTCSF = 3, SW1 = 1
5–9	L = 0, U = 4, TTCSF = 3, NPETB = 2
5–10	L = 0, U = 4, TTCSF = 3, SW1 = 1, NPETB = 2

Student Performance Model

Figure B-1 presents a formal flow diagram of the model of teacher-student interaction used to produce the results discussed in Chapter Seven. The symbols used are explained in the section preceding Appendix A.

The equations for the model, presented in the DYNAMO notation also explained prior to Appendix A, will be discussed here in an order that seems logical according to the flow diagram.

STUDENT BEHAVIOR

The first equation is:

SP.KL=SK.K   1, R
    SP—Student Performance (performance units)
    SK—Student Knowledge (performance units)

This rate equation indicates that the next interval of Student Performance will be calculated as equal to the present level of Student Knowledge. This equation is very simple because all other variables affecting Student Performance were omitted from the base model in order to keep the first model simple.

The next equation is:

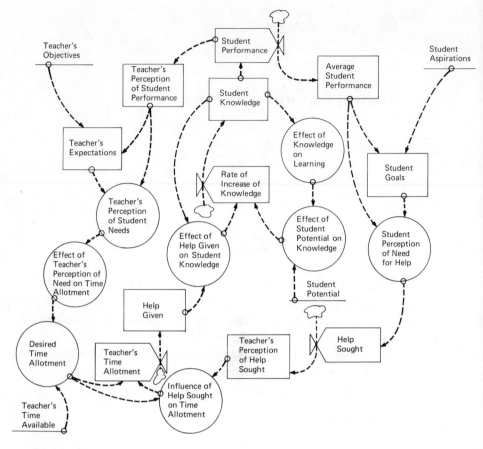

Figure B-1. Overall Flow Diagram

```
AVSP.K=AVSP.J+(DT/TAVSP) (SP.JK-AVSP.J)                          2, L
AVSP=SP                                                          2, N
TAVSP=4                                                          3, C
      AVSP—AVerage Student Performance (performance units)
      DT—Delta Time (weeks)
      TAVSP—Time for AVeraging Student Performance (weeks)
      SP—Student Performance (performance units)
```

The right-hand side of Equation 2, L calculates a first-order exponential average of Student Performance over the time period TAVSP (Time for AVeraging Student Performance). The symbol DT (Delta Time) is used here to tell the computer how often the equations are calculated. In this model DT was specified at 0.5 (every half week). The constant, TAVSP (Time for AVeraging Student Performance) is set at 4 weeks.

The next group of equations set the student's goals:

SG.K=SG.J+(DT/TCHSG) (AVSP.J–SG.J)	4, L
SG=SASP	4, N
SASP=80	5, C
TCHSG=12	6, C

      SG—Student Goals (performance units)
      TCHSG—Time for CHanging Student Goals (weeks)
      AVSP—AVerage Student Performance (performance units)
      SASP—Student ASPirations (performance units)

Student Goals is written as a level equation in the same form as
AVerage Student Performance. This form will be used for all the
level equations in the model as they are all basically averages over
time. Initially, Student Goals are equal to Student ASPirations.
In the first few runs Student ASPirations are set at a desired performance of 80 to give the student, whose initial performance is 75,
just a small goal gap. Time for CHanging Student Goals is 12 weeks.
This indicates that a student will slowly recognize when his goals are
out of line with his performance and gradually shift his goals.
    The gap between Student Goals and AVerage Student Perfor-
mance, at any point in time, will be the basis for the student seeking
help:

SPNHLP.K=SG.K–AVSP.K	7, A
HLPS.KL=TABLE(THLPS,SPNHLP.K,0,40,5)	8, R
THLPS=0/0.5/1/2/2.5/1.5/1/0.5/0	8, C
TPHLPS.K=TPHLPS.J+(DT/TTPHS) (HLPS.JK–TPHLPS.J)	9, L
TPHLPS=0	9, N
TTPHS=2	10, C

      SPNHLP—Student Perception of Need for HeLP (performance units)
      SG—Student Goals (performance units)
      AVSP—AVerage Student Performance (performance units)
      HLPS—HeLP Sought (hours/week)
      TABLE—TABLE function, special DYNAMO notation
      THLPS—Table for HeLP Sought (hours/week)
      TPHLPS—Teacher's Perception of HeLP Sought (hours/week)
      TTPHS—Time for Teacher's Perception of Help Sought (weeks)

The amount of help (in terms of hours/week) a student will seek
depends on the gap between his average performance and where he
would like his performance to be (his goals). This is expressed in
terms of a table function. Equation 8, R says that the rate at which
HeLP is Sought is a function of the Student's Perception of Need
for HeLP and covers a range of student needs from 0 to 40 perfor-

mance points, in units of 5. The next equation (8, C), a table of constants, gives the amount of help sought for each amount of perceived need. This information can be graphed as in figure B–2. This graph shows the modeled assumption that when a student perceives a 5-point gap between his performance and his goals he will seek one half-hour a week of extra help. As he perceives a larger gap, he will seek more time per week. A gap of 20 points is the largest gap the modeled student can tolerate before getting discouraged and turned off. A student perceiving that his performance is 20 points below where he would like it will seek 2½ hours/week extra help. After this point the graph turns down again, indicating the assumption that a student who perceives a 40-point gap between his goals and his performance is so discouraged that he seeks no extra help at all. This modeled graphical function can easily be changed in the computer simulation runs.

The level equation, Teacher's Perception of HeLP Sought (9, L), is again an average over time of the HeLP Sought by the student. The teacher starts with no perception of help sought by the student, but the final constant in this group of equations, Time for Teacher's

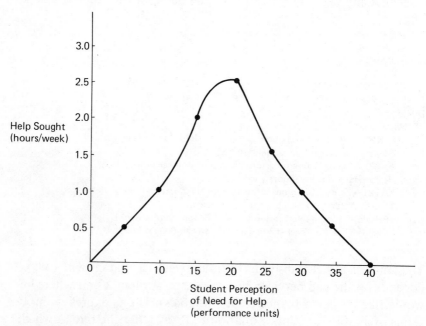

Figure B–2. Help Sought by Student

Perception of Help Sought, equals 2 weeks, indicating that the teacher responds fairly quickly to a student who is seeking extra help.

TEACHER BEHAVIOR

Now let's turn to the teacher's side of the model, which parallels the student side just discussed. The first group of equations is:

```
TPSP.K=TPSP.J+(DT/TTPSP) (SP.JK-TPSP.J)                    11, L
TPSP=SP                                                    11, N
TTPSP=4                                                    12, C
       TPSP—Teacher's Perception of Student Performance (performance units)
       TTPSP—Time for Teacher's Perception of Student Performance (weeks)
       SP—Student Performance (performance units)
```

Teacher's Perception of Student Performance is an averaging of Student Performance over time. Initially the Teacher's Perception of Student Performance will be the same as Student Performance. As the year progresses, the teacher perceives shifts in a student's average performance after about 4 weeks of changed student performance.

The next set of equations deals with how a teacher perceives a student's needs (paralleling the equations determining a student's ability to perceive his own needs).

```
TE.K=TE.J+(DT/TCHTE) (TPSP.J-TE.J)                         13, L
TE=TOBJ                                                    13, N
TOBJ=75                                                    14, C
TCHTE=8                                                    15, C
       TE—Teacher's Expectations (performance units)
       TCHTE—Time for CHanging Teacher Expectations (weeks)
       TPSP—Teacher's Perception of Student Performance (performance units)
       TOBJ—Teacher's OBJectives (performance units)
```

Teacher's Expectations is an average of Teacher's Perception of Student Performance. Initially, Teacher's Expectations are equal to Teacher's OBJectives because there is not yet any Student Performance input. In the first few computer runs described in Chapter Seven Teacher's OBJectives are set at 75. This objective would be typical of a teacher who feels that the student is about average. The teacher takes a little less time than the student for changing her expectations. Time for CHanging Teacher Expectations is initially set at 8 weeks in the model.

At any time, the gap between Teacher Expectations and Teacher's Perception of Student Performance is the basis for the Teacher's Perception of Student Needs. This is one input into the eventual decision by the teacher to allocate time to the student. This set of equations is:

TPSN.K=TE.K–TPSP.K   16, A
TTAV=10   17, C
DTA.K=(TTAV) (ETPNTA.K)   18, A
ETPNTA.K=TABLE(TEPNTA,TPSN.K,0,20,5)   19, A
TEPNTA=.01/.05/.20/.10/.03   19, C

  TPSN—Teacher's Perception of Student Needs (performance units)
  TE—Teacher's Expectations (performance units)
  TPSP—Teacher's Perception of Student Performance (performance units)
  TTAV—Teacher's Time AVailable (hours/week)
  DTA—Desired Time Allotment (hours/week)
  ETPNTA—Effect of Teacher's Perception of Need on Time Allotment
      (percentile)
  TEPNTA—Table for Effect of teacher's Perception of Need on Time
      Allotment (percentile)

Teacher's Time AVailable per week to give extra help is initially set at ten hours. The amount of time a teacher wishes to give a student (DTA) is a multiple of the amount of time she has available (TTAV) and the effect of her perception of the student's needs on the time she has available (ETPNTA). This effect is expressed as a table function with Teacher's Perception of Student Needs as the horizontal axis (figure B–3). If the teacher feels a student could be

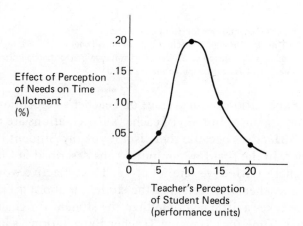

Figure B–3. Teacher's Allotment of Time

doing 10 points better than what he is currently doing, she is assumed to be willing to give him about 20 percent of the extra time
she has available. In the first few computer runs, since she has 10
hours per week available for extra help, she would therefore be
willing to give this student 2 hours/week of extra help. As the
teacher perceives a smaller or a larger gap, the percentage of her
time she is willing to give him goes down. If a teacher perceives
a 20-point gap she will get discouraged, and therefore be willing to
give the student only about 20 minutes per week of extra help.

The influences from the teacher's side of the model now join
with the influences from the student's side to determine how much
actual time the student will receive. The equations determining
Teacher's Time Allotment and therefore how much help the student
will receive are:

IHSTA.K=TABLE(TIHSTA,TPHLPS.K/DTA.K,0,3,0.5)	20, A
TIHSTA=0.10/0.75/1.00/1.10/1.25/1.35/1.40	20, C
TTA.KL=(DTA.K) (IHSTA.K)	21, R
HLPG.K=HLPG.J+(DT/THLPG) (TTA.JK−HLPG.J)	22, L
HLPG=0	22, N
THLPG=1	23, C

    IHSTA—Influence of Help Sought on Time Allotment (percentile)
    TIHSTA—Table for Influence of Help Sought on Time Allotment
        (percentile)
    TPHLPS—Teacher's Perception of HeLP Sought (hours/week)
    DTA—Desired Time Allotment (hours/week)
    TTA—Teacher's Time Allotment (hours/week)
    HLPG—HeLP Given (hours/week)
    THLPG—Time delay for HeLP Given (weeks)

The Influence of Help Sought on Time Allotment is a function of
the ratio of Teacher's Perception of HeLP Sought by the student to
the Desired Time Allotment by the teacher. Figure B–4 shows it
graphically. It indicates that when a student is looking for the same
amount of extra help per week as the teacher wishes to give him
(ratio of 1 on the horizontal axis), this amount is in fact what he
will get (multiplier of 1 on the vertical axis). When the student
wishes less help, for example half (.5) as much as the teacher wishes
to give him, he will in fact get three-fourths (.75) as much as the
teacher had wanted to give him. If the student wants no help (0), he
will still get 10 percent (.1) of what the teacher had wished. If the
student wants twice as much (2) time as the teacher wished, he will
get only 25 percent (1.25) more time from the teacher. Even when

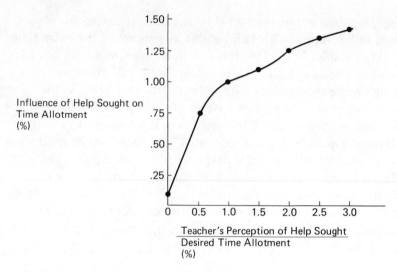

Figure B-4. Student's Influence on Teacher's Time Allotment

the student wants three times as much help as the teacher wished to give him, this will only push the teacher to give him 50 percent (1.50) more time than she had wanted. Basically this function says that the teacher will be influenced by the student's desires for help, or his lack of them, but not linearly.

The Teacher's Time Allotment is equal to her Desired Time Allotment times the just-described Influence of Help Sought on Time Allotment. If the teacher thinks a student needs an hour of extra help per week, a student very anxious for more help might influence the teacher to give 25 percent more time than she had intended, or an hour and a quarter per week. The level equation for HeLP Given is again an average over time of Teacher's Time Allotment. Initially, HeLP Given is 0. The Time delay for HeLP Given is set at one week, which says the teacher responds fairly quickly once she decides to give help to a student.

STUDENT LEARNING

The next group of equations expresses the effect of this help on the student's knowledge:

RIK.KL=(ESPOT.K) (EHGSK.K)   24, R
EHGSK.K=1+(HLPG.K) (TABLE(TEHGSK,SK.K,0,100,20))   25, A

```
TEHGSK=.010/.015/.025/.040/.080/.100                          25, C
ESPOT.K=(NORML) (EKL.K)                                        26, A
NORML=TABLE(TNORML,SPOT,80,150,10)                            27, N
TNORML=15/40/60/75/85/95/98/100                               27, C
SPOT=110                                                       28, C
EKL.K=TABLE(TEKL,SK.K/NORML,0.8,1.2,.05)                      29, A
TEKL=.80/.88/.94/.99/1.00/1.02/1.05/1.08/1.10                 29, C
```

      RIK—Rate of Increase of Knowledge (performance units)
      ESPOT—Effect of Student POTential on student knowledge (performance units)
      EHGSK—Effect of Help Given on Student Knowledge (percentile)
      HLPG—HeLP Given (hours/week)
      TEHGSK—Table for Effect of Help Given on Student Knowledge (percentile/hours/week)
      SK—Student Knowledge (performance units)
      NORML—NORMal Learning (performance units)
      EKL—Effect of Knowledge on Learning (percentile)
      TNORML—Table for NORMal Learning (performance units)
      SPOT—Student POTential (I.Q. scale)
      TEKL—Table for the Effect of Knowledge on Learning (percentile)

The Rate of Increase of Knowledge, or the student's learning rate, depends on the combination of effects of the student's I.Q. and the help he gets. Effect of Help Given on Student Knowledge is itself a function of Student Knowledge (figure B–5). When a student has little or no knowledge in an area, the effect of extra help on his learning rate is modeled as being very little. When the student's knowledge manifests itself in grades of seventy or better, the assumed effect of extra help for this student rises to a maximum

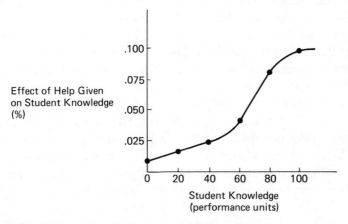

Figure B-5. Student Knowledge Accumulation

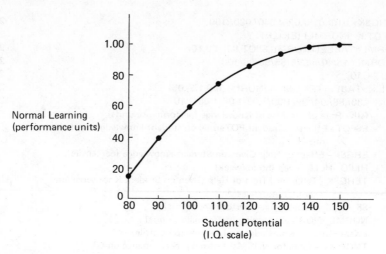

Figure B-6. Effect of I.Q.

of increasing his rate of learning by 10 percent per hour of extra help.

The output from this table is then multiplied by the actual number of hours of help given to determine the degree of enhancement of a student's learning. For example, if a student is doing 60-level work the output from the graph says he would get a 5 percent increase in his learning rate per hour of help. Two hours per week help would thus increase his normal learning rate by 10 percent (.05 × 2 = .10).

The other variable affecting learning rate is student potential (I.Q.). The Effect of Student POTential is equal to the student's NORMal Learning times the Effect of Knowledge on Learning. The student's NORMal Learning is expressed in a table as a function of Student POTential (figure B-6). That graph suggests that a student with an I.Q. of about 80 will do very poorly, performing at a grade level of about 15 in the usual classroom situation. An average suburban student (I.Q. = 110) will do work of about 75. The graph tapers off on the upper I.Q. side, showing that for an I.Q. of 130 and above the students normally will do very good work.

The Effect of Knowledge on Learning is a table expressed as a function of the ratio of Student Knowledge to NORMal Learning rate. This graph in figure B-7 shows that when a student's body of cumulative knowledge in an area is less than what is indicated by his normal learning rate (based on I.Q.), his current learning rate is

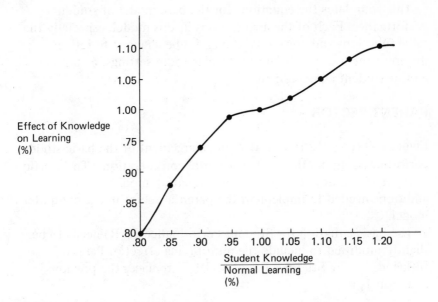

Figure B-7. Student Learning Rate

somewhat slowed. Moreover, when a student has learned more, cumulatively, than would normally be expected of him, his future learning is boosted, though not linearly. In the initial computer runs discussed in Chapter Five the constant for Student POTential was set equal to 110 (on the I.Q. Scale).

The final set of equations for this model determine student knowledge:

SK.K=SK.J+(DT/TCSK) (RIK.JK−SK.J)   30, L
SK=ISK   30, N
ISK=75   31, C
TCSK=25   32, C
        SK—Student Knowledge (performance units)
        TCSK—Time for Changing Student Knowledge (weeks)
        RIK—Rate of Increase of Knowledge (performance units)
        ISK—Initial Student Knowledge (performance units)

Student Knowledge is an equation that averages student learning rate (RIK) over time. Initially, Student Knowledge equals Initial Student Knowledge, which is set at a performance of 75 for the first few computer runs. Time for CHanging Student Knowledge (meaning having a significant impact on cumulative knowledge) is equal to 25 weeks.

This completes the equations for the base model of student performance. Each of the assumptions in this model, especially the table functions and constants, can easily be changed to reflect different theories, research results, classroom settings, or teacher and/or student characteristics.

PARENT SECTOR

Figure 7–9 (page 126) indicated an enlargement of the basic student performance model that added parental considerations. This portion of Appendix B develops the specific equation modifications and additions needed to implement the parental sector in the computer model.

The basic equation for Student Performance (1, R) needs to be slightly modified to include the multiplying effect of Parental Influence on the Student. Equation P1, R replaces the previous equation 1, R.

$$SP.KL=(SK.K)\ (PIS.K) \hspace{4cm} P1,R$$
$\quad$ SP—Student Performance (performance units)
$\quad$ SK—Student Knowledge (performance units)
$\quad$ PIS—Parental Influence on Student (percentile)

Similarly, the basic equation for Student Goals needs alteration to provide for possible influence of Parental Expectations in the formation of Student Goals. Equation P2, A replaces the previous equations 4, L and 4, N. All other equations in this sector are merely additive to the previously specified equations 1–32.

$$SG.K=(WSPG)\ (ISG.K)+(WPEG)\ (PE.K) \hspace{2cm} P2,A$$
$$WSPG=1 \hspace{6.5cm} 33,C$$
$$WPEG=0 \hspace{6.5cm} 34,C$$
$\quad$ SG—Student Goals (performance units)
$\quad$ WSPG—Weight of Student Performance on Goals (percentile)
$\quad$ ISG—Indicated Student Goals (performance units)
$\quad$ WPEG—Weight of Parental Expectations on student Goals (percentile)
$\quad$ PE—Parental Expectations (performance units)

The new goal formulation permits the weighting of two influences, the student's own performance and the persuasion of his parents. With WSPG = 1 and WPEG = 0, the student's goals are reflecting no parental influence. Setting WSPG = 0 and WPEG = 1 would entirely reverse the goal-formative influences.

ISG.K=ISG.J+(DT/TCHSG) (AVSP.J–ISG.J)   35, L
ISG=SASP   35, N
    ISG—Indicated Student Goals (performance units)
    TCHSG—Time for CHanging Student Goals (weeks)
    AVSP—AVerage Student Performance (performance units)
    SASP—Student ASPirations (performance units)

Indicated Student Goals takes on the function previously filled by
equation 4, L. It "indicates" the goal level that is consistent with
the AVerage Student Performance, changing as that average changes.
Initially, this goal indication is set equal to the Student's level of
ASPirations.

Parental Expectations similarly reflect the Student's Performance
over time, although usually they change more slowly than the
student's own self-assessment.

PE.K=PE.J+(DT/TCPE) (SP.J–PE.J)   36, L
PE=PASP   36, N
TCPE=60   37, C
PASP=80   38, C
    PE—Parental Expectations (performance units)
    TCPE—Time for Changing Parental Expectations (weeks)
    SP—Student Performance (performance units)
    PASP—Parental ASPirations (performance units)

Parental ASPirations are initially set at a desired performance of 80,
slightly above the student's previous performance level of 75.

The next equation group computes Parental SATisfaction as an
index, averaging over a brief time interval the ratio of AVerage
Student Performance to the Parental Expectations for that performance. Thus, Parental SATisfaction will be an index value of 100
percent for consistent Student Performance equal to Parental Expectations. The satisfaction index will move above or below 100
percent as that ratio goes up or down.

PSAT.K=PSAT.J+(DT/TIPS) (AVSP.J/PE.J–PSAT.J)   39, L
PSAT=AVSP/PE   39, N
TIPS=2   40, C
    PSAT—Parental SATisfaction (percentile)
    TIPS—Time to Influence Parental Satisfaction (weeks)
    AVSP—AVerage Student Performance (performance units)
    PE—Parental Expectations (performance units)

Actual Parental Influence on the Student will depend upon how the parents react to this indicated satisfaction level. Do they respond vigorously by pressuring the student for small imbalances between performance and expectations, or are their reactions modest? Whatever the parental reaction some time will elapse before parent behavior affects Student Performance. These factors are embodied in the equations below.

PPIS.K=TABHL(TPPIS,PSAT.K,0,1.4,.20)   41, A
TPPIS=.6/.65/.75/.9/.95/1/1.1/1.2   41, C
PIS.K=PIS.J+(DT/TPIS) (PPIS.J-PIS.J)   42, L
PIS=PPIS   42, N
TPIS=8   43, C
    PPIS—Potential Parental Influence on Student performance (percentile)
    TPPIS—Table for Potential Parental Influence on Student performance
        (percentile)
    PSAT—Parental SATisfaction (percentile)
    PIS—Parental Influence on Student performance (percentile)
    TPIS—Time for Parents to Influence Student performance (weeks)

The time delay for the parents' satisfaction with the student's performance to feedback to affect future student performance is initially set here at 8 weeks.

MODEL SETTINGS FOR CHAPTER SEVEN SIMULATIONS

For the reader who wishes to use the model in further study of student-teacher interactions, this final part of Appendix B lists the model settings that produced the various DYNAMO output graphs shown in Chapter Seven. As indicated below figures 7–1 through 7–6 (pages 106–121), and 7–11 (page 132), were based on the previously specified equations 1 through 32, with minor changes in values of constants. Figures 7–7 and 7–8 (pages 122 and 124) used a modified version of equation 18, with additional changes of constants. Figures 7–10 (page 130) and 7–12 through 7–15 (pages 134–141) used the model, including the parent sector modifications and additions, with changes in constants also embodied in the simulations runs.

Figure Number	*Model Form Used, Including Changes*
7–1	Student Performance Base Model
7–2	TCSK = 4, TOBJ = 80, TTAV = 20
7–3	TCSK = 4, TOBJ = 80, TTAV = 20, TCHTE = 1000, TCHSG = 1000
7–4	SPOT = 130, TOBJ = 95
7–5	SPOT = 130, TOBJ = 80, SASP = 95
7–6	SPOT = 130, TOBJ = 95, SASP = 95
7–7	DTA.K = MAX(.1, TPHLPS.K), SPOT = 130, TOBJ = 80, SASP = 95
7–8	DTA.K = MAX(.1, TPHLPS.K), SPOT = 130, TOBJ = 95
7–10	Student Performance Model with Parental Sector Modifications and Additions
7–11	Base Model, with SPOT = 130, TOBJ = 95, TCSK = 4
7–12	Parental Model, with SPOT = 130, TOBJ = 95, TCSK = 4
7–13	Parental Model, with SPOT = 130, TOBJ = 95
7–14	Parental Model, with SPOT = 130, TOBJ = 80, PASP = 95, TPPIS = .6/.65/.95/1.05/1.15/1.25/1.10/1.0
7–15	Parental Model, with SPOT = 130, TOBJ = 95, PASP = 70, TPPIS = .6/.65/.7/.75/.8/.85/.9/.95

Appendix C

Dental Manpower Model

The equations for the dental manpower model used to produce the results discussed in Chapter 9 are listed here.

The format used for the equations is the DYNAMO notation that is explained prior to Appendix A.

Although this model is only a simplified version of the dental manpower system (a far more extensive effort is presently underway by Pugh-Roberts Associates Inc., under contract from the H.E.W. Bureau of Health Manpower, Division of Dentistry[1]), the model's length discourages more amplified description than that already presented in Chapters 8 and 9. Consequently, the pages that follow have been produced by the DYNAMO DOCUMENTOR Program[2], without further comment by the authors.

1. The most recent progress report available at the time of publication of this volume is: *Examining Alternatives for Improving the Nation's Oral Health* (Cambridge: Pugh-Roberts Associates, Inc., October 1, 1975).

2. Alexander L. Pugh III, *DYNAMO II User's Manual,* Fourth Edition, (Cambridge: M.I.T. Press, 1973), pp. 77–79.

PAGE 1   FILE DENTAL   DENTAL PLANNING MODEL   12/19/75

INCIDENCE RATES

```
FNPP.K=CFNPP.K*FFF.K                                          1, A
    FNPP  - FILLINGS NEEDED PER PREVENTIVE PATIENT (T/
            PT) <1>
    CFNPP - CURRENT FILLINGS NEEDED PER PREVENTIVE
            PATIENT (T/PT) <2>
    FFF   - EFFECT OF FLUORIDATION ON THE NUMBER OF
            FILLINGS NEEDED PER PERSON (D) <4>


CFNPP.K=TABLE(TFPP,SPTI.K,0,18,6)                             2, A
TFPP=1.5/1.75/2.9/4.0 T/PT                                    2.2, T
    CFNPP - CURRENT FILLINGS NEEDED PER PREVENTIVE
            PATIENT (T/PT) <2>
    SPTI  - AVERAGE INTERVAL BETWEEN VISITS FOR
            PREVENTIVE PATIENTS (MO) <52>


FNSP.K=CFNSP*FFF.K                                            3, A
CFNSP=5 T/PT                                                  3.2, C
    FNSP  - FILLINGS NEEDED PER SYMPTOMATIC PATIENT (T/
            PT) <3>
    CFNSP - CURRENT FILLINGS NEEDED PER SYMPTOMATIC
            PATIENT (T/PT) <3.2>
    FFF   - EFFECT OF FLUORIDATION ON THE NUMBER OF
            FILLINGS NEEDED PER PERSON (D) <4>


FFF.K=1-DLINF3(.65*AFF.K,240)                                 4, A
    FFF   - EFFECT OF FLUORIDATION ON THE NUMBER OF
            FILLINGS NEEDED PER PERSON (D) <4>
    AFF   - ADDITIONAL FLUORIDATION FACTOR (D) <5>


AFF.K=STEP(SIAFF,TIAFF)                                       5, A
SIAFF=0 D                                                     5.2, C
TIAFF=12 MO                                                   5.4, C
    AFF   - ADDITIONAL FLUORIDATION FACTOR (D) <5>
    SIAFF - STEP INCREASE IN FLUORIDATION (D) <5.2>
    TIAFF - TIME FOR STEP INCREASE IN FLUORIDATION (MO)
            <5.4>


ENPP.K=CENPP.K*FFE.K                                          6, A
    ENPP  - EXTRACTIONS NEEDED PER PREVENTIVE PATIENT
            (T/PT) <6>
    CENPP - CURRENT EXTRACTIONS NEEDED PER PREVENTIVE
            PATIENT (T/PT) <7>
    FFE   - EFFECT OF FLUORIDATION ON THE AVERAGE
            NUMBER OF EXTRACTIONS NEEDED PER PATIENTS
            (D) <8>


CENPP.K=TABLE(EPP,SPTI.K,0,18,6)                              7, A
EPP=.25/.25/.62/1 EXT/PT                                      7.2, T
    CENPP - CURRENT EXTRACTIONS NEEDED PER PREVENTIVE
            PATIENT (T/PT) <7>
    SPTI  - AVERAGE INTERVAL BETWEEN VISITS FOR
            PREVENTIVE PATIENTS (MO) <52>
```

PAGE 2   FILE DENTAL   DENTAL PLANNING MODEL   12/19/75

```
FFE.K=1-DLINF3(.39*.65*AFF.K,240)                    8, A
     FFE    - EFFECT OF FLUORIDATION ON THE AVERAGE
              NUMBER OF EXTRACTIONS NEEDED PER PATIENTS
              (D) <8>
     AFF    - ADDITIONAL FLUORIDATION FACTOR (D) <5>


ENSP.K=CENSP*FFE.K                                   9, A
CENSP=2 T/PT                                         9.3, C
ENSPAS=2.0 T/PT                                      9.6, C
     ENSP   - EXTRACTIONS NEEDED PER SYMPTOMATIC PATIENT
              (T/PT) <9>
     CENSP  - CURRENT EXTRACTIONS NEEDED PER SYMPTOMATIC
              PATIENT (T/PT) <9.3>
     FFE    - EFFECT OF FLUORIDATION ON THE AVERAGE
              NUMBER OF EXTRACTIONS NEEDED PER PATIENTS
              (D) <8>
     ENSPAS - EXTRACTIONS NEEDED PER SYMPTOMATIC PATIENT
              ACCEPTING SYMPTOMATIC CARE (T/PT) <9.6>


FPPNP.K=TABLE(TFPPNP,SPTI.K,0,18,6)                  10, A
TFPPNP=.05/.05/.09/.13 D                             10.3, T
FSPNP=.23 D                                          10.4, C
BETSP=.22 T/PT                                       10.7, C
     FPPNP  - FRACTION OF PREVENTIVE PATIENTS NEEDING
              PERIODONTAL TREATMENT (D) <10>
     SPTI   - AVERAGE INTERVAL BETWEEN VISITS FOR
              PREVENTIVE PATIENTS (MO) <52>
     FSPNP  - FRACTION OF SYMPTOMATIC PATIENTS NEEDING
              PERIODONTAL TREATMENT (D) <10.4>
     BETSP  - AVERAGE NUMBER OF TEETH NEEDING ENDODONTIC
              TREATMENT PER SYMPTOMATIC PATIENT (T/PT)
              <10.7>


          SYMPTOMATIC PATIENTS


SP.K=SP.J+DT*(SGRSP*SP.J+CSPPS*(PPBS.JK-SPBP.J))     12, L
SGRSP=.00106 1/MO                                    12.3, C
     SP     - NUMBER OF SYMPTOMATIC PATIENTS (PT) <12>
     SGRSP  - GROWTH RATE OF SYMPOTOMATIC POPULATION PER
              MONTH (1/MO) <12.3>
     CSPPS  - SWITCH FOR CHANGES IN PATIENTS CARE-SEEKING
              ORIENTATION (0 = NO MOVEMENT BETWEEN
              PREVENTIVE AND SYMPTOMATIC CATEGORIES)
              <45.4>
     PPBS   - NUMBER OF PREVENTIVE PATIENTS BECOMING
              SYMPTOMATIC PATIENTS PER MONTH (PT/MO)
              <83>
     SPBP   - NUMBER OF SYMPTOMATIC PATIENTS BECOMING
              PREVENTIVE PATIENTS PER MONTH (PT/MO)
              <85>
```

PAGE 3   FILE DENTAL   DENTAL PLANNING MODEL   12/19/75

PSP.K=SP.K-SPCCP.K   13, A
PSP=NFSPPS*SP   13.3, N
NFSPPS=.66 D   13.4, C
    PSP   - NUMBER OF SYMPTOMATIC PATIENTS POTENTIALLY
          SEEKING CARE (I.E., THOSE NOT RECENTLY
          RECEIVING COMPLETE TREATMENT) (PT) <13>
    SP   - NUMBER OF SYMPTOMATIC PATIENTS (PT) <12>
    SPCCP - SYMPTOMATIC PATIENTS RECENTLY ACCEPTING
          COMPLETE CARE (PT) <29.1>
    NFSPPS - INITIAL FRACTION OF SYMPTOMATIC PATIENTS
          POTENTIALLY SEEKING CARE (D) <13.4>

SPA.K=SPADS.K+SPAPS.K+SPATS.K   14, A
    SPA   - TOTAL NUMBER OF SYMPTOMATIC PATIENTS
          ARRIVING (PT/MO) <14>
    SPADS - NUMBER OF PATIENTS ARRIVING WITH DECAY
          SYMPTOMS (PT/MO) <18>
    SPAPS - NUMBER OF PATIENTS ARRIVING WITH
          PERIODONTAL SYMPTOMS (PT/MO) <19>
    SPATS - NUMBER OF PATIENTS ARRIVING WITH TARTER AND
          STAINS (PT/MO <20>

FDSSC.K=BFD*EFASA.K*IFASA.K*BFASA.K   15, A
BFD=.055 1/MO   15.3, C
    FDSSC - FRACTION OF PATIENTS WITH DECAY SYMPTOMS
          THAT SEEK CARE PER MONTH (1/MO) <15>
    BFD   - BASE FRACTION OF PATIENTS WITH DECAY
          SYMPTOMS THAT SEEK CARE PER MONTH (1/MO)
          <15.3>
    EFASA - EFFECT OF EDUCATION OF SYMPTOMATIC PATIENTS
          ARRIVING (D) <21>
    IFASA - EFFECT OF INSURANCE ON SYMPTOMATIC PATIENTS
          SEEKING CARE (D) <22>
    BFASA - EFFECT OF BUSYNESS ON SYMPTOMATIC PATIENTS
          SEEKING CARE (D) <23>

FPSSC.K=BFP*EFASA.K*IFASA.K*BFASA.K   16, A
BFP=.042 1/MO   16.3, C
    FPSSC - FRACTION OF PATIENTS WITH PERIODONTAL
          SYMPTOMS THAT SEEK CARE PER MONTH (1/MO)
          <16>
    BFP   - BASE FRACTION OF PATIENTS WITH PERIODONTAL
          SYMPTOMS THAT SEEK CARE PER MONTH (1/MO)
          <16.3>
    EFASA - EFFECT OF EDUCATION OF SYMPTOMATIC PATIENTS
          ARRIVING (D) <21>
    IFASA - EFFECT OF INSURANCE ON SYMPTOMATIC PATIENTS
          SEEKING CARE (D) <22>
    BFASA - EFFECT OF BUSYNESS ON SYMPTOMATIC PATIENTS
          SEEKING CARE (D) <23>

PAGE 4   FILE DENTAL   DENTAL PLANNING MODEL   12/19/75

FTSSC.K=BFTS*EFASA.K*IFASA.K*BFASA.K   17, A
BFTS=.0237 1/MO   17.3, C
    FTSSC - FRACTION OF PATIENTS WITH TARTER AND STAINS
             THAT SEEK CARE PER MONTH (1/MO) <17>
    BFTS   - BASE FRACTION OF PATIENTS WITH TARTER AND
             STAINS THAT SEEK CARE PER MONTH (1/MO) <17.3>
    EFASA - EFFECT OF EDUCATION OF SYMPTOMATIC PATIENTS
             ARRIVING (D) <21>
    IFASA - EFFECT OF INSURANCE ON SYMPTOMATIC PATIENTS
             SEEKING CARE (D) <22>
    BFASA - EFFECT OF BUSYNESS ON SYMPTOMATIC PATIENTS
             SEEKING CARE (D) <23>

SPADS.K=PSP.K*FSPDS*FDSSC.K   18, A
FSPDS=.713 D   18.3, C
    SPADS - NUMBER OF PATIENTS ARRIVING WITH DECAY
             SYMPTOMS (PT/MO) <18>
    PSP   - NUMBER OF SYMPTOMATIC PATIENTS POTENTIALLY
             SEEKING CARE (I.E., THOSE NOT RECENTLY
             RECEIVING COMPLETE TREATMENT) (PT) <13>
    FSPDS - FRACTION OF SYMPTOMATIC PATIENTS WITH DECAY
             SYMPTOMS (D) <18.3>
    FDSSC - FRACTION OF PATIENTS WITH DECAY SYMPTOMS
             THAT SEEK CARE PER MONTH (1/MC) <15>

SPAPS.K=PSP.K*FSPPS*FPSSC.K   19, A
FSPPS=.271 D   19.2, C
    SPAPS - NUMBER OF PATIENTS ARRIVING WITH
             PERIODONTAL SYMPTOMS (PT/MO) <19>
    PSP   - NUMBER OF SYMPTOMATIC PATIENTS POTENTIALLY
             SEEKING CARE (I.E., THOSE NOT RECENTLY
             RECEIVING COMPLETE TREATMENT) (PT) <13>
    FSPPS - FRACTION OF SYMPTOMATIC PATIENTS WITH
             PERIODONTAL SYMPTOMS (D) <19.2>
    FPSSC - FRACTION OF PATIENTS WITH PERIODONTAL
             SYMPTOMS THAT SEEK CARE PER MONTH (1/MO)
             <16>

SPATS.K=PSP.K*FSPTS*FTSSC.K   20, A
FSPTS=.524 D   20.2, C
    SPATS - NUMBER OF PATIENTS ARRIVING WITH TARTER AND
             STAINS (PT/MO <20>
    PSP   - NUMBER OF SYMPTOMATIC PATIENTS POTENTIALLY
             SEEKING CARE (I.E., THOSE NOT RECENTLY
             RECEIVING COMPLETE TREATMENT) (PT) <13>
    FSPTS - FRACTION OF SYMPTOMATIC PATIENTS WITH
             TARTER AND STAINS (D) <20.2>
    FTSSC - FRACTION OF PATIENTS WITH TARTER AND STAINS
             THAT SEEK CARE PER MONTH (1/MO) <17>

EFASA.K=TABLE(ESA,EL.K,0,1,.2)   21, A
ESA=.96/.98/1/1.03/1.07/1.1 D   21.2, T
    EFASA - EFFECT OF EDUCATION OF SYMPTOMATIC PATIENTS
             ARRIVING (D) <21>
    EL   - EDUCATIONAL LEVEL (D) <116>

PAGE 5   FILE DENTAL   DENTAL PLANNING MODEL   12/19/75

IFASA.K=TABLE(ISA,IL.K,0,1,.2)   22, A
ISA=.95/1/1.1/1.3/1.35/1.4 D   22.2, T
   IFASA   - EFFECT OF INSURANCE ON SYMPTOMATIC PATIENTS
          SEEKING CARE (D) <22>
   IL   - LEVEL OF DENTAL INSURANCE (D) <114>

BFASA.K=TABLE(BSA,DB.K,0,5,1)   23, A
BSA=1/1/.87/.62/.25/.1 D   23.2, T
   BFASA   - EFFECT OF BUSYNESS ON SYMPTOMATIC PATIENTS
          SEEKING CARE (D) <23>
   DB   - AVERAGE DENTAL PRACTICE BUSYNESS (MO) <82>

SPACC.K=SPA.K*IFCC.K*EFCC.K*BFCC.K   24, A
   SPACC   - SYMPTOMATIC PATIENTS ACCEPTING COMPLETE
          CARE (PT/MO) <24>
   SPA   - TOTAL NUMBER OF SYMPTOMATIC PATIENTS
          ARRIVING (PT/MO) <14>
   IFCC   - EFFECT OF INSURANCE ON THE FRACTION OF
          SYMPTOMATIC PATIENTS ACCEPTING COMPLETE
          CARE (D) <25>
   EFCC   - EFFECT OF EDUCATION ON THE FRACTION OF
          SYMPTOMATIC PATIENTS ACCEPTING COMPLETE
          CARE (D) <26>
   BFCC   - EFFECT OF BUSYNESS ON THE FRACTION OF
          SYMPTOMATIC PATIENTS ACCEPTING COMPLETE
          CARE (D) <27>

IFCC.K=TABLE(ICC,IL.K,0,1,.2)   25, A
ICC=.5/.6/.7/.75/.8/.85 D   25.3, T
   IFCC   - EFFECT OF INSURANCE ON THE FRACTION OF
          SYMPTOMATIC PATIENTS ACCEPTING COMPLETE
          CARE (D) <25>
   IL   - LEVEL OF DENTAL INSURANCE (D) <114>

EFCC.K=TABLE(ECC,EL.K,0,1,.2)   26, A
ECC=1/1/1/1/1/1 D   26.3, T
   EFCC   - EFFECT OF EDUCATION ON THE FRACTION OF
          SYMPTOMATIC PATIENTS ACCEPTING COMPLETE
          CARE (D) <26>
   EL   - EDUCATIONAL LEVEL (D) <116>

BFCC.K=TABLE(BCC,DB.K,0,5,1)   27, A
BCC=1.5/1/.75/.5/.25/.1 D   27.3, T
   BFCC   - EFFECT OF BUSYNESS ON THE FRACTION OF
          SYMPTOMATIC PATIENTS ACCEPTING COMPLETE
          CARE (D) <27>
   DB   - AVERAGE DENTAL PRACTICE BUSYNESS (MO) <82>

SPECCP.KL=SPACC.K-SPBP.K   28, R
   SPECCP - NUMBER OF SYMPTOMATIC PATIENTS WHO ACCEPT
          COMPLETE CARE BUT DO NOT BECOME
          PREVENTIVE PATIENTS (PT/MO) <28>
   SPACC   - SYMPTOMATIC PATIENTS ACCEPTING COMPLETE
          CARE (PT/MO) <24>
   SPBP   - NUMBER OF SYMPTOMATIC PATIENTS BECOMING
          PREVENTIVE PATIENTS PER MONTH (PT/MO)
          <85>

SPCCP.K=SPCCP.J+DT*(SPECCP.JK-DELAY3(SPECCP.JK,   29, L
   DCC))
SPCCP=SPECCP*DCC   29.1, N
DCC=18 MO   29.4, C
   SPCCP - SYMPTOMATIC PATIENTS RECENTLY ACCEPTING
              COMPLETE CARE (PT) <29.1>
   SPECCP - NUMBER OF SYMPTOMATIC PATIENTS WHO ACCEPT
              COMPLETE CARE BUT DO NOT BECOME
              PREVENTIVE PATIENTS (PT/MO) <28>
   DCC   - DELAY IN REJOINING POOL OF SYMPTOMATIC
              PATIENTS WITH POTENTIAL SYMPTOMS AFTER
              ACCEPTING COMPLETE TREATMENT (MO) <29.4>

SPAST.K=SPA.K-SPACC.K   30, A
   SPAST - SYMPTOMATIC PATIENTS RECEIVING "
              SYMPTOMATIC" OR INCOMPLETE TREATMENT (PT/
              MO) <30>
   SPA   - TOTAL NUMBER OF SYMPTOMATIC PATIENTS
              ARRIVING (PT/MO) <14>
   SPACC - SYMPTOMATIC PATIENTS ACCEPTING COMPLETE
              CARE (PT/MO) <24>

FDSP.K=SPACC.K*FNSP.K*(1-FFEA.K)   31, A
   FDSP   - FILLINGS DEMANDED PER MONTH BY SYMPTOMATIC
              PATIENTS (FL/MO) <31>
   SPACC - SYMPTOMATIC PATIENTS ACCEPTING COMPLETE
              CARE (PT/MO) <24>
   FNSP   - FILLINGS NEEDED PER SYMPTOMATIC PATIENT (T/
              PT) <3>
   FFEA   - FRACTION FILLABLE BUT EXTRACTED ANYWAY (D)
              <32>

FFEA.K=MFFEA*BFFEA.K*IFFEA.K   32, A
MFFEA=.05 D   32.2, C
   FFEA   - FRACTION FILLABLE BUT EXTRACTED ANYWAY (D)
              <32>
   MFFEA - MAXIMUM FRACTION FILLABLE BUT EXTRACTED
              ANYWAY (D) <32.2>
   BFFEA - EFFECT OF BUSYNESS ON FILLABLE BUT
              EXTRACTED ANYWAY (D) <33>
   IFFEA - EFFECT OF INSURANCE ON FILLABLE BUT
              EXTRACTED ANYWAY (D) <34>

BFFEA.K=TABLE(BEA,DB.K,0,5,1)   33, A
BEA=0/.1/.3/.62/.95/1 D   33.2, T
   BFFEA - EFFECT OF BUSYNESS ON FILLABLE BUT
              EXTRACTED ANYWAY (D) <33>
   DB   - AVERAGE DENTAL PRACTICE BUSYNESS (MO) <82>

IFFEA.K=TABLE(IEA,IL.K,0,1,.2)   34, A
IEA=1/.95/.8/.65/.55/.5 D   34.3, T
   IFFEA - EFFECT OF INSURANCE ON FILLABLE BUT
              EXTRACTED ANYWAY (D) <34>
   IL   - LEVEL OF DENTAL INSURANCE (D) <114>

EDSP.K=SPACC.K*ENSP.K+ENSPAS*SPAST.K+OESP.K   35, A
    EDSP   - EXTRACTIONS DEMANDED PER MONTH BY
             SYMPTOMATIC PATIENTS (T/MO) <35>
    SPACC - SYMPTOMATIC PATIENTS ACCEPTING COMPLETE
             CARE (PT/MO) <24>
    ENSP   - EXTRACTIONS NEEDED PER SYMPTOMATIC PATIENT
             (T/PT) <9>
    ENSPAS - EXTRACTIONS NEEDED PER SYMPTOMATIC PATIENT
             ACCEPTING SYMPTOMATIC CARE (T/PT) <9.6>
    SPAST - SYMPTOMATIC PATIENTS RECEIVING "
             SYMPTOMATIC" OR INCOMPLETE TREATMENT (PT/
             MO) <30>
    OESP   - ORTHODONTIC EXTRACTIONS FOR SYMPTOMATIC
             PATIENTS (T/MO) <36>

OESP.K=SPEO.K*AEOSP   36, A
AEOSP=2 T/PT   36.2, C
    OESP   - ORTHODONTIC EXTRACTIONS FOR SYMPTOMATIC
             PATIENTS (T/MO) <36>
    SPEO   - SYMPTOMATIC PATIENTS ENTERING ORTHODONTIC
             TREATMENT (PT/MO) <37>
    AEOSP - AVERAGE NUMBER OF TEETH EXTRACTED PER
             PERSON ENTERING ORTHODONTIC TREATMENT FOR
             SYMPTOMATIC PATIENTS (T/PT) <36.2>

SPEO.K=SPACC.K*FSPEO.K   37, A
    SPEO   - SYMPTOMATIC PATIENTS ENTERING ORTHODONTIC
             TREATMENT (PT/MO) <37>
    SPACC - SYMPTOMATIC PATIENTS ACCEPTING COMPLETE
             CARE (PT/MO) <24>
    FSPEO - FRACTION OF SYMPTOMATIC PATIENTS ENTERING
             ORTHODONTIC TREATMENT (D) <38>

FSPEO.K=FSPNO*IFSO.K*BFSO.K   38, A
FSPNO=.05 D   38.2, C
    FSPEO - FRACTION OF SYMPTOMATIC PATIENTS ENTERING
             ORTHODONTIC TREATMENT (D) <38>
    FSPNO - FRACTION OF SYMPTOMATIC PATIENTS NEEDING
             ORTHODONTIC TREATMENT (D) <38.2>
    IFSO   - EFFECT OF INSURANCE ON SYMPTOMATIC PATIENTS
             ACCEPTING ORTHODONTIC TREATMENT (D) <39>
    BFSO   - EFFECT OF BUSYNESS ON SYMPTOMATIC PATIENTS
             ACCEPTING ORTHODONTIC TREATMENT (D) <40>

IFSO.K=TABLE(ISO,IL.K,0,1,.2)   39, A
ISO=. 1/.3/.4/.5/.6/.7 D   39.2, T
    IFSO   - EFFECT OF INSURANCE ON SYMPTOMATIC PATIENTS
             ACCEPTING ORTHODONTIC TREATMENT (D) <39>
    IL   - LEVEL OF DENTAL INSURANCE (D) <114>

BFSO.K=TABLE(BSO,DB.K,0,5,1)   40, A
BSO=1.5/1.1/.8/.5/.3/.2 D   40.2, T
    BFSO   - EFFECT OF BUSYNESS ON SYMPTOMATIC PATIENTS
             ACCEPTING ORTHODONTIC TREATMENT (D) <40>
    DB   - AVERAGE DENTAL PRACTICE BUSYNESS (MO) <82>

PAGE 8   FILE DENTAL   DENTAL PLANNING MODEL   12/19/75

ENDDSP.K=SPACC.K*BETSP   41, A
    ENDDSP - NUMBER OF TEETH TREATED THROUGH ENDODONTIC
             TREATMENT FOR SYMPTOMATIC PATIENTS (T/MO)
             <41>
    SPACC - SYMPTOMATIC PATIENTS ACCEPTING COMPLETE
             CARE (PT/MO) <24>
    BETSP - AVERAGE NUMBER OF TEETH NEEDING ENDODONTIC
             TREATMENT PER SYMPTOMATIC PATIENT (T/PT)
             <10.7>

RSPEPT.KL=FSPNP*SPACC.K   42, R
    RSPEPT - RATE OF SYMPTOMATIC PATIENTS ENTERING
             PERIODONTAL TREATMENT (PT/MO) <42>
    FSPNP - FRACTION OF SYMPTOMATIC PATIENTS NEEDING
             PERIODONTAL TREATMENT (D) <10.4>
    SPACC - SYMPTOMATIC PATIENTS ACCEPTING COMPLETE
             CARE (PT/MO) <24>

SPPP.K=SPPP.J+DT*(RSPEPT.JK-DELAY1(RSPEPT.JK,   43, L
    DSCPT))
SPPP=DSCPT*RSPEPT   43.1, N
DSCPT=8 MO   43.5, C
    SPPP   - SYMPTOMATIC PATIENTS UNDERGOING PERIODONTAL
             TREATMENT (PT) <43.1>
    RSPEPT - RATE OF SYMPTOMATIC PATIENTS ENTERING
             PERIODONTAL TREATMENT (PT/MO) <42>
    DSCPT - DELAY IN SYMPTOMATIC PATIENTS COMPLETING
             PERIODONTAL TREATMENT (MO) <43.5>

        PREVENTIVE PATIENTS

PP.K=PP.J+DT*(SGRPP*PP.J+CSPPS*(SPBP.J-PPBS.JK))   45, L
SGRPP=.00106 1/MO   45.2, C
CSPPS=1 D   45.4, C
    PP   - NUMBER OF PREVENTIVE PATIENTS (PT) <45>
    SGRPP - GROWTH RATE OF PREVENTIVE POPULATION PER
             MONTH (1/MO) <45.2>
    CSPPS - SWITCH FOR CHANGES IN PATIENTS CARE-SEEKING
             ORIENTATION (0 = NO MOVEMENT BETWEEN
             PREVENTIVE AND SYMPTOMATIC CATEGORIES)
             <45.4>
    SPBP   - NUMBER OF SYMPTOMATIC PATIENTS BECOMING
             PREVENTIVE PATIENTS PER MONTH (PT/MO)
             <85>
    PPBS   - NUMBER OF PREVENTIVE PATIENTS BECOMING
             SYMPTOMATIC PATIENTS PER MONTH (PT/MO)
             <83>

PAGE 9   FILE DENTAL   DENTAL PLANNING MODEL   12/19/75

PPA.K=PP.K*DFA*EFAPA.K*IIFAPA.K*BFAPA.K   46, A
DFA=.16667 1/MO   46.3, C
     PPA   - PREVENTIVE PATIENTS ARRIVING PER MONTH (PT/
                 MO) <46>
     PP   - NUMBER OF PREVENTIVE PATIENTS (PT) <45>
     DFA   - BASE FRACTION OF PREVENTIVE PATIENTS
                 ARRIVING PER MONTH (1/MO) <46.3>
     EFAPA - EFFECT OF EDUCATION ON PREVENTIVE PATIENTS
                 SEEKING CARE (D) <47>
     IIFAPA - EFFECT OF INSURANCE ON PREVENTIVE PATIENTS
                 SEEKING CARE (D) <48>
     BFAPA - EFFECT OF BUSYNESS ON PREVENTIVE PATIENTS
                 SEEKING CARE (D) <49>

EFAPA.K=TABLE(EPA,EL.K,0,1,.2)   47, A
EPA=.7/.7/.77/.9/.97/1 D   47.2, T
     EFAPA - EFFECT OF EDUCATION ON PREVENTIVE PATIENTS
                 SEEKING CARE (D) <47>
     EL   - EDUCATIONAL LEVEL (D) <116>

IIFAPA.K=TABLE(IPA.K,IL.K,0,1,.2)   48, A
IPA=.7/.72/.77/.88/.96/1 D   48.3, T
     IIFAPA - EFFECT OF INSURANCE ON PREVENTIVE PATIENTS
                 SEEKING CARE (D) <48>
     IL   - LEVEL OF DENTAL INSURANCE (D) <114>

BFAPA.K=TABLE(BPA,DB.K,0,5,1)   49, A
BPA=1/1/.8/.6/.25/.1 D   49.2, T
     BFAPA - EFFECT OF BUSYNESS ON PREVENTIVE PATIENTS
                 SEEKING CARE (D) <49>
     DB   - AVERAGE DENTAL PRACTICE BUSYNESS (MO) <82>

FDPP.K=PPA.K*FNPP.K   50, A
     FDPP - FILLINGS DEMANDED PER MONTH BY PREVENTIVE
                 PATIENTS (FI/MO) <50>
     PPA   - PREVENTIVE PATIENTS ARRIVING PER MONTH (PT/
                 MO) <46>
     FNPP - FILLINGS NEEDED PER PREVENTIVE PATIENT (T/
                 PT) <1>

EDPP.K=PPA.K*ENPP.K+CEPP.K   51, A
     EDPP - EXTRACTIONS DEMANDED PER MONTH BY
                 PREVENTIVE PATIENTS (T/MO) <51>
     PPA   - PREVENTIVE PATIENTS ARRIVING PER MONTH (PT/
                 MO) <46>
     ENPP - EXTRACTIONS NEEDED PER PREVENTIVE PATIENT
                 (T/PT) <6>
     OEPP - ORTHODONTIC EXTRACTIONS NEEDED BY
                 PREVENTIVE PATIENTS (T/MO) <53>

PAGE 10   FILE DENTAL   DENTAL PLANNING MODEL   12/19/75

SPTI.K=SMOOTH(PP.K/PPA.K,DSPT)   52, A
DSPT=12 MO   52.2, C
    SPTI   - AVERAGE INTERVAL BETWEEN VISITS FOR
              PREVENTIVE PATIENTS (MO) <52>
    PP   - NUMBER OF PREVENTIVE PATIENTS (PT) <45>
    PPA   - PREVENTIVE PATIENTS ARRIVING PER MONTH (PT/
              MO) <46>
    DSPT   - TIME FOR SMOOTHING INTER-VISIT TIME (MO)
              <52.2>

OEPP.K=PPEO.K*AEPO   53, A
    OEPP   - ORTHODONTIC EXTRACTIONS NEEDED BY
              PREVENTIVE PATIENTS (T/MO) <53>
    PPEO   - PREVENTIVE PATIENTS ENTERING ORTHODONTIC
              TREATMENT (PT/MO) <54>
    AEPO   - AVERAGE NUMBER OF TEETH EXTRACTED PER
              ENTERING ORTHODONTIC TREATMENT FOR
              PREVENTIVE PATIENTS (T/PT) <57.6>

PPEO.K=PPA.K*FPPEO.K   54, A
    PPEO   - PREVENTIVE PATIENTS ENTERING ORTHODONTIC
              TREATMENT (PT/MO) <54>
    PPA   - PREVENTIVE PATIENTS ARRIVING PER MONTH (PT/
              MO) <46>
    FPPEO   - FRACTION OF PREVENTIVE PATIENTS ENTERING
              ORTHODONTIC TREATMENT (D) <55>

FPPEO.K=FPPNO*IFPO.K*BFPO.K   55, A
    FPPEO   - FRACTION OF PREVENTIVE PATIENTS ENTERING
              ORTHODONTIC TREATMENT (D) <55>
    FPPNO   - FRACTION OF PREVENTIVE PATIENTS NEEDING
              ORTHODONTIC TREATMENT (D) <57.3>
    IFPO   - EFFECT OF INSURANCE ON PREVENTIVE PATIENTS
              ACCEPTING ORTHODONTIC TREATMENT (D) <56>
    BFPO   - EFFECT OF BUSYNESS ON PREVENTIVE PATIENTS
              ACCEPTING ORTHODONTIC TREATMENT (D) <57>

IFPO.K=TABLE(IPO,IL.K,0,1,.2)   56, A
IPO=.1/.3/.4/.5/.6/.7 D   56.2, T
    IFPO   - EFFECT OF INSURANCE ON PREVENTIVE PATIENTS
              ACCEPTING ORTHODONTIC TREATMENT (D) <56>
    IL   - LEVEL OF DENTAL INSURANCE (D) <114>

BFPO.K=TABLE(BPO,DB.K,0,5,1)   57, A
BPO=1.5/1.1/.8/.5/.3/.2 D   57.2, T
FPPNO=.05 D   57.3, C
AEPO=2 T/PT   57.6, C
    BFPO   - EFFECT OF BUSYNESS ON PREVENTIVE PATIENTS
              ACCEPTING ORTHODONTIC TREATMENT (D) <57>
    DB   - AVERAGE DENTAL PRACTICE BUSYNESS (MO) <82>
    FPPNO   - FRACTION OF PREVENTIVE PATIENTS NEEDING
              ORTHODONTIC TREATMENT (D) <57.3>
    AEPO   - AVERAGE NUMBER OF TEETH EXTRACTED PER
              ENTERING ORTHODONTIC TREATMENT FOR
              PREVENTIVE PATIENTS (T/PT) <57.6>

PAGE 11   FILE DENTAL   DENTAL PLANNING MODEL   12/19/75

RPPEPT.KL=FPPNP.K*PPA.K   58, R
   RPPEPT - RATE OF PREVENTIVE PATIENTS ENTERING
            PERIODONTAL TREATMENT (PT/MO) <58>
   FPPNP - FRACTION OF PREVENTIVE PATIENTS NEEDING
            PERIODONTAL TREATMENT (D) <10>
   PPA   - PREVENTIVE PATIENTS ARRIVING PER MONTH (PT/
            MO) <46>

PPPP.K=PPPP.J+DT*(RPPEPT.JK-DELAY1(RPPEPT.JK,DPPT)) 59, L
PPPP=RPPEPT*DPPT   59.1, N
DPPT=2 MO   59.4, C
   PPPP   - PREVENTIVE PATIENTS UNDERGOING PERIODONTAL
            TREATMENT (PT) <59.1>
   RPPEPT - RATE OF PREVENTIVE PATIENTS ENTERING
            PERIODONTAL TREATMENT (PT/MO) <58>
   DPPT   - DELAY IN PREVENTIVE PATIENTS COMPLETEING
            PERIODONTAL TREATMENT (MO) <59.4>

       DENTAL PRACTICE WORKLOAD

WGR.K=WF.K+WE.K+WEN.K+WP.K+WO.K+WPR.K+WPRO.K+WTPE.K 60, A
   WGR   - CURRENT DENTAL PRACTICE WORKLOAD PER MONTH
            (MIN/MO) <60>
   WF   - WORKLOAD DUE TO FILLINGS (MIN/MO) <63>
   WE   - WORKLOAD DUE TO EXTRACTIONS (MIN/MO) <64>
   WEN   - WORKLOAD DUE TO ENDODONTIC TREATMENT (MIN/
            MO) <68>
   WP   - WORKLOAD DUE TO PERIODONTAL TREATMENT (MIN/
            MO) <70>
   WO   - WORKLOAD DUE TO ORTHODONTIC TREATMENT (MIN/
            MO) <73>
   WPR   - WORKLOAD DUE TO PROSTHETIC REPLACEMENTS
            (MIN/MO) <65>
   WPRO   - WORKLOAD DUE TO PROPHYLAXIS (MIN/MO) <61>
   WTPE   - WORKLOAD DUE TO TREATMENT PLANNING AND
            EXAMINATION (MIN/MO) <62>

WPRO.K=(PPA.K+SPACC.K)*MWPRO   61, A
MWPRO=17 MIN/PT   61.2, C
   WPRO   - WORKLOAD DUE TO PROPHYLAXIS (MIN/MO) <61>
   PPA   - PREVENTIVE PATIENTS ARRIVING PER MONTH (PT/
            MO) <46>
   SPACC - SYMPTOMATIC PATIENTS ACCEPTING COMPLETE
            CARE (PT/MO) <24>
   MWPRO - MINUTES OF WORKLOAD FOR PROPHYLAXIS (MIN/
            PT) <61.2>

WTPE.K=(SPA.K+PPA.K)*MWTPE   62, A
MWTPE=10 MIN/PT   62.3, C
   WTPE   - WORKLOAD DUE TO TREATMENT PLANNING AND
            EXAMINATION (MIN/MO) <62>
   SPA   - TOTAL NUMBER OF SYMPTOMATIC PATIENTS
            ARRIVING (PT/MO) <14>
   PPA   - PREVENTIVE PATIENTS ARRIVING PER MONTH (PT/
            MO) <46>
   MWTPE - MINUTES OF WORKLOAD FOR TREATMENT PLANNING
            AND EXAMINATION (MIN/PT) <62.3>

PAGE 12   FILE DENTAL   DENTAL PLANNING MODEL   12/19/75

WF.K=(FDSP.K+FDPP.K)*MWF   63, A
MWF=10 MIN/T   63.2, C
    WF   - WORKLOAD DUE TO FILLINGS (MIN/MO) <63>
    FDSP   - FILLINGS DEMANDED PER MONTH BY SYMPTOMATIC
                PATIENTS (FL/MO) <31>
    FDPP   - FILLINGS DEMANDED PER MONTH BY PREVENTIVE
                PATIENTS (FI/MO) <50>
    MWF   - MINUTES OF WORKLOAD PER FILLING (MIN/T)
                <63.2>

WE.K=(EDSP.K+EDPP.K)*MWE   64, A
MWE=9 MIN/T   64.2, C
    WE   - WORKLOAD DUE TO EXTRACTIONS (MIN/MO) <64>
    EDSP   - EXTRACTIONS DEMANDED PER MONTH BY
                SYMPTOMATIC PATIENTS (T/MO) <35>
    EDPP   - EXTRACTIONS DEMANDED PER MONTH BY
                PREVENTIVE PATIENTS (T/MO) <51>
    MWE   - MINUTES OF WORKLOAD PER EXTRACTION (MIN/T)
                <64.2>

WPR.K=(ENSP.K*SPACC.K+EDPP.K-OEPP.K)*FETRP.K*MWPR+ 65, A
  ENSPAS*SPAST.K*FETRS.K*MWPR
MWPR=30 MIN/T   65.3, C
    WPR   - WORKLOAD DUE TO PROSTHETIC REPLACEMENTS
                (MIN/MO) <65>
    ENSP   - EXTRACTIONS NEEDED PER SYMPTOMATIC PATIENT
                (T/PT) <9>
    SPACC   - SYMPTOMATIC PATIENTS ACCEPTING COMPLETE
                CARE (PT/MO) <24>
    EDPP   - EXTRACTIONS DEMANDED PER MONTH BY
                PREVENTIVE PATIENTS (T/MO) <51>
    OEPP   - ORTHODONTIC EXTRACTIONS NEEDED BY
                PREVENTIVE PATIENTS (T/MO) <53>
    FETRP   - FRACTION OF EXTRACTED TEETH REPLACED FOR
                PREVENTIVE PATIENTS AND SYMPTCMATIC
                PATIENTS ACCEPTING COMPLTE CARE (D) <66>
    MWPR   - MINUTES OF WORKLOAD PER REPLACED TOOTH
                (MIN/T) <65.3>
    ENSPAS - EXTRACTIONS NEEDED PER SYMPTOMATIC PATIENT
                ACCEPTING SYMPTOMATIC CARE (T/PT) <9.6>
    SPAST   - SYMPTOMATIC PATIENTS RECEIVING "
                SYMPTOMATIC" OR INCOMPLETE TREATMENT (PT/
                MO) <30>
    FETRS   - FRACTION OF EXTRACTED TEETH REPLACED FOR
                SYMPTOMATIC PATIENTS ACCEPTING INCOMPLETE
                TREATMENT (D) <67>

FETRP.K=TABLE(TIFETRP,IL.K,0,1,.2)   66, A
TIFETRP=.4/.5/.6/.65/.7/.75 D   66.3, T
    FETRP   - FRACTION OF EXTRACTED TEETH REPLACED FOR
                PREVENTIVE PATIENTS AND SYMPTCMATIC
                PATIENTS ACCEPTING COMPLTE CARE (D) <66>
    IL   - LEVEL OF DENTAL INSURANCE (D) <114>

PAGE 13   FILE DENTAL   DENTAL PLANNING MODEL   12/19/75

```
FETRS.K=TABLE(TIFETRS,IL.K,0,1,.2)                         67, A
TIFETRS=.15/.25/.35/.45/.55/.65 D                          67.3, T
    FETRS  - FRACTION OF EXTRACTED TEETH REPLACED FOR
             SYMPTOMATIC PATIENTS ACCEPTING INCOMPLETE
             TREATMENT (D) <67>
    IL     - LEVEL OF DENTAL INSURANCE (D) <114>
```

```
WEN.K=ENDSP.K*MWEN                                         68, A
MWEN=44 MIN/T                                              68.2, C
    WEN    - WORKLOAD DUE TO ENDODONTIC TREATMENT (MIN/
             MO) <68>
    MWEN   - MINUTES OF WORKLOAD PER TOOTH TREATED
             THROUGH ENDODONTIC TREATMENT (MIN/T)
             <68.2>
```

```
PPP.K=SPPP.K+PPPP.K                                        69, A
    PPP    - TOTAL PATIENTS RECEIVING PERIODONTAL
             TREATMENT (PT) <69>
    SPPP   - SYMPTOMATIC PATIENTS UNDERGOING PERIODONTAL
             TREATMENT (PT) <43.1>
    PPPP   - PREVENTIVE PATIENTS UNDERGOING PERIODONTAL
             TREATMENT (PT) <59.1>
```

```
WP.K=PPP.K*MWPP                                            70, A
MWPP=30 (MIN/MO)/PT                                        70.2, C
    WP     - WORKLOAD DUE TO PERIODONTAL TREATMENT (MIN/
             MO) <70>
    PPP    - TOTAL PATIENTS RECEIVING PERIODONTAL
             TREATMENT (PT) <69>
    MWPP   - MINUTES OF WORKLOAD FOR PERIODONTAL
             TREATMENT PER PATIENT PER MONTH ((MIN/MO)
             /PT) <70.2>
```

```
RPEOT.KL=PPEO.K+SPEO.K                                     71, R
    RPEOT  - TOTAL RATE OF PATIENTS ENTERING ORTHODONTIC
             TREATMENT (PT/MO) <71>
    PPEO   - PREVENTIVE PATIENTS ENTERING ORTHODONTIC
             TREATMENT (PT/MO) <54>
    SPEO   - SYMPTOMATIC PATIENTS ENTERING ORTHODONTIC
             TREATMENT (PT/MO) <37>
```

```
POP.K=POP.J+DT*(RPEOT.JK-DELAY3(RPEOT.JK,DOT))            72, L
POP=RPEOT*DOT                                              72.1, N
DOT=36 MO                                                  72.4, C
    POP    - PATIENTS RECEIVING ORTHODONTIC TREATMENT
             (PT) <72.1>
    RPEOT  - TOTAL RATE OF PATIENTS ENTERING ORTHODONTIC
             TREATMENT (PT/MO) <71>
    DOT    - DELAY IN COMPLETING ORTHODONTIC TREATMENT
             (MO) <72.4>
```

PAGE 14   FILE DENTAL   DENTAL PLANNING MODEL   12/19/75

WO.K=POP.K*MWOP   73, A
MWOP=15 (MIN/MO)/PT   73.2, C
    WO   - WORKLOAD DUE TO ORTHODONTIC TREATMENT (MIN/
             MO) <73>
    POP   - PATIENTS RECEIVING ORTHODONTIC TREATMENT
             (PT) <72.1>
    MWOP   - MINUTES OF WORKLOAD PER MONTH PER
             ORTHODONTIC PATIENT ((MIN/MO)/PT) <73.2>

WORK.K=WORK.J+DT*(WGR.J-TDEL.J)   74, L
    WORK   - DENTAL PRACTICE WORKLOAD SCHEDULED TO BE
             PROVIDED (MIN) <74>
    WGR   - CURRENT DENTAL PRACTICE WORKLOAD PER MONTH
             (MIN/MO) <60>
    TDEL   - TREATMENT DELIVERED PER MONTH (MIN/MO) <80>

    DENTAL RESOURCES AVAILABLE FOR PROVIDING CARE

DENTIST.K=DENTIST.J+DT*(DENTIST.J*SGF)   75, L
SGF=.0009 1/MO   75.2, C
    DENTIST- NUMBER OF DENTISTS (DE) <75>
    SGF   - RATE OF GROWTH OF DENTISTS PER MONTH (1/MO)
             <75.2>

DR.K=DENTIST.K*BMA*AXAF.K   76, A
BMA=7900 (MIN/MO)/DE   76.3, C
    DR   - TOTAL MINUTES OF TIME AVAILABLE FOR
             PROVIDING DIRECT PATIENT CARE (MIN/MO)
             <76>
    DENTIST- NUMBER OF DENTISTS (DE) <75>
    BMA   - BASIC MINUTES AVAILABLE FOR DIRECT PATIENT
             CARE PER MONTH PER DENTIST ((MIN/MO)/DE)
             <76.3>
    AXAF   - EFFECT OF AUXILIARY UTILIZATION OF
             DENTISTS' PRODUCTIVITY (D) <77>

AXAF.K=TABLE(AAF,ANA.K,0,5,1)   77, A
AAF=1/1.3/1.7/2.3/2.6/2.6 D   77.2, T
    AXAF   - EFFECT OF AUXILIARY UTILIZATION OF
             DENTISTS' PRODUCTIVITY (D) <77>
    ANA   - AVERAGE NUMBER OF AUXILIARIES EMPLOYED PER
             DENTIST (AUX/DE) <78>

PAGE 15   FILE DENTAL   DENTAL PLANNING MODEL   12/19/75

ANA.K=CANA+RAMP(RIAPM,TBIA)+RAMP(-RIAPM,TEIA)   78, A
CANA=1.5 AUX/DE   78.3, C
RIAPM=0 (AUX/DE)/MO   78.6, C
TBIA=0 MO   78.8, C
TEIA=60 MO   79.1, C
    ANA   - AVERAGE NUMBER OF AUXILIARIES EMPLOYED PER
                DENTIST (AUX/DE) <78>
    CANA   - INITIAL AVERAGE NUMBER OF AUXILIARIES
                EMPLOYED PER DENTIST (AUX/DE) <78.3>
    RIAPM   - RATE OF INCREASE IN AUXILIARY UTILIZATION
                PER MONTH ((AUX/DE)/MO) <78.6>
    TBIA   - TIME FOR BEGINNING OF INCREASE IN AUXILIARY
                UTILIZATION (MO) <78.8>
    TEIA   - TIME FOR END OF INCREASE IN AUXILIARY
                UTILIZATION (MO) <79.1>

    TREATMENT DELIVERED AND DENTAL PRACTICE BUSYNESS

TDEL.K=FIFGE(DR.K,WGR.K+(WORK.K/MTDW),WGR.K+   80, A
    (WORK.K/MTDW),DR.K)
MTDW=2 MO   80.3, C
    TDEL   - TREATMENT DELIVERED PER MONTH (MIN/MO) <80>
    DR   - TOTAL MINUTES OF TIME AVAILABLE FOR
                PROVIDING DIRECT PATIENT CARE (MIN/MO)
                <76>
    WGR   - CURRENT DENTAL PRACTICE WORKLOAD PER MONTH
                (MIN/MO) <60>
    WORK   - DENTAL PRACTICE WORKLOAD SCHEDULED TO BE
                PROVIDED (MIN) <74>
    MTDW   - MINIMUM TIME TO DEPLETE WORK BACKLOG (MO)
                <80.3>

IDB.K=(MNWDB*WGR.K+WORK.K)/DR.K   81, A
IDB=NDB   81.2, N
MNWDB=1 MO   81.3, C
    IDB   - CURRENT DENTAL PRACTICE BUSYNESS (MO) <81>
    MNWDB   - MONTHS OF NEW WORKLOAD CONTRIBUTING TO
                DENTAL BUSYNESS (MO) <81.3>
    WGR   - CURRENT DENTAL PRACTICE WORKLOAD PER MONTH
                (MIN/MO) <60>
    WORK   - DENTAL PRACTICE WORKLOAD SCHEDULED TO BE
                PROVIDED (MIN) <74>
    DR   - TOTAL MINUTES OF TIME AVAILABLE FOR
                PROVIDING DIRECT PATIENT CARE (MIN/MO)
                <76>

DB.K=SMOOTH(IDB.K,TADB)   82, A
TADB=4 MO   82.2, C
    DB   - AVERAGE DENTAL PRACTICE BUSYNESS (MO) <82>
    IDB   - CURRENT DENTAL PRACTICE BUSYNESS (MO) <81>
    TADB   - TIME TO AVERAGE DENTAL PRACTICE BUSYNESS
                (MO) <82.2>

PATIENTS CHANGING THEIR CARE-SEEKING ORIENTATION

PPBS.KL=PPA.K*BFPBS.K   83, R
    PPBS   - NUMBER OF PREVENTIVE PATIENTS BECOMING
              SYMPTOMATIC PATIENTS PER MONTH (PT/MO)
              <83>
    PPA   - PREVENTIVE PATIENTS ARRIVING PER MONTH (PT/
              MO) <46>
    BFPBS   - EFFECT OF DENTAL PRACTICE BUSYNESS ON
              PREVENTIVE PATIENTS BECOMING SYMPTOMATIC
              PATIENTS (D) <84>

BFPBS.K=TABLE(BPBS,DB.K,0,5,1)   84, A
BPBS=0/.05/.10/.15/.20/.25 D   84.3, T
    BFPBS   - EFFECT OF DENTAL PRACTICE BUSYNESS ON
              PREVENTIVE PATIENTS BECOMING SYMPTOMATIC
              PATIENTS (D) <84>
    DB   - AVERAGE DENTAL PRACTICE BUSYNESS (MO) <82>

SPBP.K=SPACC.K*BFSBP.K*IFSBP.K   85, A
    SPBP   - NUMBER OF SYMPTOMATIC PATIENTS BECOMING
              PREVENTIVE PATIENTS PER MONTH (PT/MO)
              <85>
    SPACC   - SYMPTOMATIC PATIENTS ACCEPTING COMPLETE
              CARE (PT/MO) <24>
    BFSBP   - EFFECT OF DENTAL PRACTICE BUSYNESS ON
              SYMPTOMATIC PATIENTS BECOMING PREVENTIVE
              PATIENTS (D) <86>
    IFSBP   - EFFECT OF INSURANCE ON SYMPTOMATIC PATIENTS
              BECOMING PREVENTIVE PATIENTS (D) <87>

BFSBP.K=TABLE(BSBP,DB.K,0,5,1)   86, A
BSBP=.25/.165/.1/.05/.02/0 D   86.3, T
    BFSBP   - EFFECT OF DENTAL PRACTICE BUSYNESS ON
              SYMPTOMATIC PATIENTS BECOMING PREVENTIVE
              PATIENTS (D) <86>
    DB   - AVERAGE DENTAL PRACTICE BUSYNESS (MO) <82>

IFSBP.K=TABLE(ISBP,IL.K,0,1,.2)   87, A
ISBP=.85/1/1.15/1.3/1.45/1.6 D   87.2, T
    IFSBP   - EFFECT OF INSURANCE ON SYMPTOMATIC PATIENTS
              BECOMING PREVENTIVE PATIENTS (D) <87>
    IL   - LEVEL OF DENTAL INSURANCE (D) <114>

PAGE 17   FILE DENTAL   DENTAL PLANNING MODEL   12/19/75

        ORAL HEALTH MEASURES

NDT.K=FNPP.K*PP.K+FNSP.K*PSP.K+FNSRCC*SPCCP.K   88, A
FNSRCC=3 T/PT   88.2, C
    NDT   - TOTAL NUMBER OF DECAYED TEETH (T) <88>
    FNPP   - FILLINGS NEEDED PER PREVENTIVE PATIENT (T/\
              PT) <1>
    PP   - NUMBER OF PREVENTIVE PATIENTS (PT) <45>
    FNSP   - FILLINGS NEEDED PER SYMPTOMATIC PATIENT (T/
              PT) <3>
    PSP   - NUMBER OF SYMPTOMATIC PATIENTS POTENTIALLY
              SEEKING CARE (I.E., THOSE NOT RECENTLY
              RECEIVING COMPLETE TREATMENT) (PT) <13>
    FNSRCC - AVERAGE NUMBER OF FILLING NEEDED PER
              SYMPTOMATIC PATIENT RECENTLY RECEIVING
              COMPLETE TREATMENT (T/PT) <88.2>
    SPCCP   - SYMPTOMATIC PATIENTS RECENTLY ACCEPTING
              COMPLETE CARE (PT) <29.1>

SPP.K=SMOOTH(PP.K,DEL)   89, A
    SPP   - AVERAGE NUMBER OF PREVENTIVE PATIENTS (PT)
              <89>
    PP   - NUMBER OF PREVENTIVE PATIENTS (PT) <45>
    DEL   - SMOOTHING TIME DELAY (MO) <90.2>

SSP.K=SMOOTH(SP.K,DEL)   90, A
DEL=36 MO   90.2, C
AMTPP=1.5 T/PT   90.3, C
AMTSP=7 T/PT   90.5, C
    SSP   - AVERAGE NUMBER OF SYMPTOMATIC PATIENTS (PT)
              <90>
    SP   - NUMBER OF SYMPTOMATIC PATIENTS (PT) <12>
    DEL   - SMOOTHING TIME DELAY (MO) <90.2>
    AMTPP   - AVERAGE NUMBER OF MISSING TEETH PER
              PREVENTIVE PATIENT (T/PT) <90.3>
    AMTSP   - AVERAGE NUMBER OF MISSING TEETH PER
              SYMPTOMATIC PATIENT (T/PT) <90.5>

NMT.K=SPP.K*AMTPP+SSP.K*AMTSP   91, A
    NMT   - TOTAL NUMBER OF MISSING TEETH (T) <91>
    SPP   - AVERAGE NUMBER OF PREVENTIVE PATIENTS (PT)
              <89>
    AMTPP   - AVERAGE NUMBER OF MISSING TEETH PER
              PREVENTIVE PATIENT (T/PT) <90.3>
    SSP   - AVERAGE NUMBER OF SYMPTOMATIC PATIENTS (PT)
              <90>
    AMTSP   - AVERAGE NUMBER OF MISSING TEETH PER
              SYMPTOMATIC PATIENT (T/PT) <90.5>

        SUPPLEMENTARY INFORMATION

FSP.K=SP.K/(PP.K+SP.K)   92, S
    FSP   - FRACTION OF THE POPULATION THAT ARE
              SYTOMATIC PATIENTS (D) <92>
    SP   - NUMBER OF SYMPTOMATIC PATIENTS (PT) <12>
    PP   - NUMBER OF PREVENTIVE PATIENTS (PT) <45>

PAGE 18   FILE DENTAL   DENTAL PLANNING MODEL   12/19/75

FPAS.K=SPA.K/(SPA.K+PPA.K)   93, S
    FPAS   - FRACTION OF THE PATIENTS ARRIVING AT
              DENTISTS' OFFICES THAT ARE SYMPTOMATIC
              PATIENTS (D) <93>
    SPA   - TOTAL NUMBER OF SYMPTOMATIC PATIENTS
              ARRIVING (PT/MO) <14>
    PPA   - PREVENTIVE PATIENTS ARRIVING PER MONTH (PT/
              MO) <46>

FSPACC.K=IFCC.K*EFCC.K*BFCC.K   94, A
    FSPACC - FRACTION OF THE SYMPTOMATIC PATIENTS
             ARRIVING THAT ACCEPT COMPLETE TREATMENT
             (D) <94>
    IFCC   - EFFECT OF INSURANCE ON THE FRACTION OF
              SYMPTOMATIC PATIENTS ACCEPTING COMPLETE
              CARE (D) <25>
    EFCC   - EFFECT OF EDUCATION ON THE FRACTION OF
              SYMPTOMATIC PATIENTS ACCEPTING COMPLETE
              CARE (D) <26>
    BFCC   - EFFECT OF BUSYNESS ON THE FRACTION OF
              SYMPTOMATIC PATIENTS ACCEPTING COMPLETE
              CARE (D) <27>

FSPABP.K=FSPACC.K*BFSBP.K*IFSBP.K   95, S
    FSPABP - FRACTION OF THE SYMPTOMATIC PATIENTS
             ARRIVING THAT BECOME PREVENTIVE PATIENTS
             (D) <95>
    FSPACC - FRACTION OF THE SYMPTOMATIC PATIENTS
             ARRIVING THAT ACCEPT COMPLETE TREATMENT
             (D) <94>
    BFSBP   - EFFECT OF DENTAL PRACTICE BUSYNESS ON
              SYMPTOMATIC PATIENTS BECOMING PREVENTIVE
              PATIENTS (D) <86>
    IFSBP   - EFFECT OF INSURANCE ON SYMPTOMATIC PATIENTS
              BECOMING PREVENTIVE PATIENTS (D) <87>

FPPABS.K=BFPBS.K   96, S
    FPPABS - FRACTION OF THE PREVENTIVE PATIENTS
             ARRIVING THAT BECOME SYMPTOMATIC PATIENTS
             (D) <96>
    BFPBS   - EFFECT OF DENTAL PRACTICE BUSYNESS ON
              PREVENTIVE PATIENTS BECOMING SYMPTOMATIC
              PATIENTS (D) <84>

RWDRA.K=WGR.K/DR.K   97, S
    RWDRA   - RATIO OF CURRENT WORKLOAD TO DENTAL
              RESOURCES AVAILABLE FOR PROVIDING CARE
              (D) <97>
    WGR   - CURRENT DENTAL PRACTICE WORKLOAD PER MONTH
              (MIN/MO) <60>
    DR   - TOTAL MINUTES OF TIME AVAILABLE FOR
              PROVIDING DIRECT PATIENT CARE (MIN/MO)
              <76>

PAGE 19   FILE DENTAL   DENTAL PLANNING MODEL   12/19/75

PCNFR.K=(FNPP.K*PP.K+FNSP.K*PSP.K+FNSRCC*SPCCP.K)/   98, S
  (PP.K+SP.K)
    PCNFR   - AVERAGE NUMBER OF DECAYED TEETH NEEDING
                 FILLINGS PER PERSON (T/PT) <98>
    FNPP   - FILLINGS NEEDED PER PREVENTIVE PATIENT (T/
                 PT) <1>
    PP   - NUMBER OF PREVENTIVE PATIENTS (PT) <45>
    FNSP   - FILLINGS NEEDED PER SYMPTOMATIC PATIENT (T/
                 PT) <3>
    PSP   - NUMBER OF SYMPTOMATIC PATIENTS POTENTIALLY
                 SEEKING CARE (I.E., THOSE NOT RECENTLY
                 RECEIVING COMPLETE TREATMENT) (PT) <13>
    FNSRCC - AVERAGE NUMBER OF FILLING NEEDED PER
                 SYMPTOMATIC PATIENT RECENTLY RECEIVING
                 COMPLETE TREATMENT (T/PT) <88.2>
    SPCCP   - SYMPTOMATIC PATIENTS RECENTLY ACCEPTING
                 COMPLETE CARE (PT) <29.1>
    SP   - NUMBER OF SYMPTOMATIC PATIENTS (PT) <12>

TWPPA.K=MWPRO+MWTPE+FNPP.K*MWF+(ENPP.K+OEPP.K/   99, A
   PPA.K)*MWE+ENPP.K*FETRP.K*MWPR+FPPNP.K*DPPT*MWPP+
   FPPEO.K*DOT*MWOP

   TWPPA - AVERAGE WORKLOAD PER PREVENTIVE PATIENT
              ARRIVING (MIN/PT) <99>
   MWPRO - MINUTES OF WORKLOAD FOR PROPHYLAXIS (MIN/
              PT) <61.2>
   MWTPE - MINUTES OF WORKLOAD FOR TREATMENT PLANNING
              AND EXAMINATION (MIN/PT) <62.3>
   FNPP   - FILLINGS NEEDED PER PREVENTIVE PATIENT (T/
              PT) <1>
   MWF   - MINUTES OF WORKLOAD PER FILLING (MIN/T)
              <63.2>
   ENPP   - EXTRACTIONS NEEDED PER PREVENTIVE PATIENT
              (T/PT) <6>
   OEPP   - ORTHODONTIC EXTRACTIONS NEEDED BY
              PREVENTIVE PATIENTS (T/MO) <53>
   PPA   - PREVENTIVE PATIENTS ARRIVING PER MONTH (PT/
              MO) <46>
   MWE   - MINUTES OF WORKLOAD PER EXTRACTION (MIN/T)
              <64.2>
   FETRP - FRACTION OF EXTRACTED TEETH REPLACED FOR
              PREVENTIVE PATIENTS AND SYMPTOMATIC
              PATIENTS ACCEPTING COMPLTE CARE (D) <66>
   MWPR   - MINUTES OF WORKLOAD PER REPLACED TOOTH
              (MIN/T) <65.3>
   FPPNP - FRACTION OF PREVENTIVE PATIENTS NEEDING
              PERIODONTAL TREATMENT (D) <10>
   DPPT   - DELAY IN PREVENTIVE PATIENTS COMPLETEING
              PERIODONTAL TREATMENT (MO) <59.4>
   MWPP   - MINUTES OF WORKLOAD FOR PERIODONTAL
              TREATMENT PER PATIENT PER MONTH ((MIN/MO)
              /PT) <70.2>
   FPPEO - FRACTION OF PREVENTIVE PATIENTS ENTERING
              ORTHODONTIC TREATMENT (D) <55>
   DOT   - DELAY IN COMPLETING ORTHODONTIC TREATMENT
              (MO) <72.4>
   MWOP   - MINUTES OF WORKLOAD PER MONTH PER
              ORTHODONTIC PATIENT ((MIN/MO)/PT) <73.2>

PAGE 21   FILE DENTAL   DENTAL PLANNING MODEL   12/19/75

TWSPAC.K=MWPRO+MWTPE+FNSP.K*MWF+(ENSP.K+OESP.K/   100, S
    SPACC.K)*MWE+ENSP.K*FETRP.K*MWPR+BETSP*MWEN+
    FSPNP*DSCPT*MWPP+FSPEO.K*DOT*MWOP
    TWSPAC - AVERAGE WORKLOAD PER SYMPTOMATIC PATIENT
                ACCEPTING COMPLETE CARE (MIN/PT) <100>
    MWPRO   - MINUTES OF WORKLOAD FOR PROPHYLAXIS (MIN/
                PT) <61.2>
    MWTPE   - MINUTES OF WORKLOAD FOR TREATMENT PLANNING
                AND EXAMINATION (MIN/PT) <62.3>
    FNSP   - FILLINGS NEEDED PER SYMPTOMATIC PATIENT (T/
                PT) <3>
    MWF   - MINUTES OF WORKLOAD PER FILLING (MIN/T)
                <63.2>
    ENSP   - EXTRACTIONS NEEDED PER SYMPTOMATIC PATIENT
                (T/PT) <9>
    OESP   - ORTHODONTIC EXTRACTIONS FOR SYMPTOMATIC
                PATIENTS (T/MO) <36>
    SPACC   - SYMPTOMATIC PATIENTS ACCEPTING COMPLETE
                CARE (PT/MO) <24>
    MWE   - MINUTES OF WORKLOAD PER EXTRACTION (MIN/T)
                <64.2>
    FETRP   - FRACTION OF EXTRACTED TEETH REPLACED FOR
                PREVENTIVE PATIENTS AND SYMPTCMATIC
                PATIENTS ACCEPTING COMPLTE CARE (D) <66>
    MWPR   - MINUTES OF WORKLOAD PER REPLACED TOOTH
                (MIN/T) <65.3>
    BETSP   - AVERAGE NUMBER OF TEETH NEEDING ENDODONTIC
                TREATMENT PER SYMPTOMATIC PATIENT (T/PT)
                <10.7>
    MWEN   - MINUTES OF WORKLOAD PER TOOTH TREATED
                THROUGH ENDODONTIC TREATMENT (MIN/T)
                <68.2>
    FSPNP   - FRACTION OF SYMPTOMATIC PATIENTS NEEDING
                PERIODONTAL TREATMENT (D) <10.4>
    DSCPT   - DELAY IN SYMPTOMATIC PATIENTS CCMPLETING
                PERIODONTAL TREATMENT (MO) <43.5>
    MWPP   - MINUTES OF WORKLOAD FOR PERIODONTAL
                TREATMENT PER PATIENT PER MONTH ((MIN/MO)
                /PT) <70.2>
    FSPEO   - FRACTION OF SYMPTOMATIC PATIENTS ENTERING
                ORTHODONTIC TREATMENT (D) <38>
    DOT   - DELAY IN COMPLETING ORTHODONTIC TREATMENT
                (MO) <72.4>
    MWOP   - MINUTES OF WORKLOAD PER MONTH PER
                ORTHODONTIC PATIENT ((MIN/MO)/PT) <73.2>

PAGE 22   FILE DENTAL   DENTAL PLANNING MODEL   12/19/75

```
TWSPAS.K=MWTPE+ENSPAS*(MWE+FETRS.K*MWPR)                    101, A
     TWSPAS - AVERAGE WORKLOAD PER SYMPTOMATIC PATIENT
              ACCEPTING INCOMPLETE CARE (MIN/PT) <101>
     MWTPE  - MINUTES OF WORKLOAD FOR TREATMENT PLANNING
              AND EXAMINATION (MIN/PT) <62.3>
     ENSPAS - EXTRACTIONS NEEDED PER SYMPTOMATIC PATIENT
              ACCEPTING SYMPTOMATIC CARE (T/PT) <9.6>
     MWE    - MINUTES OF WORKLOAD PER EXTRACTION (MIN/T)
              <64.2>
     FETRS  - FRACTION OF EXTRACTED TEETH REPLACED FOR
              SYMPTOMATIC PATIENTS ACCEPTING INCOMPLETE
              TREATMENT (D) <67>
     MWPR   - MINUTES OF WORKLOAD PER REPLACED TOOTH
              (MIN/T) <65.3>


AFWPP.K=TWPPA.K*PPA.K/WGR.K                                 102, A
     AFWPP  - APPROX FRACTION OF WORKLOAD DUE TO
              PREVENTIVE PATIENTS (D) <102>
     TWPPA  - AVERAGE WORKLOAD PER PREVENTIVE PATIENT
              ARRIVING (MIN/PT) <99>
     PPA    - PREVENTIVE PATIENTS ARRIVING PER MONTH (PT/
              MO) <46>
     WGR    - CURRENT DENTAL PRACTICE WORKLOAD PER MONTH
              (MIN/MO) <60>


AFWSPAC.K=1-AFWPP.K-AFWSPAS.K                               103, S
     AFWSPAC- APPROX FRACTION OF WORKLOAD DUE TO
              SYMPTOMATIC PATIENTS ACCEPTING COMPLETE
              CARE (D) <103>
     AFWPP  - APPROX FRACTION OF WORKLOAD DUE TO
              PREVENTIVE PATIENTS (D) <102>
     AFWSPAS- APPROX FRACTION OF WORKLOAD DUE TO
              SYMPTOMATIC PATIENTS ACCEPTING INCOMPLETE
              CARE (D) <104>


AFWSPAS.K=TWSPAS.K*SPAST.K/WGR.K                            104, A
     AFWSPAS- APPROX FRACTION OF WORKLOAD DUE TO
              SYMPTOMATIC PATIENTS ACCEPTING INCOMPLETE
              CARE (D) <104>
     TWSPAS - AVERAGE WORKLOAD PER SYMPTOMATIC PATIENT
              ACCEPTING INCOMPLETE CARE (MIN/PT) <101>
     SPAST  - SYMPTOMATIC PATIENTS RECEIVING "
              SYMPTOMATIC" OR INCOMPLETE TREATMENT (PT/
              MO) <30>
     WGR    - CURRENT DENTAL PRACTICE WORKLOAD PER MONTH
              (MIN/MO) <60>


APPA.K=APPA.J+DT*(PPA.J-ANPLS.J*APPA.J)                     105, L
APPA=0                                                     105.1, N
     APPA   - ANNUAL NUMBER OF PREVENTIVE PATIENTS
              ARRIVING (PT) <105.1>
     PPA    - PREVENTIVE PATIENTS ARRIVING PER MONTH (PT/
              MO) <46>
     ANPLS  - ANNUAL PULSE (1/MO) <106>


ANPLS.K=PULSE(1/DT,12,12)                                   106, A
     ANPLS  - ANNUAL PULSE (1/MO) <106>
```

PAGE 23   FILE DENTAL   DENTAL PLANNING MODEL   12/19/75

```
ASPA.K=ASPA.J+DT*(SPA.J-ANPLS.J*ASPA.J)                    107, L
ASPA=0                                                     107.1, N
     ASPA   - ANNUAL NUMBER OF SYMPTOMATIC PATIENTS
                 ARRIVING (PT) <107.1>
     SPA    - TOTAL NUMBER OF SYMPTOMATIC PATIENTS
                 ARRIVING (PT/MO) <14>
     ANPLS  - ANNUAL PULSE (1/MO) <106>


ASPACC.K=ASPACC.J+DT*(SPACC.J-ANPLS.J*ASPACC.J)           108, L
ASPACC=0                                                  108.1, N
     ASPACC - ANNUAL NUMBER OF SYMPTOMATIC PATIENTS
                 ACCEPTING COMPLETE TREATMENT (PT) <108.1>
     SPACC  - SYMPTOMATIC PATIENTS ACCEPTING COMPLETE
                 CARE (PT/MO) <24>
     ANPLS  - ANNUAL PULSE (1/MO) <106>


APPBS.K=APPBS.J+DT*(PPBS.JK-ANPLS.J*APPBS.J)              109, L
APPBS=0                                                   109.1, N
     APPBS  - ANNUAL NUMBER OF PREVENTIVE PATIENTS
                 BECOMING SYMPTOMATIC (PT) <109.1>
     PPBS   - NUMBER OF PREVENTIVE PATIENTS BECOMING
                 SYMPTOMATIC PATIENTS PER MONTH (PT/MO)
                 <83>
     ANPLS  - ANNUAL PULSE (1/MO) <106>


ASPBP.K=ASPBP.J+DT*(SPBP.J-ANPLS.J*ASPBP.J)              110, L
ASPBP=0                                                   110.1, N
     ASPBP  - ANNUAL NUMBER OF SYMPTOMATIC PATIENTS
                 BECOMING PREVENTIVE (PT) <110.1>
     SPBP   - NUMBER OF SYMPTOMATIC PATIENTS BECOMING
                 PREVENTIVE PATIENTS PER MONTH (PT/MO)
                 <85>
     ANPLS  - ANNUAL PULSE (1/MO) <106>


TPPBS.K=TPPBS.J+DT*PPBS.JK                                111, L
TPPBS=0                                                   111.1, N
     TPPBS  - TOTAL NUMBER OF PREVENTIVE PATIENTS
                 BECOMING SYMPTOMATIC (PT) <111.1>
     PPBS   - NUMBER OF PREVENTIVE PATIENTS BECOMING
                 SYMPTOMATIC PATIENTS PER MONTH (PT/MO)
                 <83>


TSPBP.K=TSPBP.J+DT*SPBP.J                                112, L
TSPBP=0                                                   112.1, N
     TSPBP  - TOTAL NUMBER OF SYMPTOMATIC PATIENTS
                 BECOMING PREVENTIVE (PT) <112.1>
     SPBP   - NUMBER OF SYMPTOMATIC PATIENTS BECOMING
                 PREVENTIVE PATIENTS PER MONTH (PT/MO)
                 <85>


TSPACC.K=TSPACC.J+DT*SPACC.J                             113, L
TSPACC=0                                                  113.1, N
     TSPACC - TOTAL NUMBER OF SYMPTOMATIC PATIENTS
                 ACCEPTING COMPLETE CARE (PT) <113.1>
     SPACC  - SYMPTOMATIC PATIENTS ACCEPTING COMPLETE
                 CARE (PT/MO) <24>
```

```
IL.K=CIL+RAMP(RIILPM,TBII)+RAMP(-RIILPM,TEII)+          114, A
   STEP(SIIL,TSIIL)
CIL=.2 D                                                114.2, C
RIILPM=0                                                114.4, C
TBII=12 MO                                              114.6, C
TEII=60 MO                                              114.8, C
SIIL=0 D                                                115.1, C
TSIIL=12                                                115.3, C
     IL      - LEVEL OF DENTAL INSURANCE (D) <114>
     CIL     - INITIAL INSURANCE LEVEL (D) <114.2>
     RIILPM - RATE IN INCREASE IN INSURANCE PER MONTH (1/
               MO) <114.4>
     TBII    - TIME OF BEGINNING OF INCREASE IN INSURANCE
               (MO) <114.6>
     TEII    - TIME OF END OF INCREASE IN INSURANCE (MO)
               <114.8>
     SIIL    - STEP INCREASE IN INSURANCE LEVEL (D)
               <115.1>
     TSIIL   - TIME OF STEP INCREASE IN INSURANCE (MO)
               <115.3>

EL.K=CEL                                                116, A
CEL=.5 D                                                116.2, C
     EL      - EDUCATIONAL LEVEL (D) <116>
     CEL     - INITIAL EDUCATIONAL LEVEL (D) <116.2>

     INITIAL CONDITIONS

SP=NSP                                                  116.7, N
NSP=132E6                                               116.8, C
PP=NPP                                                  116.9, N
NPP=66E6                                                117.1, C
DENTIST=NDENT                                           117.2, N
NDENT=99180                                             117.3, C
WORK=FIFGE(0,(NDB-1)*DR,1,NDB)                          117.4, N
NDB=1.35                                                117.5, C
     SP      - NUMBER OF SYMPTOMATIC PATIENTS (PT) <12>
     PP      - NUMBER OF PREVENTIVE PATIENTS (PT) <45>
     DENTIST- NUMBER OF DENTISTS (DE) <75>
     WORK    - DENTAL PRACTICE WORKLOAD SCHEDULED TO BE
               PROVIDED (MIN) <74>
     DR      - TOTAL MINUTES OF TIME AVAILABLE FOR
               PROVIDING DIRECT PATIENT CARE (MIN/MO)
               <76>
```

PAGE 25   FILE DENTAL   DENTAL PLANNING MODEL   12/19/75

PRINT AND PLOT STATEMENTS

PRINT   PP/SP/PSP/PPA/SPA/SPACC/PCNFR/NDT/SPTI/   117.9
     (6.2)APPA,ASPA,ASPACC,APPBS
     PP   - NUMBER OF PREVENTIVE PATIENTS (PT) <45>
     SP   - NUMBER OF SYMPTOMATIC PATIENTS (PT) <12>
     PSP   - NUMBER OF SYMPTOMATIC PATIENTS POTENTIALLY
                SEEKING CARE (I.E., THOSE NOT RECENTLY
                RECEIVING COMPLETE TREATMENT) (PT) <13>
     PPA   - PREVENTIVE PATIENTS ARRIVING PER MONTH (PT/
                MO) <46>
     SPA   - TOTAL NUMBER OF SYMPTOMATIC PATIENTS
                ARRIVING (PT/MO) <14>
     SPACC   - SYMPTOMATIC PATIENTS ACCEPTING COMPLETE
                CARE (PT/MO) <24>
     PCNFR   - AVERAGE NUMBER OF DECAYED TEETH NEEDING
                FILLINGS PER PERSON (T/PT) <98>
     NDT   - TOTAL NUMBER OF DECAYED TEETH (T) <88>
     SPTI   - AVERAGE INTERVAL BETWEEN VISITS FOR
                PREVENTIVE PATIENTS (MO) <52>
     APPA   - ANNUAL NUMBER OF PREVENTIVE PATIENTS
                ARRIVING (PT) <105.1>
     ASPA   - ANNUAL NUMBER OF SYMPTOMATIC PATIENTS
                ARRIVING (PT) <107.1>
     ASPACC - ANNUAL NUMBER OF SYMPTOMATIC PATIENTS
                ACCEPTING COMPLETE TREATMENT (PT) <108.1>
     APPBS   - ANNUAL NUMBER OF PREVENTIVE PATIENTS
                BECOMING SYMPTOMATIC (PT) <109.1>

PRINT   (6.2)ASPBP/(0.4)FSP,FPAS,FSPACC,AFWEP,   118.1
     AFWSPAC,AFWSPAS/TWPPA,TWSPAC
     ASPBP   - ANNUAL NUMBER OF SYMPTOMATIC PATIENTS
                BECOMING PREVENTIVE (PT) <110.1>
     FSP   - FRACTION OF THE POPULATION THAT ARE
                SYTOMATIC PATIENTS (D) <92>
     FPAS   - FRACTION OF THE PATIENTS ARRIVING AT
                DENTISTS' OFFICES THAT ARE SYMPTOMATIC
                PATIENTS (D) <93>
     FSPACC - FRACTION OF THE SYMPTOMATIC PATIENTS
                ARRIVING THAT ACCEPT COMPLETE TREATMENT
                (D) <94>
     AFWPP   - APPROX FRACTION OF WORKLOAD DUE TO
                PREVENTIVE PATIENTS (D) <102>
     AFWSPAC- APPROX FRACTION OF WORKLOAD DUE TO
                SYMPTOMATIC PATIENTS ACCEPTING COMPLETE
                CARE (D) <103>
     AFWSPAS- APPROX FRACTION OF WORKLOAD DUE TO
                SYMPTOMATIC PATIENTS ACCEPTING INCOMPLETE
                CARE (D) <104>
     TWPPA   - AVERAGE WORKLOAD PER PREVENTIVE PATIENT
                ARRIVING (MIN/PT) <99>
     TWSPAC - AVERAGE WORKLOAD PER SYMPTOMATIC PATIENT
                ACCEPTING COMPLETE CARE (MIN/PT) <100>

PAGE 26   FILE DENTAL   DENTAL PLANNING MODEL   12/19/75

PRINT   TWSPAS/(0.4)FSPABP,FPPABS/TPPBS,TSPBP,   118.2
  TSPACC
    TWSPAS - AVERAGE WORKLOAD PER SYMPTOMATIC PATIENT
                ACCEPTING INCOMPLETE CARE (MIN/PT) <101>
    FSPABP - FRACTION OF THE SYMPTOMATIC PATIENTS
                ARRIVING THAT BECOME PREVENTIVE PATIENTS
                (D) <95>
    FPPABS - FRACTION OF THE PREVENTIVE PATIENTS
                ARRIVING THAT BECOME SYMPTOMATIC PATIENTS
                (D) <96>
    TPPBS - TOTAL NUMBER OF PREVENTIVE PATIENTS
                BECOMING SYMPTOMATIC (PT) <111.1>
    TSPBP - TOTAL NUMBER OF SYMPTOMATIC PATIENTS
                BECOMING PREVENTIVE (PT) <112.1>
    TSPACC - TOTAL NUMBER OF SYMPTOMATIC PATIENTS
                ACCEPTING COMPLETE CARE (PT) <113.1>

PRINT   DB,IDB,RWDRA/WORK,DR,WGR,WPRO,WTPE,WF,WE,   118.3
  WPR,WEN,WP,WO
    DB   - AVERAGE DENTAL PRACTICE BUSYNESS (MO) <82>
    IDB   - CURRENT DENTAL PRACTICE BUSYNESS (MO) <81>
    RWDRA - RATIO OF CURRENT WORKLOAD TO DENTAL
                RESOURCES AVAILABLE FOR PROVIDING CARE
                (D) <97>
    WORK   - DENTAL PRACTICE WORKLOAD SCHEDULED TO BE
                PROVIDED (MIN) <74>
    DR   - TOTAL MINUTES OF TIME AVAILABLE FOR
                PROVIDING DIRECT PATIENT CARE (MIN/MO)
                <76>
    WGR   - CURRENT DENTAL PRACTICE WORKLOAD PER MONTH
                (MIN/MO) <60>
    WPRO   - WORKLOAD DUE TO PROPHYLAXIS (MIN/MO) <61>
    WTPE   - WORKLOAD DUE TO TREATMENT PLANNING AND
                EXAMINATION (MIN/MO) <62>
    WF   - WORKLOAD DUE TO FILLINGS (MIN/MO) <63>
    WE   - WORKLOAD DUE TO EXTRACTIONS (MIN/MO) <64>
    WPR   - WORKLOAD DUE TO PROSTHETIC REPLACEMENTS
                (MIN/MO) <65>
    WEN   - WORKLOAD DUE TO ENDODONTIC TREATMENT (MIN/
                MO) <68>
    WP   - WORKLOAD DUE TO PERIODONTAL TREATMENT (MIN/
                MO) <70>
    WO   - WORKLOAD DUE TO ORTHODONTIC TREATMENT (MIN/
                MO) <73>

PLOT   DB=B(0,4)/FSP,FPAS,FSPACC,AFWPP,AFWSPAC,   118.4
    AFWSPAS(0,1)
       DB   - AVERAGE DENTAL PRACTICE BUSYNESS (MO) <82>
       FSP   - FRACTION OF THE POPULATION THAT ARE
                 SYTOMATIC PATIENTS (D) <92>
       FPAS   - FRACTION OF THE PATIENTS ARRIVING AT
                 DENTISTS' OFFICES THAT ARE SYMPTOMATIC
                 PATIENTS (D) <93>
       FSPACC - FRACTION OF THE SYMPTOMATIC PATIENTS
                 ARRIVING THAT ACCEPT COMPLETE TREATMENT
                 (D) <94>
       AFWPP   - APPROX FRACTION OF WORKLOAD DUE TO
                 PREVENTIVE PATIENTS (D) <102>
       AFWSPAC- APPROX FRACTION OF WORKLOAD DUE TO
                 SYMPTOMATIC PATIENTS ACCEPTING COMPLETE
                 CARE (D) <103>
       AFWSPAS- APPROX FRACTION OF WORKLOAD DUE TO
                 SYMPTOMATIC PATIENTS ACCEPTING INCOMPLETE
                 CARE (D) <104>

PLOT   PP,SP(0,160E6)/PPA,SPA,SPACC(0,12E6)   118.5
       PP   - NUMBER OF PREVENTIVE PATIENTS (PT) <45>
       SP   - NUMBER OF SYMPTOMATIC PATIENTS (PT) <12>
       PPA   - PREVENTIVE PATIENTS ARRIVING PER MONTH (PT/
                 MO) <46>
       SPA   - TOTAL NUMBER OF SYMPTOMATIC PATIENTS
                 ARRIVING (PT/MO) <14>
       SPACC   - SYMPTOMATIC PATIENTS ACCEPTING COMPLETE
                 CARE (PT/MO) <24>

SPEC   DT=2/LENGTH=120/PRTPER=4/PLTPER=4   118.6

```
U.M12127.P248.DENTAL.DYNAMO

* DENTAL PLANNING MODEL                                             00000001
NOTE                                                                00000002
NOTE               INCIDENCE RATES                                  00000003
NOTE                                                                00000004
A   FNPP.K=CFNPP.K*FFF.K               FILLINGS NEEDED PER PREVENTIVE00000010
NOTE                                   PATIENT (T/PT)               00000011
A   CFNPP.K=TABLE(TFPP,SPTI.K,0,18,6)  CURRENT FILLINGS NEEDED PER  00000020
NOTE                                   PREVENTIVE PATIENT (T/PT)    00000021
T       TFPP=1.5/1.75/2.9/4.0 T/PT                                  00000022
A   FNSP.K=CFNSP*FFF.K                 FILLINGS NEEDED PER          00000030
NOTE                                   SYMPTOMATIC PATIENT (T/PT)   00000031
C       CFNSP=5 T/PT                   CURRENT FILLINGS NEEDED PER  00000032
NOTE                                   SYMPTOMATIC PATIENT (T/PT)   00000033
A   FFF.K=1-DLINF3(.65*AFF.K,240)      EFFECT OF FLUORIDATION ON THE00000040
NOTE    NUMBER OF FILLINGS NEEDED PER PERSON (D)                    00000041
A   AFF.K=STEP(SIAFF,TIAFF)            ADDITIONAL FLUORIDATION      00000050
NOTE                                   FACTOR (D)                   00000051
C       SIAFF=0 D                      STEP INCREASE IN FLUORIDATION00000052
NOTE    (D)                                                         00000053
C       TIAFF=12 MO                                                 00000054
NOTE    TIME FOR STEP INCREASE IN FLUORIDATION (MO)                 00000055
A   ENPP.K=CENPP.K*FFE.K               EXTRACTIONS NEEDED PER       00000060
NOTE                                   PREVENTIVE PATIENT (T/PT)    00000061
A   CENPP.K=TABLE(EPP,SPTI.K,0,18,6)   CURRENT EXTRACTIONS NEEDED PER00000070
NOTE                                   PREVENTIVE PATIENT (T/PT)    00000071
T       EPP=.25/.25/.62/1 EXT/PT                                    00000072
A   FFE.K=1-DLINF3(.39*.65*AFF.K,240)                               00000080
NOTE    EFFECT OF FLUORIDATION ON THE AVERAGE NUMBER OF EXTRACTIONS 00000081
NOTE    NEEDED PER PATIENTS (D)                                     00000082
A   ENSP.K=CENSP*FFE.K                 EXTRACTIONS NEEDED PER       00000090
NOTE                                   SYMPTOMATIC PATIENT          00000091
NOTE                                   (T/PT)                       00000092
C       CENSP=2 T/PT                   CURRENT EXTRACTIONS NEEDED    00000093
NOTE                                   PER SYMPTOMATIC PATIENT      00000094
NOTE                                   (T/PT)                       00000095
C       ENSPAS=2.0 T/PT                EXTRACTIONS NEEDED PER        00000096
NOTE                                   SYMPTOMATIC PATIENT ACCEPTING 00000097
NOTE                                   SYMPTOMATIC CARE (T/PT)      00000098
A   FPPNP.K=TABLE(TFPPNP,SPTI.K,0,18,6) FRACTION OF PREVENTIVE      00000100
NOTE                                   PATIENTS NEEDING PERIODONTAL 00000101
NOTE                                   TREATMENT (D)                00000102
T       TFPPNP=.05/.05/.09/.13 D                                    00000103
C       FSPNP=.23 D                                                 00000104
NOTE    FRACTION OF SYMPTOMATIC PATIENTS NEEDING PERIODONTAL        00000105
NOTE    TREATMENT (D)                                               00000106
C       BETSP=.22 T/PT                                              00000107
NOTE    AVERAGE NUMBER OF TEETH NEEDING ENDODONTIC TREATMENT PER    00000108
NOTE    SYMPTOMATIC PATIENT (T/PT)                                  00000109
NOTE                                                                00000111
NOTE           SYMPTOMATIC PATIENTS                                 00000112
NOTE                                                                00000113
L   SP.K=SP.J+DT*(SGRSP*SP.J+CSPPS*(PPBS.JK-SPBP.J))                00000120
NOTE                                   NUMBER OF SYMPTOMATIC        00000121
NOTE                                   PATIENTS (PT)                00000122
C       SGRSP=.00106 1/MO              GROWTH RATE OF               00000123
NOTE    SYMPOTOMATIC POPULATION PER MONTH (1/MO)                    00000124
A   PSP.K=SP.K-SPCCP.K                                              00000130
```

```
U.M12127.P248.DENTAL.DYNAMO

NOTE      NUMBER OF SYMPTOMATIC PATIENTS POTENTIALLY SEEKING CARE        00000131
NOTE      (I.E., THOSE NOT RECENTLY RECEIVING COMPLETE TREATMENT) (PT)   00000132
N    PSP=NFSPPS*SP                                                       00000133
C    NFSPPS=.66 D                                                        00000134
NOTE      INITIAL FRACTION OF SYMPTOMATIC PATIENTS POTENTIALLY           00000135
NOTE      SEEKING CARE (D)                                               00000136
A    SPA.K=SPADS.K+SPAPS.K+SPATS.K          TOTAL NUMBER OF SYMPTOMATIC  00000140
NOTE                                        PATIENTS ARRIVING (PT/MO)    00000141
A    FDSSC.K=BFD*EFASA.K*IFASA.K*BFASA.K                                 00000150
NOTE      FRACTION OF PATIENTS WITH DECAY SYMPTOMS THAT SEEK CARE PER    00000151
NOTE      MONTH (1/MO)                                                   00000152
C    BFD=.055 1/MO                                                       00000153
NOTE      BASE FRACTION OF PATIENTS WITH DECAY SYMPTOMS THAT SEEK        00000154
NOTE      CARE PER MONTH (1/MO)                                          00000155
A    FPSSC.K=BFP*EFASA.K*IFASA.K*BFASA.K                                 00000160
NOTE      FRACTION OF PATIENTS WITH PERIODONTAL SYMPTOMS THAT SEEK CARE  00000161
NOTE      PER MONTH (1/MO)                                               00000162
C    BFP=.042 1/MO                                                       00000163
NOTE      BASE FRACTION OF PATIENTS WITH PERIODONTAL SYMPTOMS THAT SEEK  00000164
NOTE      CARE PER MONTH (1/MO)                                          00000165
A    FTSSC.K=BFTS*EFASA.K*IFASA.K*BFASA.K                                00000170
NOTE      FRACTION OF PATIENTS WITH TARTER AND STAINS THAT SEEK CARE PER 00000171
NOTE      MONTH (1/MO)                                                   00000172
C    BFTS=.0237 1/MO                                                     00000173
NOTE      BASE FRACTION OF PATIENTS WITH TARTER AND STAINS THAT SEEK     00000174
NOTE      PER MONTH (1/MO)                                               00000175
A    SPADS.K=PSP.K*FSPDS*FDSSC.K            NUMBER OF PATIENTS           00000180
NOTE                                        ARRIVING WITH DECAY          00000181
NOTE                                        SYMPTOMS (PT/MO)             00000182
C    FSPDS=.713 D                           FRACTION OF                  00000183
NOTE                                        SYMPTOMATIC PATIENTS WITH    00000184
NOTE                                        DECAY SYMPTOMS (D)           00000185
A    SPAPS.K=PSP.K*FSPPS*FPSSC.K            NUMBER OF PATIENTS ARRIVING  00000190
NOTE                                        WITH PERIODONTAL SYMPTOMS (PT/MO) 00000191
C    FSPPS=.271 D                           FRACTION OF                  00000192
NOTE                                        SYMPTOMATIC PATIENTS WITH    00000193
NOTE                                        PERIODONTAL SYMPTOMS (D)     00000194
A    SPATS.K=PSP.K*FSPTS*FTSSC.K            NUMBER OF PATIENTS ARRIVING  00000200
NOTE                                        WITH TARTER AND STAINS (PT/MO 00000201
C    FSPTS=.524 D                           FRACTION OF                  00000202
NOTE                                        SYMPTOMATIC PATIENTS WITH    00000203
NOTE                                        TARTER AND STAINS (D)        00000204
A    EFASA.K=TABLE(ESA,EL.K,0,1,.2)                                      00000210
NOTE      EFFECT OF EDUCATION OF SYMPTOMATIC PATIENTS ARRIVING (D)       00000211
T    ESA=.96/.98/1/1.03/1.07/1.1 D                                       00000212
A    IFASA.K=TABLE(ISA,IL.K,0,1,.2)         EFFECT OF INSURANCE ON       00000220
NOTE      SYMPTOMATIC PATIENTS SEEKING CARE (D)                          00000221
T    ISA=.95/1/1.1/1.3/1.35/1.4 D                                        00000222
A    BFASA.K=TABLE(BSA,DB.K,0,5,1)          EFFECT OF BUSYNESS           00000230
NOTE      ON SYMPTOMATIC PATIENTS SEEKING CARE (D)                       00000231
T    BSA=1/1/.87/.62/.25/.1 D                                            00000232
A    SPACC.K=SPA.K*IFCC.K*EFCC.K*BFCC.K                                  00000240
NOTE      SYMPTOMATIC PATIENTS ACCEPTING COMPLETE CARE (PT/MO)           00000241
A    IFCC.K=TABLE(ICC,IL.K,0,1,.2)          EFFECT OF INSURANCE ON       00000250
NOTE      THE FRACTION OF SYMPTOMATIC PATIENTS ACCEPTING COMPLETE        00000251
NOTE      CARE (D)                                                       00000252
T    ICC=.5/.6/.7/.75/.8/.85 D                                           00000253
```

```
J.M12127.P248.DENTAL.CYNAMO

A   EFCC.K=TABLE(ECC,EL.K,0,1,.2)              EFFECT OF EDUCATION ON         00000260
NOTE     THE FRACTION OF SYMPTOMATIC PATIENTS ACCEPTING COMPLETE            00000261
NOTE     CARE (D)                                                           00000262
T        ECC=1/1/1/1/1/1 D                                                  00000263
A   BFCC.K=TABLE(BCC,DB.K,0,5,1)              EFFECT OF BUSYNESS ON          00000270
NOTE     THE FRACTION OF SYMPTOMATIC PATIENTS ACCEPTING COMPLETE            00000271
NOTE     CARE (D)                                                           00000272
T        BCC=1.5/1/.75/.5/.25/.1 D                                          00000273
R   SPECCP.KL=SPACC.K-SPBP.K                                                00000280
NOTE     NUMBER OF SYMPTOMATIC PATIENTS WHO ACCEPT COMPLETE CARE BUT        00000281
NOTE     DO NOT BECOME PREVENTIVE PATIENTS (PT/MO)                          00000282
L   SPCCP.K=SPCCP.J+DT*(SPECCP.JK-DELAY3(SPECCP.JK,DCC))                    00000290
N   SPCCP=SPECCP*DCC                                                        00000291
NOTE                                     SYMPTOMATIC PATIENTS RECENTLY      00000292
NOTE                                     ACCEPTING COMPLETE CARE (PT)       00000293
C   DCC=18 MO                                                               00000294
NOTE     DELAY IN REJOINING POOL OF SYMPTOMATIC PATIENTS WITH POTENTIAL     00000295
NOTE     SYMPTOMS AFTER ACCEPTING COMPLETE TREATMENT (MO)                   00000296
A   SPAST.K=SPA.K-SPACC.K   SYMPTOMATIC PATIENTS RECEIVING                  00000300
NOTE     "SYMPTOMATIC" OR INCOMPLETE TREATMENT (PT/MO)                      00000301
A   FDSP.K=SPACC.K*FNSP.K*(1-FFEA.K)                                        00000310
NOTE                          FILLINGS DEMANDED PER MONTH                   00000311
NOTE                          BY SYMPTOMATIC PATIENTS (FL/MO)               00000312
A   FFEA.K=MFFEA*BFFEA.K*IFFEA.K   FRACTION FILLABLE BUT                    00000320
NOTE                          EXTRACTED ANYWAY (D)                          00000321
C   MFFEA=.05 D     MAXIMUM FRACTION FILLABLE                               00000322
NOTE                          BUT EXTRACTED ANYWAY (D)                      00000323
A   BFFEA.K=TABLE(BEA,DB.K,0,5,1)   EFFECT OF BUSYNESS ON FILLABLE          00000330
NOTE                          BUT EXTRACTED ANYWAY (D)                      00000331
T   BEA=0/.1/.3/.62/.95/1 D                                                 00000332
A   IFFEA.K=TABLE(IEA,IL.K,0,1,.2)   EFFECT OF INSURANCE ON                 00000340
NOTE                          FILLABLE BUT EXTRACTED                        00000341
NOTE                          ANYWAY (D)                                    00000342
T   IEA=1/.95/.8/.65/.55/.5 D                                               00000343
A   EDSP.K=SPACC.K*ENSP.K+ENSPAS*SPAST.K+OESP.K   EXTRACTIONS DEMANDED      00000350
NOTE                          PER MONTH BY SYMPTOMATIC                      00000351
NOTE                          PATIENTS (T/MO)                               00000352
A   OESP.K=SPEO.K*AEOSP   ORTHODONTIC EXTRACTIONS FOR                       00000360
NOTE                          SYMPTOMATIC PATIENTS (T/MO)                   00000361
C   AEOSP=2 T/PT                                                            00000362
NOTE     AVERAGE NUMBER OF TEETH EXTRACTED PER PERSON ENTERING              00000363
NOTE     ORTHODONTIC TREATMENT FOR SYMPTOMATIC PATIENTS (T/PT)              00000364
A   SPEO.K=SPACC.K*FSPEO.K   SYMPTOMATIC PATIENTS ENTERING                  00000370
NOTE                          ORTHODONTIC TREATMENT (PT/MO)                 00000371
A   FSPEO.K=FSPNO*IFSO.K*BFSO.K   FRACTION OF SYMPTOMATIC PATIENTS          00000380
NOTE                          ENTERING ORTHODONTIC TREATMENT (D)            00000381
C   FSPNO=.05 D     FRACTION OF SYMPTOMATIC PATIENTS                        00000382
NOTE                          NEEDING ORTHODONTIC TREATMENT (D)             00000383
A   IFSO.K=TABLE(ISO,IL.K,0,1,.2)   EFFECT OF INSURANCE ON SYMPTOMATIC      00000390
NOTE     PATIENTS ACCEPTING ORTHODONTIC TREATMENT (D)                       00000391
T   ISO=.1/.3/.4/.5/.6/.7 D                                                 00000392
A   BFSO.K=TABLE(BSO,DB.K,0,5,1)   EFFECT OF BUSYNESS ON SYMPTOMATIC        00000400
NOTE     PATIENTS ACCEPTING ORTHODONTIC TREATMENT (D)                       00000401
T   BSO=1.5/1.1/.8/.5/.3/.2 D                                               00000402
A   ENDDSP.K=SPACC.K*BETSP                                                  00000410
NOTE     NUMBER OF TEETH TREATED THROUGH ENDODONTIC TREATMENT               00000411
NOTE     FOR SYMPTOMATIC PATIENTS (T/MO)                                    00000412
```

```
U.M12127.P248.DENTAL.DYNAMO

R   RSPEPT.KL=FSPNP*SPACC.K       RATE OF SYMPTOMATIC PATIENTS         00000420
NOTE                             ENTERING PERIODONTAL                 00000421
NOTE                             TREATMENT (PT/MO)                    00000422
L   SPPP.K=SPPP.J+DT*(RSPEPT.JK-DELAY1(RSPEPT.JK,DSCPT))              00000430
N   SPPP=DSCPT*RSPEPT                                                 00000431
NOTE                             SYMPTOMATIC PATIENTS                 00000432
NOTE                             UNDERGOING PERIODONTAL               00000433
NOTE                             TREATMENT (PT)                       00000434
C     DSCPT=8 MO     DELAY IN SYMPTOMATIC PATIENTS                    00000435
NOTE                             COMPLETING PERIODONTAL               00000436
NOTE                             TREATMENT (MO)                       00000437
NOTE                                                                  00000438
NOTE          PREVENTIVE PATIENTS                                     00000439
NOTE                                                                  00000441
L   PP.K=PP.J+DT*(SGRPP*PP.J+CSPPS*(SPBP.J-PPES.JK))                  00000450
NOTE                             NUMBER OF PREVENTIVE PATIENTS (PT)   00000451
C     SGRPP=.00106 1/MO     GROWTH RATE OF                           00000452
NOTE       PREVENTIVE POPULATION PER MONTH (1/MO)                     00000453
C     CSPPS=1 D                                                      00000454
NOTE       SWITCH FOR CHANGES IN PATIENTS CARE-SEEKING ORIENTATION   00000455
NOTE       (0 = NO MOVEMENT BETWEEN PREVENTIVE AND SYMPTOMATIC CATEGORIES)00000456
A   PPA.K=PP.K*DFA*EFAPA.K*IIFAPA.K*BFAPA.K                          00000460
NOTE                             PREVENTIVE PATIENTS ARRIVING         00000461
NOTE                             PER MONTH (PT/MO)                    00000462
C     DFA=.16667 1/MO   BASE FRACTION OF PREVENTIVE PATIENTS ARRIVING 00000463
NOTE       PER MONTH (1/MO)                                           00000464
A   EFAPA.K=TABLE(EPA,EL.K,0,1,.2)   EFFECT OF EDUCATION             00000470
NOTE       ON PREVENTIVE PATIENTS SEEKING CARE (D)                    00000471
T     EPA=.7/.7/.77/.9/.97/1 D                                       00000472
A   IIFAPA.K=TABLE(IPA.K,IL.K,0,1,.2)                                 00000480
NOTE       EFFECT OF INSURANCE ON PREVENTIVE PATIENTS SEEKING         00000481
NOTE       CARE (D)                                                   00000482
T     IPA=.7/.72/.77/.88/.96/1 D                                     00000483
A   BFAPA.K=TABLE(BPA,DB.K,0,5,1)   EFFECT OF BUSYNESS               00000490
NOTE       ON PREVENTIVE PATIENTS SEEKING CARE (D)                    00000491
T     BPA=1/1/.8/.6/.25/.1 D                                         00000492
A   FDPP.K=PPA.K*FNPP.K             FILLINGS DEMANDED                00000500
NOTE                               PER MONTH BY PREVENTIVE           00000501
NOTE                               PATIENTS (FI/MO)                  00000502
A   EDPP.K=PPA.K*ENPP.K+OEPP.K      EXTRACTIONS DEMANDED PER         00000510
NOTE                               MONTH BY PREVENTIVE PATIENTS (T/MO)00000511
A   SPTI.K=SMOOTH(PP.K/PPA.K,DSPT)                                   00000520
NOTE       AVERAGE INTERVAL BETWEEN VISITS FOR PREVENTIVE PATIENTS (MO)00000521
C     DSPT=12 MO                                                     00000522
NOTE       TIME FOR SMOOTHING INTER-VISIT TIME (MO)                   00000523
A   OEPP.K=PPEO.K*AEPO             ORTHODONTIC EXTRACTIONS NEEDED     00000530
NOTE                               BY PREVENTIVE PATIENTS (T/MO)     00000531
A   PPEO.K=PPA.K*FPPEO.K           PREVENTIVE PATIENTS ENTERING      00000540
NOTE                               ORTHODONTIC TREATMENT (PT/MO)     00000541
A   FPPEO.K=FPPNO*IFPO.K*BFPO.K    FRACTION OF PREVENTIVE            00000550
NOTE                               PATIENTS ENTERING ORTHODONTIC     00000551
NOTE                               TREATMENT (D)                     00000552
A   IFPO.K=TABLE(IPO,IL.K,0,1,.2)     EFFECT OF INSURANCE ON         00000560
NOTE       PREVENTIVE PATIENTS ACCEPTING ORTHODONTIC TREATMENT (D)    00000561
T     IPO=.1/.3/.4/.5/.6/.7 D                                        00000562
A   BFPO.K=TABLE(BPO,DB.K,0,5,1)      EFFECT OF BUSYNESS ON          00000570
NOTE       PREVENTIVE PATIENTS ACCEPTING ORTHODONTIC TREATMENT (D)    00000571
```

```
U.M12127.P248.DENTAL.DYNAMO

T       BPO=1.5/1.1/.8/.5/.3/.2 D                                            00000572
C       FPPNO=.05 D                              FRACTION OF PREVENTIVE      00000573
NOTE                                             PATIENTS NEEDING            00000574
NOTE                                             ORTHODONTIC TREATMENT (D)   00000575
C       AEPO=2 T/PT                                                          00000576
NOTE       AVERAGE NUMBER OF TEETH EXTRACTED PER ENTERING ORTHODONTIC       00000577
NOTE       TREATMENT FOR PREVENTIVE PATIENTS (T/PT)                         00000578
R       RPPEPT.KL=FPPNP.K*PPA.K                  RATE OF PREVENTIVE          00000580
NOTE                                             PATIENTS ENTERING           00000581
NOTE                                             PERIODONTAL TREATMENT (PT/MO) 00000582
L       PPPP.K=PPPP.J+DT*(RPPEPT.JK-DELAY1(RPPEPT.JK,DPPT))                  00000590
N       PPPP=RPPEPT*DPPT                                                     00000591
NOTE                                             PREVENTIVE PATIENTS UNDERGOING 00000592
NOTE                                             PERIODONTAL TREATMENT (PT)  00000593
C       DPPT=2 MC                                DELAY IN PREVENTIVE         00000594
NOTE       PATIENTS COMPLETEING PERIODONTAL TREATMENT (MO)                  00000595
NOTE                                                                         00000596
NOTE          DENTAL PRACTICE WORKLOAD                                       00000597
NCTE                                                                         00000598
A       WGR.K=WF.K+WE.K+WEN.K+WP.K+WO.K+WPR.K+WPRO.K+WTPE.K                  00000600
NOTE       CURRENT DENTAL PRACTICE WORKLOAD PER MONTH (MIN/MO)              00000601
A       WPRO.K=(PPA.K+SPACC.K)*MWPRO             WORKLOAD DUE TO             00000610
NOTE                                             PROPHYLAXIS (MIN/MO)        00000611
C       MWPRO=17 MIN/PT                          MINUTES OF WORKLOAD         00000612
NOTE                                             FOR PROPHYLAXIS (MIN/PT)    00000613
A       WTPE.K=(SPA.K+PPA.K)*MWTPE               WORKLOAD DUE TO             00000620
NOTE                                             TREATMENT PLANNING AND      00000621
NOTE                                             EXAMINATION (MIN/MO)        00000622
C       MWTPE=10 MIN/PT                          MINUTES OF WORKLOAD FOR     00000623
NOTE                                             TREATMENT PLANNING AND      00000624
NOTE       EXAMINATION (MIN/PT)                                             00000625
A       WF.K=(FDSP.K+FDPP.K)*MWF                 WORKLOAD DUE                00000630
NOTE                                             TO FILLINGS (MIN/MO)        00000631
C       MWF=10 MIN/T                             MINUTES OF WORKLOAD PER     00000632
NOTE                                             FILLING (MIN/T)             00000633
A       WE.K=(EDSP.K+EDPP.K)*MWE                 WORKLOAD DUE TO             00000640
NOTE                                             EXTRACTIONS (MIN/MO)        00000641
C       MWE=9 MIN/T                              MINUTES OF WORKLOAD PER     00000642
NOTE                                             EXTRACTION (MIN/T)          00000643
A       WPR.K=(ENSP.K*SPACC.K+EDPP.K-OEPP.K)*FETRP.K*MWPR+                   00000650
X       ENSPAS*SPAST.K*FETRS.K*MWPR                                         00000651
NOTE       WORKLOAD DUE TO PROSTHETIC REPLACEMENTS (MIN/MO)                 00000652
C       MWPR=30 MIN/T                            MINUTES OF WORKLOAD         00000653
NOTE                                             PER REPLACED TOOTH (MIN/T)  00000654
A       FETRP.K=TABLE(TIFETRP,IL.K,0,1,.2)       FRACTION OF EXTRACTED       00000660
NOTE       TEETH REPLACED FOR PREVENTIVE PATIENTS AND SYMPTOMATIC           00000661
NOTE       PATIENTS ACCEPTING COMPLTE CARE (D)                              00000662
T       TIFETRP=.4/.5/.6/.65/.7/.75 D                                       00000663
A       FETRS.K=TABLE(TIFETRS,IL.K,0,1,.2)       FRACTION OF EXTRACTED       00000670
NOTE       TEETH REPLACED FOR SYMPTOMATIC PATIENTS ACCEPTING                00000671
NOTE       INCOMPLETE TREATMENT (D)                                         00000672
T       TIFETRS=.15/.25/.35/.45/.55/.65 D                                   00000673
A       WEN.K=ENDSP.K*MWEN                       WORKLOAD DUE TO             00000680
NOTE                                             ENDODONTIC TREATMENT (MIN/MO) 00000681
C       MWEN=44 MIN/T                            MINUTES OF WORKLOAD PER     00000682
NOTE       TOOTH TREATED THROUGH ENDODONTIC TREATMENT (MIN/T)               00000683
A       PPP.K=SPPP.K+PPPP.K                      TOTAL PATIENTS RECEIVING    00000690
```

```
U.M12127.P248.DENTAL.DYNAMO

NOTE                                    PERIODONTAL TREATMENT (PT)    00000691
A   WP.K=PPP.K*MWPP                     WORKLOAD DUE TO               00000700
NOTE      PERIODONTAL TREATMENT (MIN/MO)                             00000701
C         MWEP=30 (MIN/MC)/PT               MINUTES OF WORKLOAD FOR   00000702
NOTE      PERIODONTAL TREATMENT PER PATIENT PER MONTH ((MIN/MO)/PT)  00000703
R   RPEOT.KL=PPEO.K+SPEO.K              TOTAL RATE OF PATIENTS        00000710
NOTE                                    ENTERING ORTHODONTIC          00000711
NOTE                                    TREATMENT (PT/MO)             00000712
L   POP.K=POP.J+DT*(RPEOT.JK-DELAY3(RPEOT.JK,DOT))                   00000720
N       POP=RPEOT*DOT                                                00000721
NOTE                                    PATIENTS RECEIVING            00000722
NOTE                                    ORTHODONTIC TREATMENT (PT)    00000723
C         DOT=36 MO                     DELAY IN COMPLETING           00000724
NOTE                                    ORTHODONTIC TREATMENT (MO)    00000725
A   WO.K=POP.K*MWOP                     WORKLOAD DUE TO               00000730
NOTE                                    ORTHODONTIC TREATMENT (MIN/MO) 00000731
C         MWOP=15 (MIN/MC)/PT               MINUTES OF WORKLOAD PER   00000732
NOTE                                    MCNTH PER ORTHODONTIC         00000733
NOTE                                    PATIENT ((MIN/MO)/PT)         00000734
L   WORK.K=WORK.J+DT*(WGR.J-TDEL.J)                                  00000740
NOTE      DENTAL PRACTICE WORKLOAD SCHEDULED TO BE PROVIDED (MIN)    00000741
NOTE                                                                 00000742
NOTE      DENTAL RESOURCES AVAILABLE FOR PROVIDING CARE              00000743
NOTE                                                                 00000744
L   DENTIST.K=DENTIST.J+DT*(DENTIST.J*SGF)                           00000750
NOTE                                    NUMBER OF DENTISTS (DE)       00000751
C         SGF=.0009 1/MO                                             00000752
NOTE      RATE OF GROWTH OF DENTISTS PER MONTH (1/MO)                00000753
A   DR.K=DENTIST.K*BMA*AXAF.K                                        00000760
NOTE      TOTAL MINUTES OF TIME AVAILABLE                            00000761
NOTE      FOR PROVIDING DIRECT PATIENT CARE (MIN/MO)                 00000762
C         BMA=7900 (MIN/MO)/DE              BASIC MINUTES AVAILABLE   00000763
NOTE      FOR DIRECT PATIENT CARE PER MONTH PER DENTIST ((MIN/MO)/DE) 00000764
A   AXAF.K=TABLE(AAF,ANA.K,0,5,1)                                    00000770
NOTE      EFFECT OF AUXILIARY UTILIZATION OF DENTISTS' PRODUCTIVITY (D) 00000771
T   AAF=1/1.3/1.7/2.3/2.6/2.6 D                                     00000772
A   ANA.K=CANA+RAMP(RIAPM,TBIA)+RAMP(-RIAPM,TEIA)                    00000780
NOTE                                    AVERAGE NUMBER OF             00000781
NOTE      AUXILIARIES EMPLOYED PER DENTIST (AUX/DE)                  00000782
C         CANA=1.5 AUX/DE                                            00000783
NOTE      INITIAL AVERAGE NUMBER OF AUXILIARIES EMPLOYED PER DENTIST 00000784
NOTE      (AUX/DE)                                                   00000785
C         RIAPM=0 (AUX/DE)/MO     RATE OF INCREASE IN AUXILIARY UTILIZATION 00000786
NOTE      PER MONTH ((AUX/DE)/MO)                                    00000787
C         TBIA=0 MO    TIME FOR BEGINNING OF INCREASE IN AUXILIARY   00000788
NOTE      UTILIZATION (MO)                                           00000789
C         TEIA=60 MO    TIME FOR END OF INCREASE IN AUXILIARY UTILIZATION 00000791
NOTE      (MO)                                                       00000792
NOTE                                                                 00000793
NOTE      TREATMENT DELIVERED AND DENTAL PRACTICE BUSYNESS           00000794
NOTE                                                                 00000795
A   TDEL.K=FIFGE(DR.K,WGR.K+(WORK.K/MTDW),WGR.K+(WORK.K/MTDW),DR.K)  00000800
NOTE                                    TREATMENT DELIVERED           00000801
NOTE                                    PER MONTH (MIN/MO)            00000802
C         MTDW=2 MO                     MINIMUM TIME TO DEPLETE WORK  00000803
NOTE                                    BACKLOG (MO)                  00000804
A   IDB.K=(MNWDB*WGR.K+WORK.K)/DR.K                                  00000810
```

```
U.M12127.P248.DENTAL.DYNAMO

NOTE      CURRENT DENTAL PRACTICE BUSYNESS (MO)                            00000811
N      IDB=NDB                                                             00000812
C      MNWDB=1 MO                          MONTHS OF NEW WORKLOAD          00000813
NOTE                               CONTRIBUTING TO DENTAL BUSYNESS (MO)    00000814
A    DB.K=SMOOTH(IDB.K,TADB)                                               00000820
NOTE      AVERAGE DENTAL PRACTICE BUSYNESS (MC)                            00000821
C      TADB=4 MO                           TIME TO AVERAGE DENTAL          00000822
NOTE        PRACTICE BUSYNESS (MO)                                         00000823
NOTE                                                                       00000824
NOTE        PATIENTS CHANGING THEIR CARE-SEEKING ORIENTATION              00000825
NOTE                                                                       00000826
R    PPBS.KL=PPA.K*BFPBS.K                                                 00000830
NOTE      NUMBER OF PREVENTIVE PATIENTS BECOMING SYMPTOMATIC PATIENTS      00000831
NOTE      PER MONTH (PT/MO)                                               00000832
A    BFPBS.K=TABLE(BPBS,DB.K,0,5,1)                                        00000840
NOTE      EFFECT OF DENTAL PRACTICE BUSYNESS ON PREVENTIVE PATIENTS        00000841
NOTE      BECOMING SYMPTOMATIC PATIENTS (D)                               00000842
T    BPBS=0/.05/.10/.15/.20/.25 D                                         00000843
A    SPBP.K=SPACC.K*BFSBP.K*IFSBP.K                                        00000850
NOTE      NUMBER OF SYMPTOMATIC PATIENTS BECOMING PREVENTIVE PATIENTS      00000851
NOTE      PER MONTH (PT/MO)                                               00000852
A    BFSBP.K=TABLE(BSBP,DB.K,0,5,1)                                        00000860
NOTE      EFFECT OF DENTAL PRACTICE BUSYNESS ON SYMPTOMATIC PATIENTS       00000861
NOTE      BECOMING PREVENTIVE PATIENTS (D)                                00000862
T    BSBP=.25/.165/.1/.05/.02/0 D                                         00000863
A    IFSBP.K=TABLE(ISBP,IL.K,0,1,.2)            EFFECT OF INSURANCE ON    00000870
NOTE      SYMPTOMATIC PATIENTS BECOMING PREVENTIVE PATIENTS (D)            00000871
T    ISBP=.85/1/1.15/1.3/1.45/1.6 D                                       00000872
NOTE                                                                       00000873
NOTE            ORAL HEALTH MEASURES                                       00000874
NOTE                                                                       00000875
A    NDT.K=FNPP.K*PP.K+FNSP.K*PSP.K+FNSRCC*SPCCP.K                         00000880
NOTE      TOTAL NUMBER OF DECAYED TEETH (T)                               00000881
C      FNSRCC=3 T/PT                                                       00000882
NOTE      AVERAGE NUMBER OF FILLING NEEDED PER SYMPTOMATIC PATIENT         00000883
NOTE      RECENTLY RECEIVING COMPLETE TREATMENT (T/PT)                    00000884
A    SPP.K=SMOOTH(PP.K,DEL)                                                00000890
NOTE      AVERAGE NUMBER OF PREVENTIVE PATIENTS (PT)                       00000891
A    SSP.K=SMOOTH(SP.K,DEL)                                                00000900
NOTE      AVERAGE NUMBER OF SYMPTOMATIC PATIENTS (PT)                      00000901
C      DEL=36 MO                           SMOOTHING TIME DELAY (MO)       00000902
C      AMTPP=1.5 T/PT                                                      00000903
NOTE      AVERAGE NUMBER OF MISSING TEETH PER PREVENTIVE PATIENT (T/PT)    00000904
C      AMTSP=7 T/PT                                                        00000905
NOTE      AVERAGE NUMBER OF MISSING TEETH PER SYMPTOMATIC PATIENT (T/PT)   00000906
A    NMT.K=SPP.K*AMTPP+SSP.K*AMTSP                                         00000910
NOTE      TOTAL NUMBER OF MISSING TEETH (T)                               00000911
NOTE                                                                       00000912
NOTE            SUPPLEMENTARY INFORMATION                                  00000913
NOTE                                                                       00000914
S    FSP.K=SP.K/(PP.K+SP.K)                                                00000920
NOTE      FRACTION OF THE POPULATION THAT ARE SYMPTOMATIC PATIENTS (D)     00000921
S    FPAS.K=SPA.K/(SPA.K+PPA.K)                                            00000930
NOTE      FRACTION OF THE PATIENTS ARRIVING AT DENTISTS' OFFICES THAT     00000931
NOTE      ARE SYMPTOMATIC PATIENTS (D)                                    00000932
A    FSPACC.K=IFCC.K*EFCC.K*BFCC.K                                         00000940
NOTE      FRACTION OF THE SYMPTOMATIC PATIENTS ARRIVING THAT ACCEPT        00000941
```

```
U.M12127.P248.DENTAL.DYNAMO

NOTE      COMPLETE TREATMENT (D)                                          00000942
S  FSPABP.K=FSPACC.K*BFSBP.K*IFSBP.K                                      00000950
NOTE      FRACTION OF THE SYMPTOMATIC PATIENTS ARRIVING THAT BECOME       00000951
NOTE      PREVENTIVE PATIENTS (D)                                         00000952
S   FPPABS.K=BFPBS.K                                                      00000960
NOTE      FRACTION OF THE PREVENTIVE PATIENTS ARRIVING THAT BECOME        00000961
NOTE      SYMPTOMATIC PATIENTS (D)                                        00000962
S  RWDRA.K=WGR.K/DR.K                                                     00000970
NOTE      RATIO OF CURRENT WORKLOAD TO DENTAL RESOURCES AVAILABLE FOR     00000971
NOTE      PROVIDING CARE (D)                                             00000972
S  PCNFR.K=(FNPP.K*PP.K+FNSP.K*PSP.K+FNSRCC*SPCCP.K)/(PP.K+SP.K)          00000980
NOTE      AVERAGE NUMBER OF DECAYED TEETH NEEDING FILLINGS PER PERSON     00000981
NOTE      (T/PT)                                                         00000982
A  TWPPA.K=MWPRO+MWTPE+FNPP.K*MWF+(ENPP.K+OEPP.K/PPA.K)*MWE+              00000990
X    ENPP.K*FETRP.K*MWPR+FPPNP.K*DPPT*MWPP+FPIEO.K*DOT*MWOP               00000991
NOTE      AVERAGE WORKLOAD PER PREVENTIVE PATIENT ARRIVING (MIN/PT)       00000992
S  TWSACC.K=MWPRO+MWTPE+FNSP.K*MWF+(ENSP.K+OESP.K/SPACC.K)*MWE+           00001000
X    ENSP.K*FETRP.K*MWPR+BETSP*MWEN+FSPNP*DSCPT*MWPP+FSPEO.K*DOT*MWOP     00001001
NOTE      AVERAGE WORKLOAD PER SYMPTOMATIC PATIENT ACCEPTING              00001002
NOTE      COMPLETE CARE (MIN/PT)                                          00001003
A  TWSPAS.K=MWTPE+ENSPAS*(MWE+FETRS.K*MWPR)                               00001010
NOTE      AVERAGE WORKLOAD PER SYMPTOMATIC PATIENT ACCEPTING              00001011
NOTE      INCOMPLETE CARE (MIN/PT)                                        00001012
A  AFWPP.K=TWPPA.K*PPA.K/WGR.K            APPROX FRACTION OF WORKLOAD     00001020
NOTE      DUE TO PREVENTIVE PATIENTS (D)                                  00001021
S  AFWSPAC.K=1-AFWPP.K-AFWSPAS.K          APPROX FRACTION OF WORKLOAD     00001030
NOTE      DUE TO SYMPTOMATIC PATIENTS ACCEPTING COMPLETE CARE (D)         00001031
A  AFWSPAS.K=TWSPAS.K*SPAST.K/WGR.K       APPROX FRACTION OF WORKLOAD     00001040
NOTE      DUE TO SYMPTOMATIC PATIENTS ACCEPTING INCOMPLETE CARE (D)       00001041
L  APPA.K=APPA.J+DT*(PPA.J-ANPLS.J*APPA.J)                                00001050
N     APPA=0                                                              00001051
NOTE      ANNUAL NUMBER OF PREVENTIVE PATIENTS ARRIVING (PT)              00001052
A  ANPLS.K=PULSE(1/DT,12,12)                                              00001060
NOTE      ANNUAL PULSE (1/MO)                                             00001061
L  ASPA.K=ASPA.J+DT*(SPA.J-ANPLS.J*ASPA.J)                                00001070
N     ASPA=0                                                              00001071
NOTE      ANNUAL NUMBER OF SYMPTOMATIC PATIENTS ARRIVING (PT)             00001072
L  ASPACC.K=ASPACC.J+DT*(SPACC.J-ANPLS.J*ASPACC.J)                        00001080
N     ASPACC=0                                                            00001081
NOTE      ANNUAL NUMBER OF SYMPTOMATIC PATIENTS ACCEPTING COMPLETE        00001082
NOTE      TREATMENT (PT)                                                  00001083
L  APPBS.K=APPBS.J+DT*(PPBS.JK-ANPLS.J*APPBS.J)                           00001090
N     APPBS=0                                                             00001091
NOTE      ANNUAL NUMBER OF PREVENTIVE PATIENTS BECOMING SYMPTOMATIC (PT)  00001092
L  ASPBP.K=ASPBP.J+DT*(SPBP.J-ANPLS.J*ASPBP.J)                            00001100
N     ASPBP=0                                                             00001101
NOTE      ANNUAL NUMBER OF SYMPTOMATIC PATIENTS BECOMING PREVENTIVE (PT)  00001102
L  TPPBS.K=TPPBS.J+DT*PPBS.JK                                             00001110
N     TPPBS=0                                                             00001111
NOTE      TOTAL NUMBER OF PREVENTIVE PATIENTS BECOMING SYMPTOMATIC (PT)   00001112
L  TSPBP.K=TSPBP.J+DT*SPBP.J                                              00001120
N     TSPBP=0                                                             00001121
NOTE      TOTAL NUMBER OF SYMPTOMATIC PATIENTS BECOMING PREVENTIVE (PT)   00001122
L  TSPACC.K=TSPACC.J+DT*SPACC.J                                           00001130
N     TSPACC=0                                                            00001131
NOTE      TOTAL NUMBER OF SYMPTOMATIC PATIENTS ACCEPTING COMPLETE CARE    00001132
NOTE      (PT)                                                            00001133
```

```
U.M12127.P248.DENTAL.DYNAMO

A   IL.K=CIL+RAMP(RIILPM,TBII)+RAMP(-RIILPM,TEII)+STEP(SIIL,TSIIL)   00001140
NOTE     LEVEL OF DENTAL INSURANCE (D)                                00001141
C     CIL=.2 D                                                        00001142
NOTE     INITIAL INSURANCE LEVEL (D)                                  00001143
C     RIILPM=0                                                        00001144
NOTE     RATE IN INCREASE IN INSURANCE PER MONTH (1/MO)               00001145
C     TBII=12 MO                                                      00001146
NOTE     TIME OF BEGINNING OF INCREASE IN INSURANCE (MO)              00001147
C     TEII=60 MO                                                      00001148
NOTE     TIME OF END OF INCREASE IN INSURANCE (MO)                    00001149
C     SIIL=0 D                                                        00001151
NOTE     STEP INCREASE IN INSURANCE LEVEL (D)                         00001152
C     TSIIL=12                                                        00001153
NOTE     TIME OF STEP INCREASE IN INSURANCE (MO)                      00001154
A   EL.K=CEL                                                          00001160
NOTE     EDUCATIONAL LEVEL (D)                                        00001161
C     CEL=.5 D                                                        00001162
NOTE     INITIAL EDUCATIONAL LEVEL (D)                                00001163
NOTE                                                                  00001164
NOTE         INITIAL CONDITIONS                                       00001165
NOTE                                                                  00001166
N     SP=NSP                                                          00001167
C     NSP=132E6                                                       00001168
N     PP=NPP                                                          00001169
C     NPP=66E6                                                        00001171
N     DENTIST=NDENT                                                   00001172
C     NDENT=99180                                                     00001173
N     WORK=FIFGE(0,(NDB-1)*DR,1,NDB)                                  00001174
C     NDB=1.35                                                        00001175
NOTE                                                                  00001176
NOTE PRINT AND PLOT STATEMENTS                                        00001177
NOTE                                                                  00001178
PRINT PP/SP/PSP/PPA/SPA/SPACC/PCNFR/NDT/SPTI/(6.2)APPA,ASPA,ASPACC,APPBS00001179
PRINT (6.2)ASPBP/(0.4)FSP,FPAS,FSPACC,AFWPP,AFWSPAC,AFWSPAS/TWPPA,TWSPAC00001181
PRINT TWSPAS/(0.4)FSPA3P,FPPABS/TPPBS,TSPBP,TSPACC                    00001182
PRINT DB,IDB,RWDRA/WORK,DR,WGR,WPRO,WTPE,WF,WE,WPR,WEN,WP,WO          00001183
PLOT DB=B(0,4)/FSP,FPAS,FSPACC,AFWPP,AFWSPAC,AFWSPAS(0,1)             00001184
PLOT PP,SP(0,160E6)/PPA,SPA,SPACC(0,12E6)                            00001185
SPEC DT=2/LENGTH=120/PRTPER=4/PLTPER=4                               00001186
```

About the Authors

Gilbert Levin is associate professor of psychiatry and community health at the Albert Einstein College of Medicine. He graduated from the University of Michigan and received a Ph.D. in clinical and social psychology from Boston University. He has conducted research at the Harvard Medical School and taught at Carnegie-Mellon University. At Einstein since 1963, he teaches and conducts research on social and community psychiatry and consults to industrial and health organizations. He is best known for his contributions to the development and evaluation of community mental health practices and has published many articles and two books in this field.

Edward B. Roberts is the David Sarnoff Professor of the Management of Technology at the M.I.T. Alfred P. Sloan School of Management. He received four degrees from M.I.T., including a Ph.D. in economics. On the M.I.T. faculty since 1961, Dr. Roberts was a founding member of what is now the System Dynamics Group. He helped organize and direct the M.I.T. Research Program on the Management of Science and Technology, and now chairs the Technology and Health Management area at the Sloan School.

Dr. Roberts has been active as a consultant and lecturer to government, industry and universities. He is co-founder and president of Pugh-Roberts Associates, Inc., and a director of several other firms. For several years he was a member of the U.S. Air Force Scientific Advisory Board and the Commerce Technical Advisory Board, and also served as a consultant to the President's Advisory Council on Management Improvement. An author of several books and numerous articles, Dr. Roberts has also consulted to the Association of American Medical Colleges and the American College of Physicians.

Gary B. Hirsch is Senior Consultant at Pugh-Roberts Associates, Inc., a Cambridge-based management consulting firm, and directs the firm's activities in the areas of health and social systems. Recipient of the bachelor's and master's degrees from the M.I.T. Sloan School of Management, Hirsch has led major projects on human service delivery systems, including criminal justice, welfare and health care. His extensive publications in the health field include works on manpower planning, medical education, dental care, mental health, and HMO planning. He is co-author with Drs. Levin and Roberts of *The Persistent Poppy: A Computer-Aided Search for Heroin Policy.*

Deborah S. Kligler is assistant dean and assistant professor of psychiatry at the Albert Einstein College of Medicine. After graduating from Smith College she received an M.A. in Economics from Columbia University and a Ph.D. in Sociology from Yale. At Einstein, after participating in the research and demonstration programs of the Division of Social and Community Psychiatry, she became a staff member of a pioneering community mental health center affiliated with the medical school. Dr. Kligler's special interest there was in evaluation activities and in the development of a management information system which, as associate director of the center, she sought to integrate into the administration and operations of the agency.

Jack F. Wilder is Associate Dean for Planning and Operations and associate professor of psychiatry at the Albert Einstein College of Medicine. He graduated from Yale University, received an M.A. in clinical psychology from Columbia University and an M.D. from New York University School of Medicine. A member of the faculty at AECOM since 1960, Dr. Wilder has served as Acting Chairman of the Department of Psychiatry and developed and directed a model urban mental health center, the Sound View-Throgs Neck Community Mental Health Center. He has consulted and published widely in the areas of management of mental health services, and partial hospitalization and rehabilitation programs. He is a member of the Editorial Board of *Hospital & Community Psychiatry.*

Nancy Roberts is a Lecturer at Lesley College, Graduate School of Education. After graduating from Boston University in history and political science, she taught in the elementary schools for several years, returning to Boston University for an Ed.M. and Ed.D. in elementary education. She is actively engaged in the application of system dynamics to educational problems while also working on the development of system dynamics curricula. Dr. Roberts is currently heading a project team in the M.I.T. System Dynamics Group that is creating teaching materials for the elementary and secondary school levels. She is also collaborating with faculty of several Boston-area universities to integrate systems approaches into more traditional course structures, and has published several articles on her systems studies.